Latinx Encounters

LATINX HISTORIES

Lori Flores and Michael Innis-Jiménez, editors

This series features innovative historical works that push boundaries in the study of race, ethnicity, sexuality, gender, migration, and nationalism within and around Latinx communities, premised on the view that Latinx histories are essential to understanding the full sweep of history in the United States, the Americas, and the world.

A complete list of books published in Latinx Histories is available at https://uncpress.org/series/latinx-histories.

Latinx Encounters

How Mexicans, Mexican Americans, and Puerto Ricans Made the Modern Midwest

Juan Ignacio Mora

The University of North Carolina Press CHAPEL HILL

Set in Merope Basic by Westchester Publishing Services

Library of Congress Cataloging-in-Publication Data
Names: Mora, Juan Ignacio author
Title: Latinx encounters : how Mexicans, Mexican Americans, and Puerto Ricans made the modern Midwest / Juan Ignacio Mora.
Other titles: Latinx histories
Description: Chapel Hill : The University of North Carolina Press, 2026. | Series: Latinx histories | Includes bibliographical references and index.
Identifiers: LCCN 2026018183 | ISBN 9781469693842 cloth | ISBN 9781469693859 paperback | ISBN 9781469693866 epub | ISBN 9781469693873 pdf
Subjects: LCSH: Migrant agricultural laborers—Middle West—History—20th century | Agricultural laborers—Labor unions—Organizing—Middle West—History—20th century | Mexican Americans—Middle West—Social conditions—20th century | Puerto Ricans—Middle West—Social conditions—20th century | Mexicans—Middle West—Social conditions—20th century | BISAC: SOCIAL SCIENCE / Ethnic Studies / American / Hispanic American Studies | HISTORY / United States / State & Local / Midwest (IA, IL, IN, KS, MI, MN, MO, ND, NE, OH, SD, WI)
Classification: LCC HD1527.M54 M67 2026 | DDC 331.5/440977—dc23/eng/20260422
LC record available at https://lccn.loc.gov/2026018183

Cover photograph: *Agricultural Workers at the Airport in Puerto Rico*, 1948, by Louise Rosskam. Courtesy of Archivo General de Puerto Rico, Colección Departamento de Instrucción Pública, Fotografía Oficina de Información de Fortaleza / Gobierno de Puerto Rico.

Portions of Chapter One were derived in part from Mora, Juan Ignacio, "Managing the Migration: Latino Intermediaries and the Expansion of United States Migratory Labor from World War I through the Bracero Program." *Journal of American Ethnic History* 42, no. 3 (1 April 2023). Used by permission of the University of Illinois Press.

For product safety concerns under the European Union's General Product Safety Regulation (EU GPSR), please contact gpsr@mare-nostrum.co.uk or write to the University of North Carolina Press and Mare Nostrum Group B.V., Doelen 72, 4831 GR Breda, The Netherlands.

This book is dedicated to
my mom, dad, grandparents, and family.
Your endless support, love, and stories made this possible.
I hope you see a bit of yourselves when you see this book.

Contents

Acknowledgments

Finding the words to start writing these acknowledgments have probably been the most difficult words to write in this book. It's difficult to figure where to start and in what order to give thanks. Generally, this book would not have been possible without the endless support from family, friends, colleagues, librarians, and archivists—each of whom shaped the development of this book in unique ways. I owe such an immense debt of gratitude to so many individuals that it feels improbable that I will remember everyone who is deserving of credit.

As I began my path through higher education with a bachelor's degree in history and Latina/Latino studies at the University of Illinois, Urbana-Champaign and completed it with a doctoral degree from the Department of History at the University of Illinois, there is an extensive list of people from there deserving of recognition. Special thanks belong to my dissertation advisor, Adrian Burgos Jr., who has long served as a model for innovative scholarship and committed mentorship. Beginning with undergraduate coursework, supervising part of the undergraduate thesis, having faith in my capacity to pursue a PhD, supporting the early ideas of this project, and guiding the dissertation to completion, Adrian was there every step of the way.

During graduate school, I had the privilege of being mentored and guided by several other faculty members from Illinois's Department of History. Augusto Espiritu, Marc Hertzman, and Kathy Oberdeck were instrumental to the development of this project during graduate school. While Kathy sadly passed away in 2022, I hope she would be proud of this Midwestern labor history book. I cannot thank Adrian, Augusto, Marc, and Kathy enough for their role in shaping how I think about researching, teaching, and mentoring. Lilia Fernández joined the dissertation committee toward the end of the process, but I will never forget how Lilia generously provided line-by-line feedback and edits for the dissertation. Their influence on the intellectual development of the project extends far beyond that as *Brown in the Windy City* contributed to my desire to understand the intertwined histories of Mexicans, Mexican Americans, and Puerto Ricans in the Midwest.

A heartfelt note of appreciation goes out to Jim Barrett and Mireya Loza. Jim's research and teaching inspired my interest in the working-class history of the Midwest and was a constant source of support. Alongside Adrian, Mireya has been my longest-standing mentor from my time at Illinois. As an undergraduate student, I took pride in almost taking all the classes Mireya taught at Illinois. I'm grateful for Mireya's committed mentorship and friendship. The Department of Latina/Latino Studies was a special place for me during my time at Illinois. In addition to all of the wonderful LLS faculty and postdoctoral fellows that I had the opportunity to learn from and interact with, Laura Castañeda and Alicia Rodriguez were two of the most amazing people I had the pleasure of meeting in Urbana-Champaign. Not only have Alicia and Laura been such valuable resources at Illinois, but they are also wonderful friends. Alicia and Laura were there for me during a tough time in graduate school, so I will never forget their generosity and compassion.

This book could not have been written without the expertise and generosity of archivists and librarians throughout North America. Archivists at the *Archivo General de la Nación* and *Archivo Histórico de la Secretaría de Relaciones Exteriores* in Mexico City, the Bancroft Library, the Bentley Historical Library, the Harry S. Truman Presidential Library, the Library of Congress, the National Archives and Records Administration, and the Center for Puerto Rican Studies Archives at Hunter College were the facilitators to finding the collections and documents needed to pursue this project. The Archives of Labor and Urban Affairs at the Walter P. Reuther Library was the most influential archive to the development of this project. It was the archive where this project started and no matter how many times I went to Reuther, I always found myself making the trip back to Detroit. Kristen Chinery, the reference archivist at the Reuther, has been an invaluable resource for navigating their immense collections. While I was in graduate school, historian Eileen Findlay was incredibly generous and selfless for sharing some of the records they collected from *Archivo General de Puerto Rico* at a time when it was impossible for me to access materials there immediately following Hurricane Maria. Finally, one of the most challenging aspects of completing the manuscript was securing the image reproduction rights for the photos that appear in the book. For their assistance with this, I want to thank Elizabeth Clemens and Dawn Lawson at the Reuther Library; Aníbal Arocho and Grace McKenna at the Center for Puerto Rican Studies Archives; Julio Yamil Mercado Avila with the *Universidad de Puerto Rico—Recinto de Río Piedras's Archivo Fotográfico Periódico El Mundo*; María I. Rodríguez Matos at the *Archivo General de Puerto Rico*; Jill Gregg Clever at the Toledo Lucas County Public Library; Laurie Austin at the Harry S. Truman Library; and Analiese Oetting at the National Museum of American History. I'd also like to thank Baldemar Velásquez, President of the Farm Labor Organizing Committee, for giving permission to use certain photos in the last chapter.

Conducting extensive research indeed takes time and funding, so this book has benefited from a number of different fellowships and grants. As a graduate student, these included the University of Illinois Department of History's summer research travel grant and Dickerson ABD Fellowship, and the Center for Latin American and Caribbean Studies' Tinker Fellowship. As a postdoctoral fellow and assistant professor at Indiana University, the Walter P. Reuther Library's Sam Fishman Research Grant, the Nettie Lee Benson Latin American Collection's Center for Mexican American Studies Research Fellowship, the Mauricio Gastón Institute for Latino Community Development and Public Policy's Andrés Torres Paper Series Award, the Center for Research on Race and Ethnicity in Society's Faculty Seed Grant, and the College of Arts and Humanities Institute's Faculty Research Travel Grant all generously supported the research that appears in this book.

I have been fortunate to work with the University of North Carolina Press to see this book come to fruition. I am thankful for everyone in the Latinx Histories series team, particularly the series editors, Lori Flores and Michael Innis-Jiménez, who had faith in this project early on and helped guide it to this point. My appreciation for Debbie Gershenowitz, who shepherded this book through almost every stage of the process, cannot be fully expressed. The meals, cocktails, and conversations about our respective times in Bloomington have easily been one of my favorite parts about working with UNCP. With Debbie now at Bloomsbury, I am grateful for having had the opportunity to work with Dawn Durante to complete this process. Emily Spangenberg and many others at UNCP are also deserving of recognition for their role in the publication of this book. I hired Jessica Newman at the last minute for assistance with formatting and editing. I'm immensely appreciative of her expertise and wizardry in these areas. Finally, I am indebted to the anonymous reviewers who provided incisive feedback for proposal and sample chapters, and then again with the full manuscript. They improved the quality of this book in immeasurable ways. If there are any errors in this book, the fault lies with me.

Throughout the years in Champaign-Urbana, Bloomington, and at various conferences, I have been lucky to meet some of the most amazing and supportive people. At the University of Illinois, it was a true joy to enter the PhD program with Brian Campbell, Eliza Dreier, Leanna Duncan,

Marco Jaimes, and Thais Rezende Da Silva De Sant'ana. Outside of this cohort and across campus, Olivia Hagedorn, Liz Matsushita, Peter Wright, Catherine Corr, and Gabriela Vargas have remained close friends. Through the Latina/Latino Studies Postdoctoral Fellowship program, I was introduced to brilliant friends like Eddie Bonilla and Yuridia Ramírez. A shared intellectual interest in the Latinx Midwest has led to amazing friendships with the likes of Emiliano Aguilar, Mike Amezcua, Delia Fernández-Jones, Sergio González, Carolina Ortega, Nico Soto, Michael Staudenmaier, Antonio Ramirez, and Bryan Winston. Many of these friends have been the basis for far too many group chats. Whether from receiving conference and workshop feedback or sharing meals and drinks, I am appreciative of individuals like Gabriela Arredondo, Katherine Bynum Chávez, René Cordero, Lilia Fernández, Lori Flores, Adam Goodman, Martha Guerrero, Perla Guerrero, Felipe Hinojosa, Michael Innis-Jiménez, Benjamin Johnson, Jorge Leal, Verónica Martínez-Matsuda, Sarah McNamara, Kristy Nabhan-Warren, Ivón Padilla-Rodríguez, Stephen Pitti, Andrew Sandoval-Strausz, Jorge Ramirez-Lopez, ToniAnn Treviño, and Audrey Danielle Winston.

When I moved to Bloomington, Indiana, to begin a Postdoctoral Fellowship at IU's Center for Research on Race and Ethnicity in Society (CRRES), it was the first time I had lived outside of Illinois as an adult. The community I have found among CRRES leadership, current and past postdocs, faculty affiliates, and graduate students has been indescribable. Dina Okamoto, Michelle Moyd, Sylvia Martinez, and Sonia Lee have been exemplary leaders of the center. CRRES's cohort model allowed me to start the postdoctoral fellowship alongside Aleshia Barajas, and I've had the fortune of developing friendships with the postdocs that have followed, which include Olivia Ekeh, Joseph Wei, Lucía Stavig, and Ramón Resendiz.

Throughout the Department of History, the Latino Studies Program, other units across campus, and elsewhere in Bloomington, I have found dear colleagues, mentors, and friends. As faculty mentors in the department or through other campus programs, Peter Guardino, Alex Lichtenstein, and Ellen Wu have shared their wisdom, institutional knowledge, and friendship with me. As chair of the Department of History when I arrived, Michael McGerr ensured that I felt like a valued member of the department, stewarded my retention process, and helped recruit Carolina Ortega to IU. Colleagues in History, Latino Studies, and American Studies like Cara Caddoo, Thomas Chan, Arlene Díaz, Jeff Gould, Michael Dodson, Janine Giordano Drake, Clare Griffin, Karen Inouye, Ben Irvin, Sarah Knott, Lara Kriegel, Eunice

Lee, Meredith Lee, Sonia Lee, Jason McGraw, Amrita Chakrabarti Myers, John Nieto-Phillips, Solimar Otero, Roberta Pergher, Judy Rodriguez, Olga Rodriguez-Ulloa, Mark Roseman, and Alberto Varon have all opened their homes to Carolina and I during the time we have been here in Bloomington. Elsewhere across campus or in Bloomington, Hayden Blankenship, Claire Cumberland, Kathy Darragh, Leslie Del Carpio, Monica Heilman, Max Jack, Mackenzie Mills, Nancy Nguyen, and Mariana Stavig have been wonderful friends. The Thursday and Sunday soccer games at BUGS have been a welcome reprieve from the stresses of work and life and let me meet people I otherwise might not have had the chance to. This is far from an exhaustive list of all of the amazing people I have had the good fortune of meeting here in Bloomington and I wish I could mention everyone. Nevertheless, all of you have made Bloomington home.

As I was finishing the book revisions and securing image rights, I had the distinct privilege of doing so in Washington, DC, as a postdoctoral fellow with the Latino Museum Studies Program at the Smithsonian Institution's National Museum of American History and National Museum of the American Latino. I am thankful to both the NMAH and NMAL for this unique opportunity. This experience afforded me the occasion to conduct research, revise the book, and become immersed in the museum world. Diana Bossa Bastidas, Verónica Méndez, and Steve Velasquez are due particular recognition for their support and guidance during my time in DC. While it otherwise would have been a lonely summer being away from Bloomington for the better part of three months, the time spent with Mike Amezcua and Mireya Loza in DC helped remedy that. Whether going to a weekend of punk shows and grabbing beers with Mike or going to Judy's with Mireya, I am deeply appreciative of them for their friendship.

Raquel Escober is entitled to her own part here. She took me under her wing from the day I started graduate school and has since been one of my longest-standing friends. She has always loved to watch baby birds as they learn to fly. Graduate school would not have been the same without the advice and guidance she offered, the laughter we shared, and our adventures throughout Champaign. Since then, we have made it a point to hang out wherever we can: in Chicago, Bloomington, Chapel Hill, and even Treasure Beach, Jamaica. Wherever they were, Raquel and Peter never hesitated to open their home. Words are insufficient to describe how important Raquel has been to my academic and personal journey these past ten-plus years, and I know this will only continue on.

The last words here are saved for my family. My acknowledgments would not be complete without underscoring their endless support. My mom, Lorraine Chavez, and dad, Juan Mora-Torres, have been constant sources of encouragement, advice, and love. They have each inspired me and taught me in so many unique ways. This book is in no small part due to their confidence in me and their reassurance over the years. I can never repay you for everything you have done for me, but I at least know how proud both of you will be to say that your son has written a book.

I have always been awed by the creativity and imagination of my twin sister, Magdalena Mora. You have so many qualities that seem so natural to you, but I know how hard you work at everything you do. This has always motivated me to do the same. Even though I had a ten-minute head start on you, you are clearly the more prolific author-illustrator. At least I can say I have one book. Marcos has been a source of joy, youth, and admiration throughout my adult years. My grandparents and abuelitos endured much throughout their lives, and their sacrifices continue to inspire me. To Irene Chavez, Martin Pimsler, Magdaleno Mora, and Esther Torres, I am thankful for the care and love you have provided me from the day I was born. From my mom's side of the family, I would like to thank Catherine, John, Dennis, Ambrose, Garrison, and Serafina. From my dad's side, I would like to thank Carmelo, Gregorio, Hugo, Magdalena, Nacho, Gloria, Rosa, Hugito, Moctezuma, Samuel, Solomon, and Xavy. Everyone mentioned here is deserving of thanks and so much more, but for now, all I have to offer are these words. For the family of Carolina, my wife, *gracias por aceptarme como a uno más de su propia familia. Nunca he dejado de sentirme parte de esta grande familia*. To Carolina's niece, Jasmine, you know you're always welcome wherever we are.

The final words here could only be reserved for my best friend, my intellectual partner, and my wife: Carolina Ortega. We met in graduate school and shared a nerdy fascination about the history of Latinxs in the Midwest. This shared interest and friendship eventually blossomed into something indescribable. We have been there for each other during the best of times and the most challenging of times. I know that will never change. You have been my biggest supporter, and I will always be yours. Living these years alongside such a compassionate, brilliant, and loving person has been the best part of my life. We've been lucky enough to also spend many of these years alongside our two cats, Chico and Mihca, and our dog, Chuy. Chico passed away as this book was being finished, but I know he'll always be on the couch armrest. We've been through graduate school together, long distance for two years while Carolina was in Corpus Christi, and now together in Bloomington. I can't wait for more travels together, nightly movies, spontaneous adventures, and a lifetime of love. I'll do my best to never be late for lunch again. I could go on for pages and still never convey how much you mean to me. So, I will just end it with this: *Mi querida Carolina,* I love you with all of my heart.

Latinx Encounters

Introduction

Migrant Farmworkers and the Modern Midwest

In the May 1971 edition of *CREEM* magazine, Dave Marsh wrote about attending a show by a niche Michigan band, Question Mark and the Mysterians (or ? and the Mysterians), who had a fleeting moment of commercial success in 1966. With Marsh reliving his near-euphoric experience of seeing the band reunited and play, the young music critic wrote, "I couldn't imagine it happening but there I was—swaggering, and jiving, again like I did at Mt. Holly back in '66—and there HE was, swagging and jiving, again like HE did at Mt. Holly back in '66."[1] The "HE" was the band's lead singer, Question Mark, and the place that Marsh was referring to was Mt. Holly Ski Resort. About halfway between Flint and Detroit, Michigan, Mt. Holly doubled as a music venue for bands in the mid-to-late 1960s. As the *Detroit Free Press* remarked about the importance of this venue for emerging artists and teenage music enthusiasts, "Mt. Holly between '64 and '70 was where such groups as Alice Cooper, Question Mark and the Mysterians, the Bob Seger System, and Grand Funk Railroad made their pre-big-time debuts as new groups." Or as other reporters characterized it, in 1967 at Mt. Holly, Question Mark and the Mysterians were "practically the house band."[2]

Marsh, who would eventually become a prolific and renowned music critic, is popularly recognized as introducing the term "punk rock" into the musical lexicon after attending the band's reunion show and writing about it in the *CREEM* article.[3] Even after the exhaustion of watching Tina Turner perform for the past two nights, Marsh had no intentions of missing a chance to watch Question Mark and the Mysterians perform again. "Needless to say, it was impossible . . . to miss such a landmark exposition of punk-rock," wrote Marsh. A captive to Question Mark's enchanting stage presence, the music critic wrote, "Down on his back, legs flailing the air . . . Then up again, a threat to the audience, dancing like a maniac and all of a sudden, he's doing the knee-drop, and the splits and every other James Brown move. He's the only one in punk-rock who's still got 'em."[4] There, Marsh uses the phrase again. Five years prior to this article, Question Mark and the Mysterians were at the height of their musical success. With a catchy chorus and repetitive Farfisa organ hook, this group of Mexican American teenagers' hit song "96 Tears" soared to *Billboard*'s Hot 100 #1 spot on October 29, 1966. Altogether, the song spent a total of fifteen weeks on the charts.[5] Often derided as being a "one-hit wonder," this Latinx band out of the Midwest had an overlooked, but profound, impact on US popular culture.[6]

Before "96 Tears" would sell over one million records and propel Question Mark and the Mysterians to fleeting musical stardom, the band was just a group of teenage musicians from Michigan's Tri-Cities (Saginaw, Bay City, and Midland). The designation of being the first "punk-rock" band may suggest a ragtag set of circumstances that brought these group members together. Yet, their convergence in the Midwest, and Michigan more specifically, was actually the result of a distinct set of processes that brought Mexican, Mexican American, and Puerto Rican migrant farmworkers to the region—often times temporarily, but sometimes permanently.

Regarding their settlement in the Midwest, Question Mark and the Mysterians were the result of what could be called the "harvest route." This harvest route encompasses the range of migratory experiences that farmworkers encountered in agricultural settings before they set down permanent roots in cities or semi-urban areas. The time that agricultural migrants spent in the fields proved to be formative to the political, social, and cultural development of the Latinx Midwest. The core members of Question Mark and the Mysterians achieved various levels of education and possessed assorted musical backgrounds by the time they joined the band, and their parents found permanent employment in different industries, but there was one constant that connected them to the Saginaw Valley area: The families of the band members came from backgrounds as migrant agricultural workers.[7] However, not all of the interactions between Mexicans, Mexican Americans, and Puerto Ricans in the Midwest's fields would be as harmonious as the melodies of the band.

Labor Migrations

For over one hundred years, the fields and orchards of the Midwest offered seasonal agricultural work for countless Latinx migrant families and single men who came on their own. Throughout the twentieth century, a mix of formal and informal labor migration efforts recruited hundreds of thousands, if not millions, of Mexican, Mexican American (including Mexican Americans from Texas, or Tejanos), and Puerto Rican migrants for work in the Midwest's agricultural industry. Amid the tail end of World War I, Midwestern sugar beet companies began recruiting ethnic Mexicans (Mexican

Americans and Mexican nationals) from the Texas-Mexico borderlands for employment as *betabeleros*, or sugar beet workers, in 1918.[8] Since these Mexican American farmworkers from Texas who came to the Midwest were interstate migrants, this would not be considered a formal labor migration program, yet they were still participating in a seasonal migratory stream that was shaping the region's agricultural industry. Marc Simon Rodriguez appropriately describes this process, writing, "Thrust into migration by changes in the North American labor market and agricultural economy that often pitted them against Mexican workers, Tejanos fashioned flexible labor, economic, and social networks that functioned for much of the twentieth century."[9] Rodriguez characterizes this broader process as the "Tejano diaspora." As Rodriguez suggests, growers in the Midwest and beyond coveted both groups of ethnic Mexicans, Tejanos and Mexican nationals, as invaluable sources of seasonal labor.

The United States's entrance into World War I would mark the beginning of the first Mexican guestworker program. While the United States formally entered World War I in 1917 and the war was over by the end of 1918, the labor recruitment program lasted until 1922. During this period, scholars estimate that employers recruited between 73,000 and 80,000 Mexicans for work in agricultural, railroad, mining, and construction industries. While the World War II Bracero Program has overshadowed the more modest World War I version, the first Mexican guestworker program still set an important precedent. Lori Flores and Mireya Loza show that the initial Mexican contract labor program provided future employers and government officials with clarity regarding how to structure and implement this type of guestworker program, and cemented their appetite for low-wage, Mexican workers with contracts that could be loosely upheld, if at all.[10] As Loza concludes, "During this first program, growers learned how to utilize strategic noncompliance and manage migrants in ways that deployed the power of deportation." Furthermore, it cemented the perspective that "there was no need for farm workers to be year-round, permanent, and full-fledged members of the communities where they worked."[11] Just as the first Mexican guestworker program was proposed as a temporary war measure that eventually exceeded its initial justification, so too would the World War II Bracero Program, except on a much larger scale.

On August 7, 1942, the *Chicago Tribune* announced that the United States had entered into an agreement with Mexico whereby "this country's southern border can be opened for temporary immigration of Mexican farm workers, under stipulated conditions, as a means of making certain that an agricultural labor shortage does not blight the 'food for victory' program."[12] As millions of Americans joined the country's armed forces, both voluntarily and through the draft, millions more sought defense jobs in the country's industrialized areas. With farmworkers abandoning the fields in favor of more lucrative industrial jobs or enlisting in the army, growers and government representatives exhorted the necessity of temporary, contract laborers as the solution. Agreed to just months after Pearl Harbor and the United States's entrance into World War II, through various agreements, both governments would continually renew this binational contract labor program until 1964. While the wartime effort activated the recruitment of Mexican workers to mitigate the agricultural and railroad industry's labor shortages, it was growers' intensifying dependency and enduring demand for inexpensive, migratory farmworkers that propelled the program's numerous extensions over the course of two decades.[13]

In total, around 4.6 million contracts were issued, with many Mexican men returning several times on different contracts. As half a million Mexicans received contracts during the height of the program, this made for the largest guestworker program in US history.[14] With the Farm Security Administration (FSA) overseeing the certification process for US farmers to obtain guestworkers, the first waves of *braceros* were initially contracted to farms in the Southwest. Yet, as Lilia Fernández shows, it would not be long before braceros began working in Midwestern fields and orchards, some arriving as early as 1944. Incidentally, with braceros, as well as unsanctioned Mexican workers, arriving in the Southwest in greater numbers, many Tejanos decided to seek agricultural work elsewhere. "Mexican American migrant farm laborers, including many who had worked the seasonal circuit from Texas to the Midwest (Michigan, Ohio, Wisconsin, Indiana, Illinois), were particularly compelled to head north by the competition from the very braceros that farmers began hiring for lower wages," writes Fernández.[15] In addition to the Bracero Program directly bringing Mexican workers to the Midwest, as well as indirectly encouraging increasing amounts of Mexican American migrants to follow the harvest route north, the World War II and postwar period would birth another state-sponsored migration program that would continue to transform the region's ethnoracial dynamics.

Mexican American and Mexican farmworkers were but two parts of the Latinx migrant farmworker triad that would shape the mid-twentieth-century development of the Midwest's agricultural industry. Explaining the evolution of Grand Rapids, Michigan's Latinx community and the introduction of Puerto Rican migrants into this equation, Delia Fernández-Jones

An official collects documents from braceros, Mexico City, Mexico. Leonard Nadel Photographs and Scrapbooks, Archives Center, National Museum of American History, Smithsonian Institution.

contends that "state-sponsored migration experiments devised originally to promote Puerto Rican temporary relocation to the mainland combined to facilitate a socially engineered Latino diaspora to the Midwest."[16] As scholars of Puerto Rico's colonial relationship to the United States have shown, the 1917 Jones-Shafroth Act, typically referred to as just the "Jones Act," granted US citizenship to Puerto Ricans. This was a measure that fundamentally altered Puerto Rican migratory practices, especially after World War II.[17] Coinciding with the United States's entrance into World War II was the beginning of Puerto Rico's implementation of Operation Bootstrap, the archipelago's large-scale economic development, industrialization, and "modernization" program.[18]

Beyond attracting foreign investment to finance export-oriented industrialization, Operation Bootstrap's other main component was to fuel Puerto Rican migration to the mainland. This aspect was intended to help resolve the "overpopulation" and unemployment on the islands. Teodoro Moscoso, an architect of Operation Bootstrap and administrator of the Economic Development Administration, captured all of these aspects when they stated that barring a "vast program of emigration to more promising lands, coupled with an intense program of industrialization and birth control, Puerto Rico's greatest problem will never be resolved."[19] 1947 was a pivotal moment for these efforts. With regard to the former, the Puerto Rican legislature passed the Industrial Incentives Act (IIA). Luis Muñoz Marín, the populist leader of the *Partido Popular Democrático* (PPD) and soon to become Puerto Rico's first elected governor in 1948, worked closely with the US federal government to design this law that would provide considerable tax breaks and economic incentives for US corporations. The main feature of the IIA was that these corporations would be completely exempt from Puerto Rican income and property taxes, as well as most excise taxes, municipal taxes, and license fees. In combination with sections of the US Tax Code, this essentially produced a tax holiday for US corporations that invested in the archipelago.[20]

In addition to the passage of the IIA, 1947 also marked the year that the Puerto Rican legislature would pass and provide funding for Public Law 89 (PL89). This law authorized the Commissioner of Labor to "regulate the contracts for workmen or employees whose services are to be used in State of the American Union, in territories thereof, or in any foreign country."[21] This broad range of oversight included monitoring the sourcing and adherence of labor contracts, ensuring the welfare of Puerto Rican migrants, and requiring prospective employers seeking to recruit migrant workers to receive approval from the Department of Labor. Furthermore, PL89's third article required compliance with Public Law 417, which was enacted to regulate private employment agencies that sought to operate in Puerto Rico. With an ideological framework that promoted Puerto Rican migration to the mainland and an administrative structure to oversee the contracting of migrant laborers, the first groups of contract workers sponsored by the Puerto Rican Department of Labor (PRDL) made their way to the United States in the summer of 1947.[22]

The Encounters

Alongside these mid-twentieth-century state-sanctioned contract labor programs that facilitated the deployment of Mexican and Puerto Rican migrant workers to different parts of the United States were the Mexican American migrant farmworkers from Texas that followed the harvest route north or who were recruited by employment agencies. The three strands of Latinx migrants were coming from backgrounds that often overlapped, as well as diverged from one another—these lines included ethnicity, race, gender, citizenship status, age, and language, among other aspects. Depending on the circumstances, these characteristics could breed camaraderie, confrontation, or some combination of both. Ultimately, it was in the fields of the Midwest where these different groups of Latinx migrant farmworkers converged with one another.

References to the US Midwest as "the heartland" in popular culture, national politics, and mass media evoke a romanticized regional past where the descendants of European settlers and immigrants populated rural towns and sowed the seeds of small, family farms. What this perspective elides is the fact that, for over a century, Latinx migrants have performed some of the most grueling and strenuous manual labor needed to sustain an industry that was vital to the regional economy. One state in particular was a dominant force in agribusiness and the recruitment of migratory labor—Michigan. While *Latinx Encounters* does extend beyond Michigan in its treatment of the Midwest, this state's agricultural industry does require particular emphasis. In a 1947 report on the state's World War II Emergency Farm Labor Program prepared by Michigan State College's Extension Service, the analysts plainly demonstrate the importance of Michigan's agricultural industry to the country, as well as the centrality of migrant workers to that sector.[23] This report, produced by A. B. Love, Michigan's Emergency Farm Labor Supervisor, and H. P. Gaston, a horticulturalist at Michigan State, noted that the state's

Lee, Russell. Mexican sugar beet workers, Saginaw Farms, Michigan. Library of Congress, Prints & Photographs Division, FSA/OWI Collection, LC-USF34-063704-D [P&P] LOT 1054.

agricultural industry "markets annually over 500 million dollars' worth of crops, livestock, and livestock products."[24] While much of the work producing small grains, livestock, dairy products, poultry, and eggs was done by the aforementioned small, family farmers, fruit and vegetable farmers often depended on the labor of migrant farmworkers.[25]

In 1954, the Governor's Study Commission on Migratory Labor clarified the extent to which Michigan required out-of-state and foreign agricultural workers. This report, "Migrants in Michigan," stated, "Many areas have crop production patterns with periods of peak labor requirements that cannot be supplied entirely from local sources. The production of these commercial fruits and vegetables is dependent upon seasonal laborers."[26] In 1952, Michigan was the highest producer of sour cherries in the country; second in producing plums, peaches, and blueberries; third in grapes; fourth in sweet cherries and pears; and fifth in commercial apples. The state was also a top producer of cucumbers, canning beets, asparagus, sugar beets, celery, onions, strawberries, carrots, tomatoes, and several other crops. "The care and harvesting of some 30 commercial fruits, vegetables and other crops require the employment of over 100,000 seasonal workers, a majority of whom are from out-of-state," concluded the report.[27] As Michigan also had the fourth highest rate of population growth in the country, members of the commission—who ranged from academics to religious leaders, union representatives, farmers, growers' associations, and medical doctors—predicted that migratory labor would be increasingly crucial to meeting the commercial fruit and vegetable needs of the rising population.[28] Consistent with that expectation, Michigan's peak level of seasonal workers ballooned to 125,000 in 1957, the highest in the country after only Texas and California.[29]

Despite advancements in farm mechanization, the reliance upon migrant farmworkers in Michigan, and the greater Midwest, continued into the 1960s, even as the Bracero Program was officially terminated. In their 1965 report on migratory farm labor in the state, Michigan's Legislative Service Bureau determined that the 1964 seasonal labor force peaked at 98,000, a number consistent with that from the early 1950s. The state continued to rank third nationally in the number of migrant workers the agricultural industry used.[30] In 1968, the Michigan Civil Rights Commission (MCRC) interviewed over 1,100 workers and almost 200 growers as part of their report on the "Status of Migratory Farm Labor in Michigan." The MCRC calculated that farmers employed around 80,000 out-of-state workers, which according to their assessment, made the state the second largest user of migrant farmworkers in the country.[31] Given the importance of migratory laborers to various sectors of the industry, agriculturalists, academics, and government agencies semi-regularly expressed at least nominal concern over the rights and conditions of migrant farmworkers.

Even as early as the 1947 report on Michigan's World War II Emergency Farm Labor Program, analysts predicted that issues surrounding labor would be paramount to the development of the industry, stating, "A new day in farm labor is rapidly approaching." They continued, "The most important factor in the farming of the future is probably the farmers' ability to get along with their help." Possibly grasping to some of the optimism of New Deal legislation from the prior decade, the analysts were confident that worker's compensation, unemployment compensation, and other benefits were "just around the corner."[32] The assurance was that organized labor would be making a more concerted effort to unionize agricultural workers, despite the fact that New Deal labor laws were not extended to farmworkers. As Verónica

Martínez-Matsuda writes, "The National Industrial Recovery Act of 1933, the National Labor Relations Act and Social Security Act of 1935, and the Fair Labor Standards Act of 1938 all failed to guarantee farmworkers the same benefits it did urban industrial workers."[33] By the 1960s, the emergence of the Agricultural Workers Organizing Committee (AWOC) and the National Farm Workers Association (NFWA) in California—and their eventual unification as the United Farm Workers Organizing Committee (UFWOC or just UFW)—was elevating the farmworker justice movement to the national stage.[34]

Still, farmworkers faced an uphill battle in their efforts to organize. Federal labor laws continued to exclude agricultural workers from the collective bargaining rights possessed by workers in most other industries. At the state level, Michigan's lawmakers upheld legislation that explicitly excluded farmworkers from basic labor protections. The state's Minimum Wage Law of 1964, an act that intended to "fix minimum wages for employees within this state" and to "prohibit wage discrimination," continued to rely on the argument that farm work functioned independently of most other forms of wage labor. Michigan's 1964 law declared, "This act does not apply to agricultural fruit growers, pickle growers and tomato growers, or other agricultural employees who traditionally contract for harvesting on a piecework basis."[35] At the same time that the federal and state governments denied migrant farmworkers the protections of the National Labor Relations Act and the State Labor Mediation Act, respectively, farmers and consumers continued to demonstrate their dependency on Mexican, Mexican American, and Puerto Rican farmworkers. While migrants were essential to the operations of growers, their labor also proved increasingly indispensable to the pocketbooks of Americans. In 1947, the average US consumer spent 25.7 percent of their disposable income on food. Two decades later, that average was down to 17.2 percent. As farmers often housed their migrant laborers in converted sheds, decrepit shacks, and farmhouses, and paid workers according to a piecework basis, the Michigan Civil Rights Commission determined that "the poverty of these agricultural workers and their families is living evidence that the low food prices have been gained, partially, at the expense of these workers."[36] These elements—Latinx migratory labor, the rights of farmworkers, and the food industry—are at the core of this book.

While the increased visibility of Latinxs in recent decades has led to their portrayal as a "new" group of migrants to the Midwest, they have had a sustained presence in the region for over a century. For the past one hundred years, Midwestern Latinxs have been laborers, community builders (and sustainers), cultural producers, enterprising business owners, consumers, labor activists, and political organizers, among other roles. The core question guiding *Latinx Encounters* is: How did agricultural workers in the Midwest redefine migrant power, justice, and rights throughout the twentieth century? This book argues that migrants coveted more power and autonomy as agricultural workers, in an industry with notoriously dismal working conditions, toothless government protections, and fierce hostility to organizing efforts. These desires of Latinx farmworkers came into direct conflict with the objectives of state officials, Midwestern agribusiness, and even other Latinx migrants. This pursuit of migrant justice tells a larger story about the twentieth-century history of US immigration, transnational politics, and labor organizing.

Latinx Encounters is set between the tail end of World War I, when sugar beet companies and agricultural employers began recruiting ethnic Mexicans from the Texas-Mexico borderlands, and the late 1980s, when the Farm Labor Organizing Committee (FLOC) secured several collective bargaining contracts. Within this periodization, *Latinx Encounters* shows how Mexicans, Mexican Americans, and Puerto Ricans used postwar migration, temporary guestworker programs, and agricultural labor to forge national and transnational networks throughout the Midwest. The mid-twentieth-century confluence of the US-Mexico Bracero Program, Puerto Rico's Farm Labor Program, and the interstate migration of Mexican Americans within the region generated a tapestry of both conflict and collaboration between these three groups of migrants. There is a vibrant literature, particularly in the Midwest, on the possibilities of panethnic or pan-Latinx coalition building and identity.[37] Whether exploring the conflicts that arose between Mexican American crew leaders (or "Latinx intermediaries" as I term them) and the ethnic Mexican workers that they were supervising or dissecting how Puerto Rican migrants and ethnic Mexicans were alternatively racialized during the 1950 Truman Commission on Migratory Labor, this book challenges the inevitability of pan-Latinx solidarity.

Latinx Encounters tells a new history of the post-World War II farmworker justice movement. Specifically, it questions the center of labor organizing among farmworkers. While names like César Chávez and Dolores Huerta understandably sit at the center of our collective memory as people who challenged the indignities of migrant farmwork, this book tells a different story about the farmworker justice movement. This is a story where ordinary individuals, like Francisco Espinosa and Uvaldo García, used letter writing and engagement with a broader public sphere to challenge agribusiness's exploitative labor conditions and the negligence of government officials.[38]

In addition to scrutinizing the motivations and actions of individual migrant farmworkers, *Latinx Encounters* is also a study that examines the collective organizing efforts of migratory laborers. Although still immensely impactful, the contributions of the better-known United Farm Workers (UFW) are sidelined here. Instead, the history of the Farm Labor Organizing Committee is brought from the periphery to the center of the Midwest's farmworker justice movement. As FLOC's accomplishments in the 1980s transformed the landscape of organized labor and agribusiness in the Midwest, the entire periodization of the postwar farmworker struggle must be rewritten when FLOC is elevated to a position of prominence within this movement.

For far too long, the Midwest as a region has been on the margins of Latinx history. Over the past several years though, historians of the Latinx Midwest have conveyed the value, urgency, and possibilities of underscoring the region. In *Strangers No Longer*, Sergio M. González writes, "For decades, histories of Latino communities have focused disproportionately on California, Texas, and New York, while paying insufficient attention to the development of Latino populations in the Midwest."[39] Traditionally, historians of Latinxs in California and Texas have typically focused on Mexican Americans and Mexicans, while those analyzing communities along the Atlantic Coast have largely concentrated on Puerto Ricans, Cubans, and Dominicans. Yet, as the works of Lilia Fernández, Delia Fernández-Jones, and González demonstrate, the Midwest is perhaps the ideal site for braiding together the histories of migration and settlement of the two largest Latinx groups in the country: Mexicans and Puerto Ricans.[40]

In their description of how the experiences of these groups became intertwined, Mike Amezcua states, "Imperialist and colonialist hegemony over the Americas, along with US capitalism's thirst for unregulated labor, impelled state bureaucrats and influential lobbyists to turn Mexico and Puerto Rico into distribution centers for migratory labor. This created diasporic nodes of workers in Chicago and the greater Midwest."[41] As Chicago and other urban-industrial areas have produced the most visible Latinx communities in the Midwest, it is understandable that these locations have been the primary setting for these histories in the region.[42] *Latinx Encounters* makes the case for why the twentieth-century rural and agricultural Midwest provides a unique lens for analyzing shifting agrarian labor regimes, the development or fracturing of emerging Latinx communities, breakthroughs in American popular culture, and the challenges facing organized labor. By focusing on the migrant workers that fueled a robust and lucrative agricultural industry, this book traces the relationship of the Midwest to the Texas-Mexico borderlands, to Mexico's interior, and to the colonial archipelago of Puerto Rico. While this is a story of the Midwest, it is a vast one that spans multiple borderlands.

Book Structure

To best explore the different groups of Latinxs, the intersecting labor recruitment programs, and the diverse ways that migrant farmworkers articulated their vision of justice, the five chapters here follow a chronological structure; they sometimes overlap but are primarily organized around a series of interrelated topics. Chapter 1 charts the migration of ethnic Mexican agricultural workers to the Midwest in the years following the United States's entrance into World War I, the formalization of an interstate labor recruitment infrastructure, and the role of ethnic intermediaries. This chapter introduces the term "Latinx intermediary," which is used to describe the Mexican American truckers and crew leaders who most directly upheld the Midwest's agricultural industry. Latinx intermediaries straddled the line between serving the interests of growers, other ethnic Mexican migrant workers, and themselves. While some intermediaries developed profitable business operations, their success often came at the expense of other Latinx migrant agricultural workers. This chapter ends in 1949, seven years after the start of the Bracero Program and on the eve of Puerto Rico's Farm Labor Program. This periodization provides an opportunity to chart the emergence of Latinx intermediaries and to examine how Mexican Americans navigated the arrival of Mexican braceros.

Chapter 2 is an episodic one that focuses on the introduction of Puerto Rican migrant farmworkers to Michigan's fields. In 1950, Michigan growers recruited 5,300 Puerto Rican migrants, which was touted as one of the largest civilian airlifts ever.[43] A few months later, President Harry S. Truman's Commission on Migratory Labor held hearings in Saginaw, Michigan. This chapter argues that the Truman Commission hearings became a forum for debating the racialization of Mexican, Mexican American, and Puerto Rican migrants. In *Making the Latino South*, Cecilia Márquez writes, "By tracing the shifting racial categorizations of Latino people from the 1940s to the present, we can see how race and racism are formed and reformed under demographic, cultural, social, and economic pressures."[44] This chapter pinpoints the moment that these three groups of Latinxs converged with one another and demonstrates how migrant work became racialized. While the concept of migrant work is assumed to be noncitizen labor, this chapter illustrates how agribusiness drew from networks of Latinxs who were US citizens—a fact that pushes us to interrogate constructions of foreignness and citizenship.

Chapter 3 conceptualizes a framework for understanding how Latinx migrant farmworkers confronted uneven power dynamics within the Midwest's agricultural industry, even without collective bargaining protections. This chapter examines how farmworkers organized themselves and advocated for labor rights independently of well-known labor leaders. I use the term "migrant public sphere" to describe the process by which Latinx migrants sustained a transnational circulation of information through their travels, correspondence, and the print press during the 1950s and 1960s—the height of the Bracero Program and Farm Labor Program. While the US, Mexican, and Puerto Rican governments often neglected worker grievances or misled the public about agricultural labor conditions, migrants utilized their personal experiences and historical memory to act as a counterbalance to official state narratives.

Returning to the vignette that began the introduction, Chapter 4 maps the trajectory of the band Question Mark and the Mysterians and their hit song "96 Tears." As migrant workers and their families followed the seasonal harvest route, some ended up exiting it and settling permanently. While some migrant farmworkers inevitably identified Detroit as a place where they could find well-paid industrial labor, others chose places like Saginaw and Bay City. The early members of the band were Mexican American teenagers, who were the children of migrant farmworkers that eventually settled in Michigan's Tri-Cities (Saginaw-Midland-Bay City). I demonstrate that the Mysterians' *Billboard* Hot 100 #1 record was the result of the intersections between Texas's Mexican American music industry, agricultural labor, and the post-World War II migration of Latinxs to the Midwest. By historicizing the first "punk rock" band, this chapter emphasizes the interstate cultural infrastructure that was created and demonstrates the cultural significance of a band that was the result of migratory farmwork.

The final chapter of *Latinx Encounters* is on the history of the Farm Labor Organizing Committee. In 1967, one year after AWOC and the NFWA merged into the UFW, Baldemar Velásquez and a small cadre of midwestern migrant farmworkers formed FLOC. Throughout the 1970s and 1980s, FLOC successfully challenged some of the United States's most powerful food corporations—Campbell Soup Company and Heinz. FLOC's accomplishments in the 1980s transformed the landscape of organized labor and agribusiness in the Midwest. By the late 1970s, the UFW was in a state of decline—a current that would only continue in the 1980s as the union was weakened by internal disagreements, the loss of leadership, and the depletion of union contracts. However, it was precisely during that period that FLOC began to establish a foothold in the Midwest and secure the first three-way collective bargaining agreements between the farmworker organization, local growers, and corporate food processors.

Ultimately, this book bridges the fields of Latinx, labor, migration, and agricultural history. It shows how Mexican, Mexican American, and Puerto Rican migrant workers shaped the labor regimes, culture, and politics of the twentieth-century US Midwest. Given the multiple groups of people, the broad geographic scale, and the thematic range, there are inevitably aspects of these histories that will not make it into the book. Nevertheless, it is my sincere hope that *Latinx Encounters* energizes further attention to the Latinx Midwest, particularly its agricultural areas.

CHAPTER ONE

Harvesting Power

Latinx Intermediaries and Midwest Migratory Labor, 1917–1949

During the spring of 1947, labor agents and truckers in Texas were preparing for their annual operation of contracting, transporting, and facilitating the migration of ethnic Mexicans to work in the Midwest's sugar beet fields. For the past three decades, the approach of the harvest season meant that San Antonio's *La Prensa* newspaper would be filled with daily advertisements for labor agencies and sugar processing companies. But on April 1, 1947, *La Prensa* took a much different course of action. In the plainly titled article "Important Notice to Beet Workers," *La Prensa* reported on concerning information they were receiving from *La Unión Cívica Mexicana* (Mexican Civic Union) in Saginaw, Michigan. By detailing how migrant workers are recruited for Midwestern sugar beet labor, this article describes a process whereby the sugar companies set up employment offices across the state of Texas, but the foundations of the operation are truckers and other intermediary figures. As described in the article, the *troqueros* (truckers) hire labor recruiters who then hire the crews of migrant workers, "often irresponsibly, since they [truckers and recruiters] resort to all sorts of deceitful means to take people to the beet fields, since they earn a commission for each individual they transport."[1] Given how these Mexican American crew leaders and truckers were interstitially situated between ethnic Mexican migrant workers and the growers or sugar processing companies who relied on their labor, I am terming these figures "Latinx intermediaries."

By occupying a variety of roles, such as labor contractor or recruiter, trucker, and crew leader, Latinx intermediaries were central to the maintenance and expansion of the agricultural labor system in the years and decades following the Great Depression. Although numerous scholars have emphasized the role of labor contractors or "emigrant agents" on the migratory stream of ethnic Mexicans that flowed outward from South Texas to the Midwest, and all other parts of the United States for that matter, historians have been less successful in developing a nuanced understanding of the truckers and crew leaders who were most directly responsible for managing the agricultural labor system and mediating the relationship between the migrant workers and Michigan's growers and sugar companies.[2] Often times, after the migrant workers arrived in the Midwest, the *troqueros* would then assume the role of crew leader, field instructor, or translator. This was similar to Cindy Hahamovitch's characterization of immigrant *padrones* as "ambiguous and dynamic" individuals that "might play the role of taskmaster, shop steward, or indifferent mediator, depending on his interests of the moment."[3] Because these individuals functioned as the central cog of the Midwestern agricultural industry, some intermediaries achieved a significant amount of power that they then leveraged into profitable business operations.[4] Although not always the case, the Latinx intermediaries' use of their influence for personal gain was frequently predicated on the exploitation of Tejano and Mexican migrant farmworkers. Thus, the role of these figures underscores the need for a better understanding of the emerging ethnic and class conflicts that were developing within migrant agricultural labor groups.

Throughout this chapter, I refer to the truckers and crew leaders as "Latinx intermediaries," even though most of the cases involved Tejano crew leaders managing other Tejano fieldworkers. In addition to these episodes though, there are instances where I focus on the relationship between Tejano crew leaders that supervised Mexican braceros. The *Bracero History Archive* is replete with further examples of former braceros who described their experiences working for Mexican American foreman or crew leaders, as well as oral histories with Mexican Americans that managed crews of braceros. Absent from this chapter, but present in the *Bracero History Archive*, are examples of braceros who were originally fieldworkers, but eventually became the crew leaders of other braceros.[5] Although outside the periodization of this chapter, there are cases of ethnic Mexican intermediaries that oversaw Puerto Rican migrants in Michigan during the 1950s and 1960s.[6] Thus, the main reason for using "Latinx intermediary" is that the applicability of this term will be more generative than the more specific, but possibly limiting, "Tejano intermediary." Using "Tejano intermediary" conceals the full breadth of ethnicity- and labor-based power dynamics that were developing in the Midwest's agricultural industry during this period.

The introduction of the term "Latinx intermediary" expands upon and contributes to the broader literature on the intersections of ethnicity, migration, and labor. Foundational works on the history of Latinxs in the

Midwest, particularly Dionicio N. Valdés's *Al Norte* and Zaragosa Vargas's *Proletarians of the North*, have highlighted how, during World War I, recruiters (*enganchistas*) facilitated the often-informal contracting of ethnic Mexicans from the Texas-Mexico border to Michigan's sugar beet fields with promises of higher wages and better working conditions. Although Vargas is primarily concerned with the settlement and industrial labor of Mexicans in Detroit, he is mindful of the impact that recruiters, agricultural labor, and seasonal migration had on the eventual settlement of Mexicans in the urban Midwest.[7] In *Al Norte*, Valdés comes the closest to conceptualizing these Latinx intermediaries, stating, "The *troquero* system removed growers and companies from direct involvement with fieldworkers and it redirected worker conflict from the real employers, the companies and growers, to the hired *troqueros*. Worker complaints went through the *troquero*, who tried to resolve them." Furthermore, Valdés characterizes many of the *troqueros* as "honest, capable, and dedicated," but acknowledges that they had a tendency to take advantage of the other migrant workers.[8] Even then, the vital role of these individuals in sustaining the everyday operations of the Midwestern agricultural industry is undersold as Valdés is mainly assessing these figures in relation to the concerns that social reformers had about "the migrant problem."[9]

In addition to Midwest Latinx history, examining these intermediaries amplifies the findings of other scholars that have emphasized the importance of migrant brokers who aided co-ethnics and the employers of various industries (agricultural, railroad, auto, and meatpacking) alike in navigating the social and economic contours of labor mobility. A comparable and useful framework for understanding the importance of Latinx intermediaries is provided by the immigrant *padrones* who guided co-ethnics to specific industries and employers during the late nineteenth and early twentieth centuries. Historians Cindy Hahamovitch and Gunther Peck provide instructive studies of ethnic intermediaries that created profitable business operations by recruiting workers to various industries, financing their travels, and supervising various aspects of the migratory labor experience (including, but not limited to, living accommodations, provisions, and the actual work). Yet, there are important distinctions between the Latinx intermediaries here and the *padrones* described in those works.[10]

First, by the turn of the twentieth century and during the first two decades of it, Hahamovitch and Peck are generally describing a gradual erosion in the influence of immigrant *padrones*. This was due to the efforts of the migrant workers themselves, the sharp reduction of European immigration, the interventions of government agencies and reformers, and the onset of the Great Depression. Hahamovitch notes that "US Congress had impoverished the profits of international and metropolitan labor contractors," and Peck concludes that "A brief examination of the whereabouts of [Roman] Gonzalez, [Antonio] Cordasco, and [Leon] Skliris in 1930 confirms the view that padrones had indeed vanished."[11] Contrary to this, it was during the 1910s–1920s that we witness the formal emergence of ethnic Mexican labor recruiters, and it would be in the subsequent decades that the role of Latinx intermediaries in managing the migratory labor force would expand exponentially. Second, the mobility of Tejanos and Mexicans shifted the role and responsibilities of Latinx intermediaries from those of earlier European immigrant *padrones*. This is something Peck recognizes, stating, "Mexican sojourners consequently succeeded better than Greeks or Italians in maintaining control over their mobility and in offsetting some of the more coercive aspects of padrone authority and corporate power in the West."[12] Time and again, ethnic Mexican migrant farmworkers demonstrated their resolve to abandon contracts at sites where they deemed the work conditions to be inadequate or abusive, a feature that would become even more common with the greater availability of cars and trucks in the 1930s.[13] Thus, contending with the mobility of ethnic Mexican workers served as an additional arena of conflict that Latinx intermediaries were forced to grapple with.

By exploring the conflicts that arose between Tejano crew leaders and the ethnic Mexicans that they were supervising (both other Tejanos and braceros), this chapter challenges any inevitability of a pan-Latinx identity or comradery. In *Grounds for Dreaming*, Lori A. Flores triangulates the histories of three groups of co-ethnics—Mexican Americans, braceros, and undocumented migrants—in California's Salinas Valley. By assessing the tensions between these groups, Flores argues, "It rubs against the common story of Latino community formation and solidarity to explain why, in an agricultural economy and context, some Latino communities did *not* get formed or took [a] much longer time to evolve compared with urban centers."[14] Just as growers possessed the ability to exploit Latinx migrant farmworkers, so did the Latinx intermediaries that served as crew leaders in the fields. While the field of Latinx studies has provided important works on Latinx panethnic identity, a focus on Latinx intermediaries highlights some of the complications and challenges to achieving this.[15] When considering the intersections of migration, ethnicity, and labor in the United States, scholars must continue to account for the enduring role of intermediaries who use their liminal position to broker these connections. In the case of the

Latinx intermediaries who rose to prominence following the United States's entry into World War I, a combination of national and regional developments shaped the conditions under which they operated.

National and Regional Transformations in Labor and Immigration: World War I through the Bracero Program

Upon the United States's formal entrance into World War I, growers across the Southwest sought increasing amounts of Mexican farmworkers, while growers in the Midwest turned to this same labor source to meet their demands for sugar beets and other agricultural goods. In South Texas, John Weber notes that farmers of the area reaped the rewards of this wartime prosperity in ways that were unimaginable in the years leading up to World War I. Contributing to the fortunes of the South Texas farmers was the continuous influx of Mexican immigrants. As Weber explains, "this wartime economic boom did not extend to Mexico, which continued to suffer under severe economic conditions brought by the continued instability of the [Mexican] Revolution, so the waves of immigration did not slow down."[16] In terms of the Michigan side of this equation, lacking any sizable Mexican population before World War I, historians identify 1918 as the first year that Midwestern sugar beet companies would formally recruit ethnic Mexican labor. Linking Michigan's sugar companies' pursuit of Mexican labor to the desire of Texas's industries to preserve their reservoir of Mexican labor, Zaragosa Vargas states, "Recruitment by northern employers helped break the virtual quarter-century monopoly on Mexican labor held by Southwest farmers, railroads, and mining companies."[17] With the end of World War I, the United States descended into an economic depression between 1920 and 1921 that disrupted the Midwest's developing transformation from a European to a Mexican farmworking population. Yet, following this brief downturn, growers in Michigan would once again turn toward ethnic Mexican labor to sustain the agricultural industry.

European workers returned to Michigan's sugar beet fields during the postwar depression, but by the late 1920s ethnic Mexican migrants had largely supplanted European immigrant families as the main source of labor in Michigan's sugar beet growing regions.[18] Kathleen Mapes notes, "As early as 1922, Michigan's sugar beet companies [once again] began recruiting Mexican workers, and by 1927 Mexicans and Mexican Americans would make up 75 percent of that force."[19] This transformation where Michigan's agricultural industry went from reviving its interest in ethnic

Mexican workers to solidifying them as the prevailing source of farm labor in the region was, at least partially, shaped by the monumental 1924 Johnson-Reed Act. As Mae Ngai and other immigration historians have shown, the Johnson-Reed Act placed a numerical restriction on annual immigration through national quotas. This system severely limited the more recent, but "undesirable," immigration of individuals from Southern and Eastern European countries. Furthermore, because of the provision that excluded individuals who were racially ineligible for US citizenship, it was nearly impossible for immigrants from Asia and Africa to attain legal entry into the country. Significantly, restrictive quotas were not placed on the countries of the Western Hemisphere, which included Mexico.[20] By curtailing immigration from Eastern and Southern European countries, which made up a large segment of Michigan's pre-World War I farm labor, and by exempting Mexico from these restrictions, the Johnson-Reed Act cemented the understanding that ethnic Mexicans were the ideal source of farm labor for the Midwest's agricultural industry.[21]

Five years after the passing of the Johnson-Reed Act, the United States entered the Great Depression. Characterized by the 1929 stock market crash, the Dust Bowl, record levels of unemployment, and devastating poverty, there were tumultuous consequences of the Great Depression—one of which was the deportation and repatriation of Mexicans and Mexican Americans. As Francisco E. Balderrama and Raymond Rodríguez thoroughly account in *Decade of Betrayal*, "Americans, reeling from the economic disorientation of the depression, sought a convenient scapegoat. They found it in the Mexican community."[22] In the years leading up to the Depression, Mexicans were deemed necessary for the labor they provided to the agricultural industry. But as fears of them becoming a "public charge" grew and as their presence was interpreted as a contributing factor to the unemployment of "actual" Americans, coordinated efforts by local, state, and national governments, as well as the Mexican government, resulted in the repatriation of between 400,000 and 2 million ethnic Mexicans, many of whom were US citizens.[23] With the decimation of ethnic Mexican communities across the United States during the early 1930s, particularly those in major cities, it would be years before any semblance of a restoration developed.

Despite the deportation and repatriation campaigns that occurred throughout the Midwest and the rest of the country during the Great Depression, the onset of Franklin Delano Roosevelt's New Deal offered some limited hope of broader inclusion for ethnic Mexicans in the United States.[24] If the New Deal era provided some optimism that the federal government would recognize and offer protections to agricultural workers, its implementation was uneven at best. During a half decade of powerful labor legislation—which included the National Industrial Recovery Act, National Labor Relations Act, Social Security Act, and the Fair Labor Standards Act—Congress purposefully excluded farmworkers and failed to deliver them the same benefits afforded to industrial workers. Even in the face of these efforts to deny farmworkers the right to organize and strike, nascent agricultural unionizing was already underway. Michigan's first union of sugar beet workers surfaced in 1935, amid the New Deal labor legislation.[25]

In Blissfield, Michigan, a multiethnic cast of 700 sugar beet workers organized and joined the American Federation of Labor's (AFL) Agricultural Workers Union (AWU) Local 19994.[26] This eclectic group was comprised of around 400 men and 300 women, included Hungarians, Bohemians, Romanians, Germans from Russia, Mexicans, and Mexican Americans. While the US Department of Labor (USDL) disputed the strength of the union, the diverse group of beet workers assembled a clear-cut list of demands, including: a flat rate of $23 per acre, having staggered plantings so that the beets did not need picking all at once, equal distribution of acreage among workers, and a closed-field clause (which stated that only union members could work in the fields and that the grower could not bring in outside labor if it was available locally). In short, the Blissfield beet workers wanted a fair wage and allocation of acreage, as well as a harnessing of the growers' abilities to recruit migratory labor. Local 19994's list of demands was presented to the Blissfield Beet Growers Association (BBGA), a growers' organization that was created to challenge the overwhelming power of the sugar manufacturing companies they supplied their beets to. Following pleas from Local 19994's president, Fred Schmidt, USDL secretary Frances Perkins sent J. E. O'Conner to mediate this standoff. While the union did not obtain all their demands, they did force the growers to make important concessions. The "Blissfield agreement," as it would be known, between the area's growers and the resident beet workers, secured the workers a standard wage increase to $19 per acre, acreage allotments per worker nearly double the prior year's, union recognition, and the closed-field clause. Despite the promise of the 1935 agreement for the Blissfield workers and other aspiring agricultural unions, the following years' organizing efforts would be filled with obstacles.[27]

In 1938, the consolidated actions of Michigan's sugar companies fundamentally changed the landscape of labor recruitment and power relations in the agricultural industry. When it came time to negotiate a contract for the 1938 harvest season, Local 19994 encountered their strongest opposition yet. Rather than having to bargain directly with the BBGA, as they did a few years prior, negotiations took place with the recently established Great Lakes Growers' Employment Corporation (a combination of the Great Lakes Sugar Company and the Lake Shore Sugar Company). This autonomous "corporation" was responsible for reorganizing methods of migratory labor recruitment and the setting of wages. As Mapes states, "Though this employment corporation was little more than a piece of paper . . . legally it moved the question of labor relations from a three-way relationship between the sugar manufacturers, the growers, and the workers, to a two-way relationship between the labor corporation and the workers."[28] In 1935 and 1936, when Local 19994 was clashing with the growers, the BBGA was managing their own agitation with the sugar processing companies and the factory-dominated Farmers and Manufacturers Beet Sugar Association (F&M). Thus, from the farmworkers' perspective, there was some hope that workers and growers could mobilize against the sugar processing companies. Ultimately, the fealty of growers to the sugar companies in the form of a united labor corporation allowed them to collectively leverage their power against the beet workers' union. In 1935 the farmworkers negotiated with the growers who were in separate negotiations with sugar manufacturers. By 1938, the growers and companies effectively united their interests against those of the workers.[29]

Intensifying the impact of the formation of the Great Lakes Growers' Employment Corporation was the creation of the Beet Growers' Employment Committee (BGEC) that same year. The BGEC was comprised of the beet growers' associations who delivered to the Michigan Sugar Company. An officer of the BGEC was in residence nearby all six of the Michigan Sugar Company's plants, with the responsibility of maintaining communication with the smaller farmers about their labor needs.[30] Taken together, 1938 marked a significant restructuring of Michigan's agricultural industry. Highlighting the importance of this development, Valdés states that even though Michigan's sugar beet growers and processing companies brought in a small number of ethnic Mexican workers from Texas in 1936 and 1937, the real transformation would occur in 1938. He writes, "During the nadir of the depression, there was little outside recruitment of beet field workers into the Midwest. . . . In 1938, the corporations, claiming a shortage of workers, used their newly formed committees to initiate massive recruitment of Tejano (Texas-born) *betabeleros* to Michigan and Ohio."[31] The creation of growers' employment corporations reduced the liability of the sugar processing companies and modernized the methods of recruiting migrant laborers. With growers' organizations and sugar processing companies working in unison, the mechanisms for recruiting and managing migratory seasonal labor became increasingly efficient. The resurfacing in the late 1930s of the relationship between ethnic Mexicans, the migratory labor apparatus, and Michigan's agricultural industry became even more complex with the beginning of the Bracero Program.

On August 4, 1942, the United States and Mexico entered what would be known as the Bracero Program. Lasting until 1964, 4.6 million Mexican workers would come to the United States throughout the duration of the program.[32] Following several amendments and extensions, the wartime phase of the program effectively ended in 1947. During this first phase of the Bracero Program, the Mexican government would not provide legal contracts for their nationals to find employment in Texas, but that did not stop Texas's growers from employing unauthorized Mexican migrants. Despite the "blacklisting" of Texas from Bracero Program contracts, by 1949, Texas had 46 percent of all the Mexican nationals under contract.[33] Assessing how this process shaped the migration of Tejanos out of the state, Weber states, "While Mexican braceros poured into South Texas during the peak years of the international agreement, Mexican Americans poured out. An increase in out-of-state migration occurred during World War II as many Mexican Americans left Texas for employment in the booming war industries and the fields of the Midwest and West. Rather than decreases after the war, however, the number of out-of-state migrants who registered with the state jumped from 22,460 in 1945 to 39,801 in 1947 and 71,353 in 1949, not to mention the unknown number who left without registering."[34] As the number of bracero contracts ballooned during the mid-twentieth century, increasing amounts of Mexican Americans in Texas sought out farm labor in Midwestern fields. With the arrival of braceros, growers and agricultural companies required Latinx intermediaries that could help manage the migration of these two groups of ethnic Mexicans. Therefore, the growth of the Bracero Program, as well as the accompanying rise in undocumented migration, encouraged tens of thousands of Mexican Americans in Texas to find agricultural work elsewhere, which fueled the out-of-state migration. One of the deepest ironies here is that while architects of the Bracero Program envisioned an efficient and orderly system for supplying workers to growers in need, the migratory labor apparatus became inadvertently more reliant on intermediaries who were sometimes capable of acting in all sorts of unpredictable ways.

From Texas to Michigan: Labor Contractors and Interstate Migration

Throughout the 1930s and 1940s, Frank Cortez operated a variety of businesses out of 508 El Paso Street in San Antonio, Texas. Throughout most of the year, the main commercial operation at that location was "*La Guadalupana*," a full-service funeral parlor. With advertisements for *La Guadalupana* regularly appearing in San Antonio's *La Prensa*, then one of the most widely circulated Spanish-language newspapers in the United States, thirty-five dollars covered the cost of the coffin, grave, carriage, chapel, and a cross. Aside from offering these funeral services, Cortez also operated an ambulance and served as a notary public.[35] Toward the end of the 1930s, Cortez began an additional venture out of 508 El Paso Street: a labor contracting agency. Carey McWilliams interviewed Cortez in October 1940 for his study, *Ill Fares the Land*. Describing the scene that developed around March of each year outside of *La Guadalupana*, McWilliams writes, "Once recruiting starts on El Paso Street, Mr. Cortez is a busy man. Workers begin to arrive from all over Texas. The flow of traffic around the funeral parlor is so heavy that special police traffic squads have to be called to maintain some degree of order in the neighborhood. At four o'clock in the morning, the line begins to form outside the office."[36] On February 6, 1940, the Cortez Employment Agency entered into a contractual agreement with the Beet Growers Employment Committee in Saginaw, Michigan.[37]

According to the agreement signed between Cortez and the BGEC, Cortez was authorized to find and contract sugar beet workers in Texas for employment in Michigan and he would receive a dollar per worker successfully contracted for work in Michigan. Furthermore, Cortez was to supply the workers to the BGEC exclusively. When the harvest season was approaching, the recruitment of prospective beet workers could occur in several ways: the labor contractor might pass it down the grapevine, work crews might be personally invited back if they had previously worked for a particular grower, and advertisements would also be made on the radio and in newspapers, like *La Prensa*. Once the prospective workers arrived at the labor contracting office, they would be asked a series of questions regarding their prior experience working with sugar beets and the size of their work crew or family. For the potential migrant workers who passed through this screening process, the final step before receiving a contract was the medical exam.[38]

The physical exam, which included testing for sexually transmitted infections and a fluoroscopic exam for tuberculosis, determined whether migrant workers and families would be able to receive a formal labor contract from Michigan growers' organizations, such as the BGEC. An indicator of the extensive Tejano migratory presence in Michigan during the sugar beet season is that the Michigan State Department of Health was actually responsible for conducting these exams in Texas. This clinic operated for about two weeks along El Paso Street, the same street where Cortez operated his funeral parlor and labor contracting agency. Because of a Michigan law requiring that hospitals provide care for all persons with tuberculosis, at the expense of the state, the physical exams conducted by Michigan's Department of Health functioned to prevent the entrance of workers with these infections. In short, the Department of Health deemed it more cost effective to screen all potential workers in San Antonio than it was to treat any cases that might emerge in Michigan. As M. C. Gonzales, the lawyer for San Antonio's Mexican Consul, aptly put it, "the State of Michigan decided it was a lot cheaper to send a doctor down to Texas and pay him quarter apiece to examine them."[39] The expense that Gonzales is referring to is the cost of the physical, which actually cost fifty cents, but was split between the Michigan Department of Health and the BGEC. However, the BGEC would deduct the cost of the exam from the workers' paychecks, thus absolving themselves of any cost. Once the physical exam was passed, the migrant workers would prepare for the over-1,400-mile trek north to Michigan.[40]

Max Henderson, executive secretary of the Michigan Field Crops, Inc. (MFCI), during his statement to the Harry S. Truman Commission on Migratory Labor, offered insight into how the MFCI and other agricultural employers or organizations utilized Latinx intermediaries. Often, these Tejanos functioned as remote liaisons for specific growers, growers' organizations, and sugar processing companies. The role of crew supervisor required the Latinx intermediaries to be attentive and observant of the migrant labor groups in the fields. As Max Henderson explains, "[Texas Mexicans] are the folks who keep the pulse on the labor end of it. If there are complaints, the Mexican goes to another Mexican more quickly than he goes to anyone else. They are on our payroll and they keep us posted."[41] The position of the crew leader was slightly different depending on whether an individual grower or a larger growers' organization employed them. For many crew supervisors, their pay was separate from that of the migrants who were working under them. Whereas growers typically compensated fieldworkers on a piecework basis, employers typically paid Latinx intermediaries a fixed wage for managing the crew. In other instances, if these intermediaries were not receiving a wage for overseeing a crew, they negotiated for the grower to hire them for a less demanding position, such as being responsible for delivering the picked produce to stores in the area. For the Tejano crew leaders working for a single grower, their primary role was to supervise the workers they contracted in Texas. If working for a growers' organization with a more expansive operation, Latinx intermediaries fulfilled a different type of managerial role. For example, as an employee of the MFCI, crew leaders could supervise an entire sugar beet district or area, which might include several different Latinx work crews in the fields. These Latinxs reported to a manager of a specific sugar company and were responsible for responding to any labor issues that arose among Latinx migrant workers in the area.[42]

Depending on their employer, the range of responsibilities for a crew leader could be enormous. If employed by a larger organization, intermediaries might also assist in coordinating the transferal of workers from one crop area to another (i.e., sugar beets to cucumbers or cherries) once the harvest season for a specific crop was over. Henderson explained a process where employers send their crew leaders into the fields near the end of a crop's harvesting period to interview and make contractual agreements with the migrant workers so that they can be rehired or recontracted for the next employing crop.[43] And in some cases, Tejano crew leaders also turned into crop-picking instructors. In short, from the recruitment of migrant workers to their transportation, to their supervisory roles, Latinx intermediaries were integral to the operation and growth of Michigan's agricultural industry.[44]

The influence of Latinx intermediaries on Michigan agriculture extended far beyond the realm of labor—these individuals also proved to be pivotal in shaping access to social services and migrant cultural life. This was made evident when "Mrs. Carl Gladstone," chairman of the Marshall Migrant Committee (MMC), stated, "Company Field Man [William Lopez] is member of the Migrant Committee and very helpful in planning for welfare of migrant people. We are very proud of the work done each summer among our migrants and can see a changed attitude toward them by the community in general."[45] As local reformers were often concerned with a range of aspects related to the "migrant problem," the MMC was a religious-based organization that provided a vast array of summer programming, including health exams, church services, and recreational activities. Their programming even included bringing in Saul Contreras from Los Angeles's Spanish-American Baptist Seminary to coordinate the afternoon school for the "older children" at the labor camp. Their curriculum consisted of health, handicraft, art, spelling, math, geography, English, and reading. At some point of the

Lee, Russell. Mexican labor contractor and inspectors in the fields, La Pryor, Texas. Library of Congress, Prints & Photographs Division, FSA/OWI Collection, LC-USF33- 012049-M4 [P&P] LOT 602.

harvest season, William Lopez, the crew leader, even sent a letter to the Migrant Committee that included a $55 donation raised by the migrant workers. Although it was not common for crew leaders to be this invested in local organizations and services, Latinx intermediaries managed a range of relationships and acted as influential liaisons between migrant workers, growers, social service organizations, and local communities. It was precisely this type of influence that Latinx intermediaries wielded, which allowed them to transform their liminal position into a profitable business operation.[46]

The Business of Migration

Following Max Henderson's statement to the Truman Commission on Migratory Labor, William Leiserson asked him a series of follow-up questions. Leiserson was an influential US labor figure who had served on the National Mediation Board (NMB) and the National Labor Relations Board (NLRB).[47] As Leiserson's time on the NMB largely concentrated on the railroad industry, they fittingly asked Henderson whether recruited migratory workers arrived in Michigan via railroad, bus, truck, or jalopy. Henderson explained that while a greater volume of migrants used to come by train or bus, the more recent trend was for the labor to arrive in personal vehicles or in the trucks of labor contractors. According to Henderson, there were groups of Tejanos who used the booming World War II economy to create and expand their crew leader operations. Describing the process by which a class of Tejanos utilized the flourishing economy, Henderson states, "during the war years when wages were up and they were in great demand there was quite a lot of racketeering that went on between themselves, and some were able to accumulate quite a lot of money, and the first thing a Texas Mexican does in this area when he gets sufficient money is to buy a truck. . . . [They] now have bought themselves something and are in business in a little different way."[48] The process Henderson described highlights how, in some cases, the improved World War II economy provided new opportunities for burgeoning intermediaries.

While their business was already operational, not to mention sizable, before the United States entered World War II, S. P. Acosta was Texas's most prominent authorized labor recruiter. Usually in mid-April, the Midwestern beet growers' associations informed Acosta of how many workers they would require for the upcoming season. Then, sugar manufacturing companies would provide funds to the growers' associations to pay the Acosta Employment Agency, who was also responsible for handling money advances to the migrant workers. In 1941 alone, Acosta's labor agency recruited 7,600 migrant workers for sugar beet work in Michigan and Ohio. The following year, Acosta directed one of only four licensed agencies in Texas that were legally authorized to recruit workers for employment in other states. As one might imagine, the job of recruiting and transporting thousands of migrant workers to the Midwest and the Mountain states was too tall of an order for a single person to handle. Based out of 812 Buena Vista Street in San Antonio, Acosta employed an army of sub-agents throughout the state. According to the *Valley Morning Star,* the Acosta Employment Agency utilized 108 sub-agents. Although Acosta's lucrative enterprise predated the United States's official involvement in World War II, other aspiring intermediaries had to use the wartime economic boom to break into the industry.[49]

There was a contingent of intermediaries who emerged in the postwar years as upwardly mobile crew leaders and truckers. Most of these Tejanos had previously worked the fields as typical migratory farmers, but, as Henderson described it, they now participated in the agricultural labor industry "in a little different way." For the Latinx intermediaries that were able to make a profit from their business operations, they identified Michigan and the greater Midwest's reliance on migrant agricultural workers from the Texas-Mexico borderlands, then found a way to capitalize off it. During the summer of 1948, the National Council on Agricultural Life and Labor conducted a series of questionnaires throughout Michigan regarding migratory labor. These surveys consisted of questions regarding transportation methods, piecework rate, nationality of workers, living conditions, and resources for migrants. One of these surveys took place at the Calhoun County Pickle Company. Regarding the transportation of workers, the representative stated, "Spanish Speaking Americans (Mexican Percentage) [were] brought from Texas by truck by a foreman of Company who has 'risen from the ranks' of migrants by his own ability."[50] There did indeed exist a handful of Tejano crew leaders and truckers who were able to develop profitable business operations; however, emphasizing the experiences of those individuals would distort the reality of other Latinx intermediaries and of the migrant agricultural industry more broadly.

On some of the rare occasions that the *Detroit Free Press* took notice of migrant farmworkers in the state, they did so to frame Tejano crew leaders as embracers of capitalist attitudes. Often, there was an association between migrant agricultural laborers and "premodern" tendencies. During the Truman Commission's hearings, Harry Markle, executive director of the Michigan Unemployment Compensation Commission, stated that Benton Harbor's housing for migrants possessed all the necessary appliances and amenities they would need. Markle presents this information to argue that the housing for migrant workers became decrepit because of the migrants' "lack of education" and a tendency to "destroy property."[51] This was a general perception that some Latinx migrants were acutely aware of. In 1948, the *Detroit Free Press* published an article providing a range of opinions that migrant workers held about agricultural labor in Saginaw, which concluded with a Señora Garcia showing a picture of a Mexican pulling a donkey and then commenting, "See. That's what I mean. We are always shown like that—bad clothes—barefooted."[52] In contrast to this portrayal, journalists frequently presented Latinx intermediaries as the antithesis of this "typical" migrant worker. That same article began by narrating the experiences of Emilio Zamora, a Tejano crew leader who is described as "a capitalist among his people. He owns a stake truck and transports other migrants from Texas to Michigan. He is the captain of his crew. His commands are law."[53] Tejano crew leaders were often referred to in ways that symbolized authority and power.[54] Far from destroying or lacking appreciation for property, the occupation of crew leader depended on possessing and maintaining property. Thus, this portrait of Latinx intermediaries was, at least in some part, due to their capitalist ambitions to possess property and create their own businesses.[55]

However, journalistic and government agency portrayals of Latinx intermediaries were not singularly complimentary. At times, the financial self-interest of intermediaries also resulted in their representation as exploitative, careless, and greedy figures. This tendency was visible at various House of Representatives committee investigations during the early 1940s. At the 1940 Oklahoma City hearings for the Select Committee to Investigate the Interstate Migration of Destitute Citizens, Robert M. McKinley, Farm Placement Supervisor for the Texas State Employment Service, was critical of crammed vehicles that labor contractors used to move Mexican American farmworkers to Michigan. McKinley testified, "The truck drivers go in pairs, and there will be two truck drivers in one truck, but those people will be stacked up in the trucks like cattle standing up. 35 to 40 people in one truck, and they drive straight through just as rapidly as they can go." Following this description of conditions that were likened to those used for transporting livestock, McKinley continued by providing an example of the discrepancy in earnings between the intermediaries and the migrant farmworkers. "Very few of them [the migrant workers] come back with any money," stated McKinley. "The truck drivers make plenty of money out of it; one truck driver was reported to Mr. Banks [E. H. Banks, Farm Placement Supervisor] as having made $3,000 for hauling Mexicans to Michigan last year; he charged about $11 a head and he takes 35 or 40 at a trip and makes 3 or 4 trips."[56] As Texas agribusiness and government agencies had long attempted to control the mobility of the state's ethnic Mexican labor, McKinley's motivations for this characterization do require us to approach his statement with a pinch of skepticism.

In 1929, the legislature of Texas took a considerable step toward protecting the state's supply of ethnic Mexican workers: the Emigrant Labor Agency Laws (also commonly referred to as the Emigrant Agent Act). Introduced by state representative Andrew Percy (A. P.) Johnson and with the support of the South Texas Chamber of Commerce, the Winter Garden Chamber of Commerce, and the West Texas Chamber of Commerce, this law unambiguously sought to limit the ability of labor agents to recruit individuals for out-of-state work. These various attempts to extinguish the presence of labor recruiters—including the implementation of a state license tax, a county license tax, and the posting of a bond to guarantee the return transportation of contracted workers back to Texas—constituted what David Montejano called a "web of labor controls."[57] House Bill No. 207, which was introduced by Johnson to "define and license emigrant agents," levied a $5,000 annual license tax for labor agent, a $2,500 tax for use of that license in the county, and a $5,000 return bond. H. B. 207 was approved on May 17, 1929, but within one week, attorneys for Michigan Sugar Co. intervened.[58]

In order to halt their ability to enforce this law, Michigan Sugar Co. filed for a temporary injunction against Texas governor Dan Moody, the state's attorney general, commissioner of labor, and the district attorneys of Dallas and Bexar County. The sugar refining company argued that the Emigrant Agent Act was unconstitutional on the grounds that it taxed interstate commerce. By June 1, the Federal District Court granted Michigan Sugar Co. their temporary injunction, but the Texas Legislature responded within ten days by amending and passing a new bill that abandoned the $7,500 in occupation taxes and replaced it with a reduced range of fees. This included a $1,000 occupation tax, a county tax of $100–$300 depending on the county, a $150 employment agency license, and a $10 license fee.[59] While these fees would have certainly proven to be prohibitive for many prospective labor contractors, one of the most contentious components of the bill was the $5,000 return bond. Labor agents were required to post this bond before they started operating as an "agent," which was intended to guarantee that all migrant workers who left the state would be provided with or arranged to have transportation back to Texas.[60] As a result of the Michigan Sugar Co.'s lawsuit against Governor Moody, the Federal District Court for the Northern District of Texas made a ruling on the two primary points of contention: the $5,000 return bond and the occupation taxes. The judges ruled the $5,000 return bond to be unconstitutional, but as to the amended occupation taxes ($1,000 for state and $100–$300 for county), "the court held that they were not an illegal and oppressive exercise of sovereign power of the State of Texas."[61] As this fierce struggle between the State of Texas and the Michigan Sugar Co. demonstrates, controlling the mobility of ethnic Mexican labor was a fraught struggle for several different parties.

With this longer struggle over ethnic Mexican mobility in mind, McKinley's comments at the hearings on the Interstate Migration of Destitute Citizens were shaped by his irritation with the Latinx intermediaries that were selectively "taking" Texas's labor supply. The Farm Placement Service, for which McKinley was a supervisor, was responsible for ensuring that the state's farmers had sufficient workers, primarily by coordinating a pool of agricultural workers that could be dispersed according to growers' needs.[62] It is from this position that McKinley disdainfully stated, "Well, those people [prospective migratory workers] are gathered together and examined, and they [labor contractors] leave us the weak, sickly ones; they cull them out and take the best labor all to Michigan."[63] While clearly frustrated that labor intermediaries and Midwestern agribusiness were successfully enticing workers to leave the state, McKinley was not alone in characterizing Latinx intermediaries as exploitative and greedy.

A month before the Oklahoma City hearings, Vincent Neira testified before the same committee in Chicago. Neira, a twenty-six-year-old migrant from San Antonio, was contracted for beet work by none other than Frank Cortez of the Cortez Employment Agency. Neira described a trip north that lasted around forty hours, with no stops aside from a quick meal. The drivers shuttled Neira and a group of twenty-five to thirty other migrant workers in a stake-body truck covered by a tarp. When asked by the committee about the conditions of the ride, Neira responded, "We was very uncomfortable, because, you see, it was loaded up with a lot of stuff. . . . At night I took my shoes off. In the morning when I went to put them back my feet was so swollen I couldn't put them on."[64] Neira later describes that while the truckers make money for each worker they bring up to Michigan, the workers themselves end up in a more precarious financial position. On the way back to San Antonio, Neira encountered other migrant families in the truck that were returning to Texas with nothing. In his telling, Neira remarked, "By the time they start working, they owe a little money, and especially if they came through the trucks. . . . That runs around $10 or $11, I think, a fare. If a family of five has to pay five fares, after what they get in groceries by the time they start working, at the end of the season they wouldn't have money left."[65] This may have been a slight exaggeration. Earlier in the testimony, Neira stated that the previous summer he and his family earned $175 after all the deductions. Nevertheless, this does not negate the general critique that Neira was making throughout the testimony—that the labor recruiters made their money regardless of whether the migrant farmworkers made any throughout the season.

It begs repeating that there were a range of Latinx intermediary figures. Neira's testimony was specifically focused on labor contractors, such as the Cortez Employment Agency. Yet, there were certainly other kinds of intermediaries, such as those that recruited, trucked, and labored among the other migrant workers. Or there were intermediaries who became crew leaders once they transported the workers to the Midwest. The focus of this chapter is largely directed toward the Latinx intermediaries that capitalized on Midwestern growers' need for labor contracting, recruitment, and management services. Still, it should be mentioned, there are nuances within this labor system that are not being fully covered here. For example, there were many recruiters who still worked as farmworkers, often recruiting from within their family and extended family network. It added an additional layer of complexity when Latinx intermediaries were recruiting and managing farmworkers that were from their own family or peer groups. Intermediaries did indeed have to purchase and maintain a minimum of one large truck in order to facilitate the migration to the Midwest. In between the different phases of sugar beet work, intermediaries were also connecting workers in Michigan to other jobs and industries in Ohio, Illinois, Wisconsin, and elsewhere. The cost of maintaining the truck to ensure that the intermediary's family and friends made it to their destinations safely could be substantial, especially when one considers the slim margins that many were operating with. For many reasons—such as overcrowded vehicles, unsurfaced roads, or just unfortunate accidents—the act of migrating to and throughout the Midwest's agricultural areas could be life threatening. Thus, their role as a recruiter or crew leader could also provide them with extra money to keep the truck functioning to avoid any unnecessary accidents.[66]

Michigan growers hired Latinx intermediaries for myriad reasons: to contract other migrant workers, to transport them, and to supervise them in the fields. Furthermore, depending on the labor crews and the grower, some intermediaries became entrusted with even more responsibilities and discretionary power—such as weighing the harvested product, dispersing earnings to workers, measuring the fields (for acreage purposes), managing wage advances, or handling the grocery shopping for the crew. For example, in 1948, Father Clement Kern of Holy Trinity Church in Detroit recorded the testimonies of numerous braceros that worked in Michigan's fields during that season but eventually made their way to the city. One of these braceros was Gerardo Hernandez Pau, who was originally coming from Tampico, Tamaulipas. Following a description of abhorrent living conditions that included "bad" water and dirty beds, Hernandez states, "A Texan, who was an employee of the farmer, told us in Spanish that we should receive $8 per acre, but the land we worked on were never measured, although we asked them to do so." Following his stay at this farm, Hernandez and the other braceros were transported in a truck to cucumber fields in Blanchard, about ninety miles east of where they originally arrived. Hernandez continues his account, "After that, they gave us some land where there [were] very few cucumbers and the Texans did not work on those fields because they were very bad. We had to do that work, although we just got $2.50 a day."[67] Hernandez's statement demonstrates the rancorous relationship that could develop between Tejanos and Mexican braceros. Furthermore, it exhibits the discretionary power that Latinx intermediaries wielded. In this case, the Tejano crew leader declined to measure the field, despite the requests of the braceros, and was able to dictate which group of ethnic Mexicans, either Tejanos or braceros, had to pick the crop. Latinx intermediaries represented several competing constituencies: the interests of the other migrant workers, the growers, and, often, their own self-interest. Because of the range of responsibilities and the competing interests of each crew leader, the ways in which they exercised their respective power also varied.

Exploitation of Power: Latinx Migrants and Abuses by Tejano Crew Leaders

As important as it is to recognize the under-acknowledged historical role of Latinx intermediaries to the apparatus of US agricultural labor, it is equally necessary to understand the frequency with which Tejano crew leaders committed abuses against other Latinx workers. During his testimony to the Truman Commission, Monsignor Harold Boulton of St. Joseph's Parish in Saginaw stated, "Rightly or wrongly, it is a fact that they [migrant workers] distrust the interpreters, the bosses [field bosses] and the others who are appointed to deal with them by employing companies."[68] Often for good reason, there was a suspicion of intermediaries whose position could allow for them to deceive workers. Thus, although Latinx intermediaries were more capable of communicating and supervising the other Latinx migrant workers, it did not mean that all workers automatically trusted them.

One tactic that Tejano crew leaders and their aides used to exploit other Latinx agricultural workers was to undercount or inaccurately weigh the amount of crops picked by the workers. Once again in 1948, Father Kern collected the testimony of a bracero who had fallen victim to this type of scheme, except this time, its occurrence was verifiable. While this incident occurred at Trailback Plantation in Essex, Missouri, the bracero brought the complaint 630 miles northeast to Detroit. It is unclear what prompted the bracero to bring their complaint to Father Kern, but Trailback Plantation does appear to have had working relationships with farms in Michigan.[69] Although Latinx intermediaries did not have a role in the contracting of braceros, many did serve as crew leaders and truckers for them. These relationships were part of a broader network of agricultural companies and organizations across the Midwestern states (i.e., Missouri, Michigan, Minnesota, and Wisconsin) that would recontract, or essentially loan out, migrant workers to each other.

The unnamed bracero who brought their complaint from Missouri to Michigan revealed a labor hierarchy where the employer or contractor was a man named Armando Salinas. Alongside Salinas was Tomas Castillo, who supervised a group of Tejano weighers. The braceros, though, were directly responsible to Castillo. The bracero writes in their statement, "To make the abuses worse[,] the weighers of Mr. Tomas Castillo, all Tejanos, robbed us of 80 to 90 pounds every day, which we discovered by accident, weighing a bundle of cotton on someone else's scale. That is how we discovered the abuses of these people."[70] In *Managed Migrations*, Cristina Salinas contextualizes the relationship between Salinas and Castillo, stating, "[They] owned three trucks, which they used to transport the workers to their destination, a location chosen after consultation with the entire group and decided upon as a group."[71] According to Salinas, they did not charge the workers for transportation or deduct anything from their wages from picking cotton because growers directly paid him fifty cents per hundred pounds of cotton picked by the crew. In September 1946, as Salinas and Castillo were set to leave Texas with a small crew of migrant workers, the deputy labor commissioner for Texas charged them with breaking the Labor Agency Law of 1943. The judge for the case ruled that Salinas was operating as a labor agent without the proper licensing. Salinas was thus ordered to pay $200, plus court fees. As Salinas and Castillo were already identified by the state of Texas as labor agents who were operating without proper licensing and as they already had connections with cotton growers outside of the state, this may have led them to believe there would be less of a liability in serving as crew leaders and weighers for braceros.[72]

This situation in Essex, Missouri—one where Tejano contractor, crew leader, and weighers were either intentionally tampering with the scales or misreporting the amount of produce so that Mexican braceros would receive less money—is almost identical to the problem in Michigan that the Mexican secretary of foreign affairs described. Placed into conversation with each other, these incidents in Missouri and Michigan indicate a broader pattern of abuse by Tejano crew leaders against Mexican braceros. Although the 1948 case at Trailback Plantation is significant for its demonstration of how Tejano migrants in positions of power attempted to take

Lee, Russell. Mexican laborer contractors employ a checker who keeps track of number of baskets cut by each cutter, La Pryor, Texas. He also okays the baskets for shipping from fields. Library of Congress, Prints & Photographs Division, FSA/OWI Collection, LC-USF33- 012043-M2 [P&P] LOT 602.

advantage of other migrant workers, particularly Mexican braceros, it also raises other equally important issues. First, why did this bracero that was working in Essex, Missouri, seek out Father Kern in Detroit? The two most likely reasons are that after leaving Trailback Plantation, they sought work in the Michigan fields and eventually made it to Detroit or that migrants were familiar with Father Kern's reputation as an official devoted to supporting Michigan's Latinx migrant laborers.[73] What is certain is that this bracero was far from being alone in their frustration with Trailback Plantation. The issue with the deceitful weighing practices was not the only major matter to cause outrage among the braceros—rain and weather conditions caused many to lose upward of twenty straight days of work. Once braceros began to run out of money, the company store stopped the lines of credit they had been offering to workers. A December 1948 telegram from the Mexican Consul in St. Louis, Missouri, to Trailback Plantation conveyed the severity of the situation, stating that "over 1000 Mexican Nationals have been abandoned by your company and refused work or transportation back."[74]

Surprisingly, the telegram in combination with the bracero letter illustrates a different dimension of the Latinx intermediary experience. After the company store discontinued the credit line to the braceros, a group of them sought out the help of Tomas Castillo, the Tejano in charge of the braceros. Believing that Castillo was their "representative," they instead found Castillo drunk. Castillo informed the workers that there was nothing that could be done for them. In fact, Castillo planned on resigning from their position because they could see how many braceros were complaining about being in this situation (at this point, that number was around 500 braceros). And this indeed happened—it was Castillo and Salinas who informed the Mexican Consulate about the 1,000 braceros stranded at Trailback Plantation.[75] While Castillo and Salinas's reasons for leaving their positions as crew leaders and alerting Mexican officials to the conditions of the braceros is unclear, one could speculate that they were motivated by feelings of guilt. Perhaps Castillo and Salinas could accept earning some extra money for themselves at the expense of the Mexican braceros, but the sight of fellow migrants without work, resources, and transportation was too large a burden. Ultimately, there is no definitive answer for why Castillo and Salinas waited for so long to report and act on the conditions at Trailback Plantation. From the perspective of growers, the presence of Latinx intermediaries allowed for a more effective relationship with workers, yet, from the perspective of other migratory workers, the significant amounts of power that Tejano crew leaders held in the landscape of migratory labor did not always benefit them.[76]

While there were likely many other Tejano migratory workers who experienced mistreatment by Latinx intermediaries, they had limited institutional recourses for their complaints. Whereas braceros at least had the option of turning to their local Mexican consulate, ordinary Tejano farmworkers lacked a definitive place to bring their complaints. Although Mexican guestworkers were often disappointed in the help they received from their government representatives in Michigan, their complaints still generated an archival paper trail of their mistreatment. Unless Tejano migrants brought their complaints to someone like Father Kern at Detroit's Holy Trinity Church or had a platform like the Truman Commission hearings, it was challenging for them to document their experiences in the fields.

It is important to acknowledge that there was no definitive standard for how they chose to manage the other migrant workers—there was great variance to how intermediaries treated their workers. Not every crew leader was intentionally under-weighing their workers' crops, managing their crew's grocery shopping, or concocting some other scheme to deceive their workers. The encounters highlighted here between migrant workers and Latinx intermediaries do complicate notions of panethnic unity. Just because a crew leader was Latinx, that did not mean that they automatically treated their fellow Latinx workers well. Because the position of crew leader was a business venture—one where earnings could be higher than through regular migratory field work—profit and self-interest often served as the main motives for intermediaries. While there were certainly honest crew leaders, it is also clear that there existed intermediaries who found the allure of profit more powerful than the fair treatment of other migratory workers. Latinx intermediaries occupied a complex positionality situated in between the Latinxs working under them and the growers or organizations that they were responsible to. Some crew leaders developed lucrative operations and it was these individuals that the press and others celebrated for being the model migrant. Yet, even when intermediaries were acting for their own benefit, it could appear that they were serving the interests of the growers.

Conclusion

Following the United States's entrance into World War I, Latinx intermediaries gradually emerged as central to the maintenance and expansion of the Midwest's agricultural industry. With Michigan's fields filled with Mexican braceros and Tejano workers, Latinx intermediaries were vital to the success of Michigan's growers and agricultural companies. Whether as truckers or crew leaders, there were distinct roles in the fields aside from picking the crops. This chapter situates the role of Latinx intermediaries within the context of World War I, postwar immigration restriction, regional agricultural developments, and the beginning of the Bracero Program. The term "Latinx intermediary" builds upon the research of US immigration, labor, and Latinx historians to provide a nuanced account of the crew leaders and truckers that managed the Midwest's migratory labor apparatus. Examining these figures exhibits the intertwined processes of expanding labor migration, the consolidation of labor recruitment efforts, and hierarchical contestations between ethnic Mexican farmworkers in the fields. Although this chapter contains references to statements provided during the Truman Commission on Migratory Labor, it is in the following one where we will more thoroughly examine the implications of these hearings. With the introduction of the Farm Labor Program and the arrival of over 5,000 Puerto Rican migrant farmworkers in 1950, Michigan's agricultural industry would be thrust into the national spotlight. While much attention surrounded this enormous airlift of Puerto Rican migrants to Michigan's fields, it was often overlooked that they were joining ethnic Mexican workers who had been working those same fields for decades. This confluence of the Bracero Program, the Farm Labor Program, and the interstate migration of Mexican Americans would result in an illuminating set of encounters.[77]

CHAPTER TWO

Sugar Beets Not So Sweet

Race, Citizenship, and the Truman Commission on Migratory Labor, 1948–1951

During the 1950 harvest season, an exceptional amount of regional and national attention concentrated on Michigan's agricultural industry. The first incident to bring the spotlight onto Michigan, and set the tone for this summer, was a tragedy. On June 6, 1950, a chartered C-46 two-engine plane carrying sixty-two Puerto Rican migrant workers to Michigan plunged into the Atlantic Ocean. The following day, the *New York Times*, *Chicago Tribune*, and *Los Angeles Times* each ran front-page coverage of the crash.[1] Two hundred and seventy-five miles off the coast of Miami, Florida, survivors spent twelve hours in the ocean before USS *Saufley* was finally able to rescue thirty-seven of the passengers that grasped to life rafts. The remaining twenty-eight died from the impact of the crash, drowning, and even shark attack.[2] The second occurrence to bring public attention to Michigan agribusiness was that Puerto Rican migrants on that plane were part of a larger contractual worker program initiated by Michigan Field Crops, Inc. (MFCI) and the Puerto Rican government. Following the crash, Luis Muñoz Marin, governor of Puerto Rico, stated that no more contracting of Puerto Rican migrants to the Michigan beet fields would occur. Yet, after negotiations between Puerto Rico's Department of Labor and the MFCI, the two parties made an emergency agreement to "save" the state's $14,000,000 sugar beet harvest.[3]

What resulted was an agreement between Puerto Rico's Migration Division of the Department Labor and Michigan Field Crops, Inc., which arranged for 5,200 Puerto Rican guestworkers to pick sugar beets and other crops in Michigan. The last event of this harvest season to thrust Michigan's agricultural industry into national focus was Harry S. Truman's Executive Order 10129, which established the President's Commission on Migratory Labor. Saginaw, Michigan, emerged as one of a handful of places that the Commission visited during the summer of 1950. In a state better known during the 1940s for its automobile industry and for being the "Arsenal of Democracy" during World War II, this was an unprecedented amount of attention on Michigan's agricultural industry.

With the large-scale introduction of Puerto Rican migrants to Michigan during the 1950 harvest season, these farmworkers entered an ethnoracial landscape that already included Mexican Americans and Mexicans, among numerous other racial and ethnic groups. Scrutinizing the exchanges between these three ethnic groups provides critical insights into the processes of racial formation, contested notions of citizenship, and ethnic identity. This chapter historicizes the migration of Puerto Ricans to the Midwest, situates the motivations and long-term implications of the Truman Commission on Migratory Labor, and examines the relational racialization of Mexicans, Mexican Americans, and Puerto Ricans. Racialized understandings of the three groups of Latinx migrant workers were fraught and inconsistent. Natalia Molina, Daniel Martinez HoSang, and Ramón A. Gutiérrez characterize relational racialization as "a dynamic and interactive process" where "group-based racial constructions are formed in relation not only to whiteness but also to other devalued and marginalized groups."[4] With the large-scale addition of Puerto Rican farmworkers to a labor regime that was already heavily reliant on ethnic Mexicans, debates revolving around growers' preferred source of labor, the public health of migrants, and agricultural workers' labor rights shifted considerably during the summer of 1950. At the heart of this transformation was the relational racialization of these three groups of Latinx migrant workers.

As Perla Guerrero notes in *Nuevo South*, the fluidity of processes of racialization allowed for a single group to be characterized in dynamic and often-competing ways.[5] In some instances, growers, politicians, and the public found it useful to group all of the Latinx migrant farmworkers together. Through racialized tropes of being innately suited for agricultural labor, Latinx migrants, at times, were racialized as an indistinguishable mass of laborers, regardless of their varying citizenship statuses, ethnicities, or places of origin. Yet, these understandings shifted as growers and the broader public found utility in distinguishing the groups from one another. Eventually, growers, residents of Michigan's agricultural areas, and migrant workers themselves had to reckon with the ethnic and racial diversity of this migratory labor force. Based on a range of conditions that included, but were not limited to, the desires of agriculturalists, legal categorizations, and the everyday rhetoric of local actors, Mexicans, Mexican Americans, and Puerto Ricans could shift in and out desirability. While their experiences in the fields were not always similar, these three groups of Latinxs were consistently racialized in relation to one another.

The racialization of these three groups derived from a range of markers, including ethnicity, citizenship status, language, class, and gender. The racialization of these groups could be shaped by media coverage, reformers, politicians, technocrats, and a myriad of other interest groups. These perceptions were capable of shaping public sympathies, producing new labor regimes, and shaping the overall experience of migratory workers in the Midwest. These circumstances culminated in a visit from President Harry S. Truman's Commission on Migratory Labor to Saginaw from September 11 to 12. The Commission's visit was highly anticipated because individuals like Detroit's Father Clement Kern, migrant workers, and other labor leaders yearned for a platform like this to express their concerns regarding the state's agricultural industry. While the Department of Labor conducted annual hearings in Detroit concerning migrant work conditions, the timing of these hearings rendered them practically useless. As the hearings were held every January, most seasonal workers had already left the area and were unavailable to present their experiences working in Michigan agribusiness. Throughout the Truman Commission proceedings, Mexican, Mexican American, and Puerto Rican migrants were referred to in varying ethnic, racial, and national terms. These representations provide insights into the racial logics that upheld the understandings of race, labor, and migration.

Truman Era, the Presidential Commission on Migratory Labor, and Public Law 78

After a brief period serving as Franklin D. Roosevelt's vice president following his election for a fourth term as president of the United States, Harry S. Truman ascended to the presidency following the death of Roosevelt in April of 1945. As the United States and the Allies were still at war with the Axis Powers, Truman also inherited the wartime efforts—one of which was the Bracero Program. Truman's tenure as president included many domestic and international policies that defined this era of politics, a number of which were related to immigration. The legislative acts passed during Truman's tenure as president included the War Brides Act of 1945, the G. I. Fiancées Act of 1946, the Luce-Cellar Act of 1946, the Displaced Persons Act of 1948, and the McCarran-Walter Immigration and Naturalization Act of 1952. The broader diplomatic policies of this period included the Truman Doctrine, the Marshall Plan, and the formation of the United Nations and the North Atlantic Treaty Organization (NATO). In the shadow of World War II ending, the formation of policies that sought to remedy some of the international ramifications of war, and the formation of these monumental intergovernmental organizations, this era also included subtle, but important, actions by the Truman administration to gather information and craft legislation around the "problem" of migratory labor in the United States.[6]

Following the beginning of the Bracero Program in 1942 and the end of its wartime phase in 1947, growers and agribusiness employers were still able to contract Mexican labor, but under a slightly different arrangement. Instead of the US Department of Agriculture contracting the workers, it was now the responsibility of the individual employer. While the future of this labor program was on shaky grounds at this moment, the passing of Public Law 78 in 1951, which amended the Agricultural Act of 1949, stabilized the presence of the Bracero Program for over a decade longer. Yet, the longevity of this program was not inevitable. After Truman's inauguration for his second term as president at the beginning of 1949, his administration began to consider establishing a prominent presidential commission that could propel legislation to reform certain aspects of agricultural labor and immigration. With those goals in mind, Truman favored legislation that would protect the usage of domestic farm labor, increase enforcement along the US-Mexico border, and adjust the terms of the Bracero Program. Truman authorized the Presidential Commission on Migratory Labor on June 3, 1950, via Executive Order 10129 to investigate a broad range of issues. Specifically, the commission was to direct their attentions toward "the social, economic, health, and education conditions among migratory workers, both alien and domestic, in the United States."[7] The bulk of the committee's work would focus on the series of public hearings they would hold throughout the country.[8]

The President's Commission on Migratory Labor consisted of Chairman Maurice T. Van Hecke, Noble Clark, William M. Leiserson, Robert E. Lucey, Peter H. Odegard, and Varden Fuller, who served as executive secretary. This commission held twelve sets of public hearings across eleven different sites.[9] Testimonies were provided by individuals representing a range of different interest groups focused on domestic labor, authorized foreign labor, and unauthorized foreign labor. One large topic of contention during the Truman Commission hearings was the rise of undocumented migrants. Although the Bracero Program sparked increased authorized migration, this also encouraged large amounts of unauthorized migration. It can be difficult to calculate the exact number of undocumented workers that arrived in the United States leading up to the hearings of the Truman Commission, but as Robert S. Robinson notes in the article "Taking the Fair Deal to the Fields,"

Braceros wait in lines based on their states of origin at the Monterrey Processing Center, Mexico. Leonard Nadel Photographs and Scrapbooks, Archives Center, National Museum of American History, Smithsonian Institution.

one way to approximate this number is to look at the number of deportations and repatriations. In 1944, two years after the start of the Bracero Program, that number was stable at 10,000. By 1950, it soared to 565,000.[10] This increase, to some extent, was the result of the arrival of more unauthorized migrants, but it likely also stemmed from a more aggressive deportation regime.

While there existed regional differences in the content probed in the hearings—for example, the migration of Puerto Rican workers to Michigan raised issues that were distinct from those in the Southwest and on the Pacific Coast, and states closer to the border might have been more concerned about unauthorized migration—there was some consistency in the tenor of the arguments presented. Generally, growers and growers' employment organizations appealed to the commission for increased access to Mexican labor and a continuation of the Bracero Program. Insisting that migratory labor was necessary to sustaining the country's agricultural industry and that participation in the Bracero Program offered Mexican workers better economic outcomes than remaining in Mexico, agribusiness interests presented guestworker programs as a win-win for all parties. Countering these arguments were different interest groups that advocated for improved opportunities for domestic laborers, restricting the number of contracts provided for foreign workers, and containing the flow of undocumented immigration into the country. These blocs ranged from academics to public health organizations, employment officials, social service and religious organizations, union officials, and even migrant workers themselves. In short, politicians and agribusiness were largely alone in their support for an expansion of the Bracero Program and having greater access to cheap migratory labor.

With almost every interest group besides the agricultural industry supporting some form of restrictions to the program and increasing the use of domestic labor, the official recommendations of the Truman Commission shared this desire to constrict the program. The commission recommended that the Bracero Program *should not* be expanded and that the agricultural industry should use domestic sources of labor more effectively, stating, "No special measures should be adopted to increase the number of alien contract laborers beyond the numbers admitted in 1950. Future efforts should be directed toward supplying agricultural labor needs with our own workers and eliminating dependence on foreign labor."[11] With 107,000 Mexicans admitted into the United States for temporary agricultural employment in 1949 and 67,500 admitted in 1950, the committee's suggested number would likely be somewhere in between.[12] Another considerable recommendation contended that "legislation is needed to make it unlawful to employ citizens who have entered the United States illegally. Legalization and contracting of aliens illegally in the United States should be discontinued and forbidden."[13] In terms of the use of foreign contract workers in the agricultural industry, the Truman Commission's recommendations can be distilled down to two main points: curtailing any future growth of the Bracero Program and criminalizing the "Wetback Invasion," the name used in the fourth chapter in the report.[14]

Ultimately, the recommendations of the Truman Commission, the wide distribution of the report, and the president's support of the recommendations were futile. With the strength of the growers' lobbies and politicians who represented the interests of growers, those in favor of increased access to foreign temporary workers proved capable of impeding any efforts to restrict the Bracero Program. Despite the dissent of organized labor, scholars, the League of United Latin American Citizens, and the G. I. Forum, these groups did not pose enough of a challenge. This was epitomized during the spring of 1951 when Senator Allen Ellender and Congressman W. R. Poage—both Democrats like Truman—introduced bills to the Senate and the House of Representatives that would usher in a new era for the Bracero Program. Public Law 78, or the Ellender-Poage Bill, ignored the recommendations of the commission, as well as Truman's second-term agenda for migratory labor. Importantly, as the Truman Commission proceeded in the summer and fall of 1950, the United States was already involved in another military conflict: the Korean War. As Robert S. Robinson precisely argues, "Much like World War II had brought to life the Bracero Program, this second conflict

[Korean War] helped make it a durable mixture of life in the United States. What critics hoped would be only a temporary advantage for growers that might subside with the end of the conflict, actually provided a moment for Public Law 78 to become settled Policy."[15] Despite the Ellender-Poage Bill's successful progression through the House and the Senate, Truman was still in a position to approve or veto the bill.[16]

Approved on July 12, 1951, Public Law 78 authorized the secretary of labor to manage the administrative execution of the program. Truman's rationale for initially approving the legislation was that if he signed the bill, while also expressing his dissatisfaction with its inadequacy, he could gain concessions when it came time to extend the program in six months. At the top of his list, Truman coveted legislation that would penalize employers who hired and transported unauthorized foreign workers, broader powers to conduct farm inspections and regulate the compliance of employers, and further funding for the Immigration and Naturalization Service (INS) and the Farm Placement Services (who could help domestic farmworkers find employment). Although the Truman Commission concentrated on a host of issues relating to migratory labor and the agricultural industry, the president's top priorities were to punish employers who used unauthorized workers and increasing resources for policing immigration in the United States. While the Truman Commission was nominally concerned with the conditions of migratory workers in the country, Truman's legislative agenda was guided by a desire to increase immigration restriction and broaden the powers of immigration enforcement agencies.[17] The Truman Commission's focus on "The Wetback Invasion" became forceful action during the Dwight D. Eisenhower administration. It begs the question then: To what extent was the Truman Commission's fixation with "wetback traffic" responsible for elevating this issue to one of national concern, eventually culminating with Operation Wetback?[18]

Ostensibly, some of Truman's target immigration reforms materialized in the form of Public Law 283. Approved on March 20, 1952, months after Truman chose not to veto PL78 and a mere six days before the agreement was to expire, PL283 sought to penalize individuals who willfully facilitated the "illegal entry of aliens" or their concealment.[19] Only officers and employees of the INS possessed the authority to make arrests, and, if punished to the full extent, offenders could receive up to a $2,000 fine and five years in prison. In short, this bill criminalized the harboring and unsanctioned recruitment of undocumented workers and expanded the powers of the INS. Senator Harley M. Kilgore, a Democrat from West Virginia, simultaneously gave life to PL283 and undermined its efficacy. Although Kilgore introduced the bill

(S. 1851) and was successfully able to push it through, he also took to the Senate floor to distinguish between employing an unauthorized foreign worker and harboring one. According to Kilgore, harboring necessitated deliberate concealing; thus, merely hiring an undocumented worker did not meet the grounds for prosecution. Somewhat predictably, this resulted in an ineffectual piece of legislation that allowed for immense legal maneuvering. In the words of historian S. Deborah Kang, "Congressional debates over S. 1851 make its intent perfectly clear: Congress passed the bill in order to ensure the continuation of the Bracero Program."[20] And that is exactly what was achieved.[21]

In 1950, the year the Truman Commission on Migratory Labor conducted their national hearings, the United States admitted 67,500 foreign workers from Mexico for temporary labor in the agricultural industry. By 1956, that number would reach 445,197. Truman certainly may have held some well-intentioned objectives for restructuring migratory labor procedures, and the immigration system more broadly, in the years immediately following the end of World War II. Although Truman intended for Public Law 78 to be a temporary measure that could eventually set in motion legislation more closely aligned with his administration's agenda of limiting the Bracero Program and criminalizing the facilitation of the employment or transportation of unauthorized foreign workers, the consequence of it was that it firmly rooted the program for over a decade longer. Between 1951 and 1963, Congress extended PL78 biennially. In 1963, with some politicians proposing a phasing out of the Bracero Program over the next three years, but with the Department of Labor and the Department of Agriculture coveting a one-year extension with modifications, the two branches of Congress eventually approved a one-year extension for 1964, which would officially mark the end of the program.[22]

Puerto Rican Migration in a Historical Context

With the signing of the 1898 Treaty of Paris, the short-lived Spanish-American War came to an end. While the Cuban War for Independence predated the intervention of the United States into this conflict, the Treaty of Paris formally established Cuba's independence from Spain and ceded Puerto Rico, Guam, and the Philippines to the United States. Shortly after the United States's acquisition of Puerto Rico, the archipelago's insular government began to encourage various forms of labor migration across the United States and the Caribbean. The option and likelihood of migration from Puerto Rico to the United States increased exponentially in 1917 with the passing of the Jones Act, which provided Puerto Ricans with formal US citizenship. As scholars such as Jorge Duany thoroughly note, for much of the twentieth century following the Jones Act, Puerto Rico's government functioned in ways that could further facilitate the process of labor migration.[23]

Despite its lack of sovereignty, the Puerto Rican government created a range of bureaus and offices that could oversee the employment of their constituents. These programs, which frequently overlapped and then replaced one another, included: the Bureau of Employment and Identification (1930–1948), Office of Information for Puerto Rico (1945–1949), Employment and Migration Bureau (1947–1951), Migration Division of the Department of Labor (1951–1989), and the Department of Puerto Rican Community Affairs in the United States (1989–1993). The actions and services of these organizations ranged from issuing identification cards for Puerto Ricans so that they could provide proof of citizenship, publicizing job opportunities in the contiguous United States, recruiting workers for available employment, helping to negotiate reduced airfares to facilitate migration, directing voter registration campaigns in US cities, and attempting to cultivate community and culture among Puerto Ricans in the diaspora. Describing the broad range of responsibilities that the Puerto Rican government undertook, Jorge Duany writes, "To my knowledge, no modern state, colonial or otherwise, has engaged in more extensive and longstanding activities concerning its expatriates than the Puerto Rican government."[24] With Operation Bootstrap functioning as the overarching logic for the "modernization" of Puerto Rico, the transformations that occurred between the 1940s and 1960s on the archipelago and among the diasporic Puerto Rican communities in the United States would be substantial.

Daniel Patrick Moynihan, oft-recognized for his pathologizing 1965 study "The Negro Family: The Case for National Action," more popularly referred to as the "Moynihan Report," published another study, *Beyond the Melting Pot,* alongside sociologist Nathan Glazer two years prior. In their chapter focusing on Puerto Ricans, Glazer and Moynihan contended that Puerto Rico needed a drastic societal restructuring and, through Operation Bootstrap, the archipelago could at long last benefit from its colonial relationship to the United States. The authors state, "Puerto Rico finally found a major virtue in its connection with America—the American market, and access to American investment capital and economic skills. Six hundred new factories were tempted to open in the island by tax exemption, government-supported economic and market analysis, and by a variety of other means."[25] They continue by lauding that this "industrialization by invitation" campaign produced 41,000 jobs in new factories, which resulted in far higher wages than what could be found doing agricultural work. With an increasing number of people veering toward industrial labor and urban settings, Glazer and Moynihan determined that there was more funding for improved health services and education, and overall, better living conditions on the islands. More delicate than the praise they heaped onto Operation Bootstrap was their acknowledgment that this transformation eliminated around the same number of jobs that it created and that agricultural mechanization steadily reduced the number of workers needed. Although certain interest groups applauded Operation Bootstrap for propelling Puerto Rico toward "modernity," this program also devastated and continued the economic marginalization of the most vulnerable sectors of Puerto Rican society. The archipelago's industrialization was one major part of Operation Bootstrap, and migration to the United States was the other.[26]

During the 1940s, large numbers of Puerto Rican workers settled in locations along the East Coast, most notably New York City. With the influx of migrants, city officials and government agencies pathologized this migration as the "Puerto Rican problem"—one characterized by high rates of unemployment, dependency on relief programs, and general impoverishment. To some extent, this is the narrative that Glazer and Moynihan are addressing in *Beyond the Melting Pot*. In 1945, commercial airplane service began from San Juan to New York City. Between 1945 and 1946, many Puerto Ricans struggled to find work on the island and decided to leave for the United States in hopes of employment and higher wages. In 1945, 13,500 new Puerto Rican migrants arrived in New York, a number that would increase to 40,000 the following year.[27] From the perspective of members of the Puerto Rican government, as well as the US government, migration was a strategy that could support economic growth and industrialization of the islands. But this also meant diverting migrants away from New York and toward other locales, both urban and rural alike. Fred L. Crawford, a Republican from Michigan's 8th District in the US House of Representatives and a former financier and operator of beet sugar mills, echoed this sentiment. During his testimony to the Truman Commission, Crawford invoked the "Puerto Rican problem" and declared the necessity of encouraging emigration from the island, stating, "They [Puerto Ricans] have a pressure of population in Puerto Rico which is no less than fantastic. They have close to 2,200,000 people at the present time, increasing at the rate of about 50,000 per annum." Crawford continued by avowing that it has been his desire for the contiguous United States to take in 25,000–50,000 Puerto Rican migratory workers annually because "anything the Puerto Ricans fail to do for themselves we, the taxpayers in the United States, must do for them."[28] With state-sanctioned migration functioning as a partial solution to the unemployment, underemployment, and low wages on the islands, Puerto Rico's *Partido Popular Democrático* (PPD; Popular Democratic Party) began to develop a bureaucratic infrastructure that could support these objectives.

Of critical importance to advancing Puerto Rico's emigration platform was the Bureau of Employment and Migration (BEM) and its Migration Division (MD), which would give rise to the Farm Labor Program (FLP). As Ismael García-Colón explains in *Colonial Migrants at the Heart of Empire*, the policy of sanctioned migration was not the result of an individual or of a single organization. Rather, it was the product of cooperation between several actors and groups, including Puerto Rican and US officials, influential politicians, intellectuals, organizations, and ultimately, migrants themselves. With the creation of the Bureau of Employment and Migration and its subsidiary Migration Division, the Puerto Rican government molded these administrative bodies in the form of the United States Employment Services (USES), which came to life through the New Deal's Wagner-Peyser Act. By successfully promoting the utility of Puerto Rican contract workers to federal and state officials, as well as growers in the United States, the BEM launched the Farm Labor Program to facilitate the contracting and migration of Puerto Rican workers to farms across the United States.[29]

Throughout the duration of the Farm Labor Program, which lasted from 1949 to 1990, 421,238 Puerto Ricans received contracts for agricultural work stateside. This made for the second-largest organized temporary labor program in US history, following only the Bracero Program. While the FLP contracted only a small number of farmworkers for labor on US farms between 1947 and 1949, the program expanded to a labor force of 8,500 in 1950—with 5,300 going to Michigan. Thus, when considering the large-scale launch of the Farm Labor Program, Michigan is the appropriate location to begin with. By 1958, Puerto Rico's Migration Division, which would administer the program, consisted of 130 staff members with a million-dollar budget.[30] The MD's Field Representatives were the delegates of the Puerto Rican government on the ground who sought to ensure the everyday

Landrón Colocación en fincas Transportación de trabajadores ca. 1952. *Archivo General de Puerto Rico, Instituto de Cultura Puertorriqueña, Colección: Departamento de Instrucción Pública, Negativos.*

execution of the program. Sometimes referred to as the "compliance man" or "trouble shooter," the field representatives strategically worked out of field offices in states with significant numbers of contracted workers so that they could reliably respond if any problems arose. While there are some comparisons to be drawn between the Latinx intermediaries of the previous chapter and the field representatives, there are also significant distinctions. The field representatives inspected housing and living arrangements, often welcomed the incoming Puerto Ricans at the local airports, familiarized the migrants with their rights as US citizens, investigated claims leveled by workers, functioned as the liaison between the laborers and their employers, and connected migrants to various resources. Nevertheless, the field representatives were not acting in this capacity as heads of a private business operation. Rather, as delegates of the Puerto Rican government, their role had more in common with Mexican Consular officials.

Fit to Be Workers? Race, Labor, and Public Health

During his statement at Saginaw's Truman Commission hearings, Representative Fred Crawford discussed the viability of using Puerto Rican labor in the Michigan fields. Crawford stated, "I would say approximately 65 cents of every dollar of the so-called national income which flows into the country [Puerto Rico] comes out of sugar operations. They are natural agriculturalists."[31] The notion that Latinx workers were more "naturally" equipped for this labor or that they were the only people who could perform stoop labor was a commonly upheld idea—by major news outlets, politicians, and ordinary residents of Michigan.[32] The prevalence of this belief was one of the primary drivers racializing Mexicans, Mexican Americans, and Puerto Ricans as a single undifferentiated group of unskilled workers.

The political and cultural economy of sugar has played a significant role in the history of the US empire in the Caribbean.[33] In Michigan, categories of race were articulated through repetitive tropes and imagery about the physical labor that Latinx workers performed in the fields. While this language was often subtle, and sometimes even complimentary, its recurring presence had the power to develop certain constructions about migrant Latinx workers. As Representative Crawford's statement to the Truman Commission suggested, Puerto Ricans, and other migrants from Latin America and the Caribbean, supposedly possessed innate and inherent capabilities for the most arduous forms of agricultural labor. During his statement, Crawford boasted, "This very past week I have picked pickles and beans with the people in the fields. I know what toil is, I know what the sweat of toil is, I know what the sweat of your own brow means."[34] Throughout his statement to the Commission, Crawford positioned himself as an expert of the sugar industry. Despite Crawford's self-professed knowledge of the sugar industry, what seems to escape Crawford's assessment is that sugar beets and cane sugar require different types of labor. The skill of harvesting sugar cane was not immediately transferrable to sugar beets.

There was nothing natural about the switch from cutting sugar cane to blocking, thinning, and picking sugar beets. Statements like this from people like Crawford, subtle as they may be, carried weight. Crawford was regarded as an authority in Michigan's sugar industry and his lobbying for Puerto Rican guestworkers played a significant role in the negotiations of Operation Operation Farmlift. In this case, Crawford's assumption that Puerto Ricans could naturally adapt to picking sugar beets could be disregarded as a misguided association between two different sugar crops. But when this language encom-

Migrant farm worker. Offices of the Government of Puerto Rico in the US (OGPRUS) Records. Migrant Farm Worker: OGPRUS_OIPR_0751. Center for Puerto Rican Studies Library & Archives, Hunter College, CUNY.

passed entire groups of Latinxs and Latin Americans, this belief contributed to the broader racialization of migrant workers and the labor they performed.

The assumption that Mexicans, Mexican Americans, and Puerto Ricans were somehow more innately suited for agricultural, or stoop, labor was based on racialized understandings of Latinxs, as well as other groups from the Global South. These tropes circulated regularly though popular and academic publications. Through Michigan State College's Section of Sociology, Dr. J. F. Thaden published a short study titled "Migratory Beet Workers in Michigan" based on interviews with over 140 sugar beet workers and investigations that were carried out over three years in twenty-eight of forty-six Michigan counties. This comprehensive study covered everything from ages, wages, migratory patterns, and the hierarchical structure of sugar beet labor. On the topic of increasing migratory fieldworkers in Michigan, Thaden writes, "Our beet growers have leaned more and more heavily on the Texas labor surplus because the Mexican, by physique and temperament, seems better suited to the job than any other available nationality group."[35] Thaden's pseudoscientific articulation that Latinxs were more naturally suited for this work legitimized that this group of migrant workers was particularly equipped to withstand the arduous labor and substandard living conditions.

As migrant groups spent more weeks, months, and eventually summers in the fields, people in Michigan began generating conflicting racialized ideas that distinguished Mexicans, Mexican Americans, and Puerto Ricans from each other. What developed in midcentury Michigan was a revolving hierarchy that categorized and tiered these Latinx groups according to various criteria. Lacking any coherence, these racial logics were equally fluid and contradictory. Racialized understandings of difference became particularly evident when Mexican Americans and Mexicans were relationally evaluated as public health risks. In terms of public health, Mexican *braceros* (non-US citizens) were interpreted as being healthier and less of a public health risk than the migrant workers that were US citizens—Mexican Americans and Puerto Ricans. As historian Deborah Cohen explains, "This concern for men's bodies and manners, like the repeated assessments of muscles, hands, and physical health during the selection process—and men's evaluation on these bases—meant that this sort of 'sizing up' was integrated into the program's daily workings."[36] Furthermore, notions of morality often informed debates about public health. While the pre-examined physicality and youth of braceros was appealing to Midwestern growers and public health officials, the morals and family structure of Mexican Americans sometimes took precedence in these considerations. These conditions made for a murky and debated understanding of the racial desirability of Latinx migrants in the fields. In the Midwest, there was debate and intrigue concerning the health of the bodies that would be sustaining the region's agricultural industry. It is no surprise then that racialized medical understandings created distinctions between different migrant groups.

When Dr. Frederick Leeder, of the Michigan State Department of Health, took the stand for the Commission on Migratory Labor, he immediately began to distinguish between the "imported labor" (Mexican braceros) and the "domestic American citizen" (Mexican Americans or Puerto Ricans). Leeder states, "Oddly enough, the imported labor does not present a health problem. They are screened at the point of origin. They are a selected group of young male adults and do not present any particular health problem. . . . The health problem revolves around the domestic American citizen who is a agricultural worker."[37] Leeder describes Mexican braceros as the ideal workers: they were pre-examined, young adults, and men. In short, they were fit for work. The medical examinations that braceros underwent to officially receive a contract were invasive and humiliating. They were forced to strip naked, have every aspect of their body inspected, and then sprayed down with DDT.[38] Although these medical examinations were invasive and sometimes seen as a violation of the body, it was these very exams at the border—and the associated clean bill of health—that provided growers and public health officials with a sense of security regarding the physicality and virility of the workers that would be making their way to the Midwestern fields.

There were moments throughout the 1950 harvest season and the Truman Commission hearings that turned into a forum for racializing Mexicans, Mexican Americans, and Puerto Ricans. Although various counties throughout Michigan began offering health services to migrant workers, it was more out of concern for the local communities than the migrants themselves. At the time of the hearing, Bay County could receive anywhere from 4,000 to 6,000 *Tejano* farmworkers. Following a discussion of the county's migrant medical program, which provided vaccinations and health exams, Dr. R. L. Loftin, the director of the Bay County Health Department, stated, "This is done because the migrants could easily act as a source of infection which will spread to our native population and so, in order to protect our native population, we must protect the migrant both against himself and against exposure to disease from our local people."[39] As historian Natalia Molina explains, public health officials and the racialized "scientific" knowledge they produced left lasting characterizations of Latinx migrants. While Molina emphasizes how dirt and disease became associated with Mexican immigrants, Mexican Americans and Puerto Ricans, despite being US citizens, were not exempt from these associations.[40]

As Operation Farmlift began to accelerate, just a week after the disastrous plane crash that claimed the lives of over two dozen Puerto Rican migrants, journalists speculated how this dramatic airlift would reshape the local communities receiving the migrant farmworkers. Frank Morris, *Detroit Times* correspondent, commented, "The biggest nonmilitary air lift in history is dumping 600 Puerto Ricans daily into the Saginaw valley, establishing a colony that is likely to become permanent." During the height of this systematic migration, flights from San Juan, Puerto Rico, arrived at Saginaw's

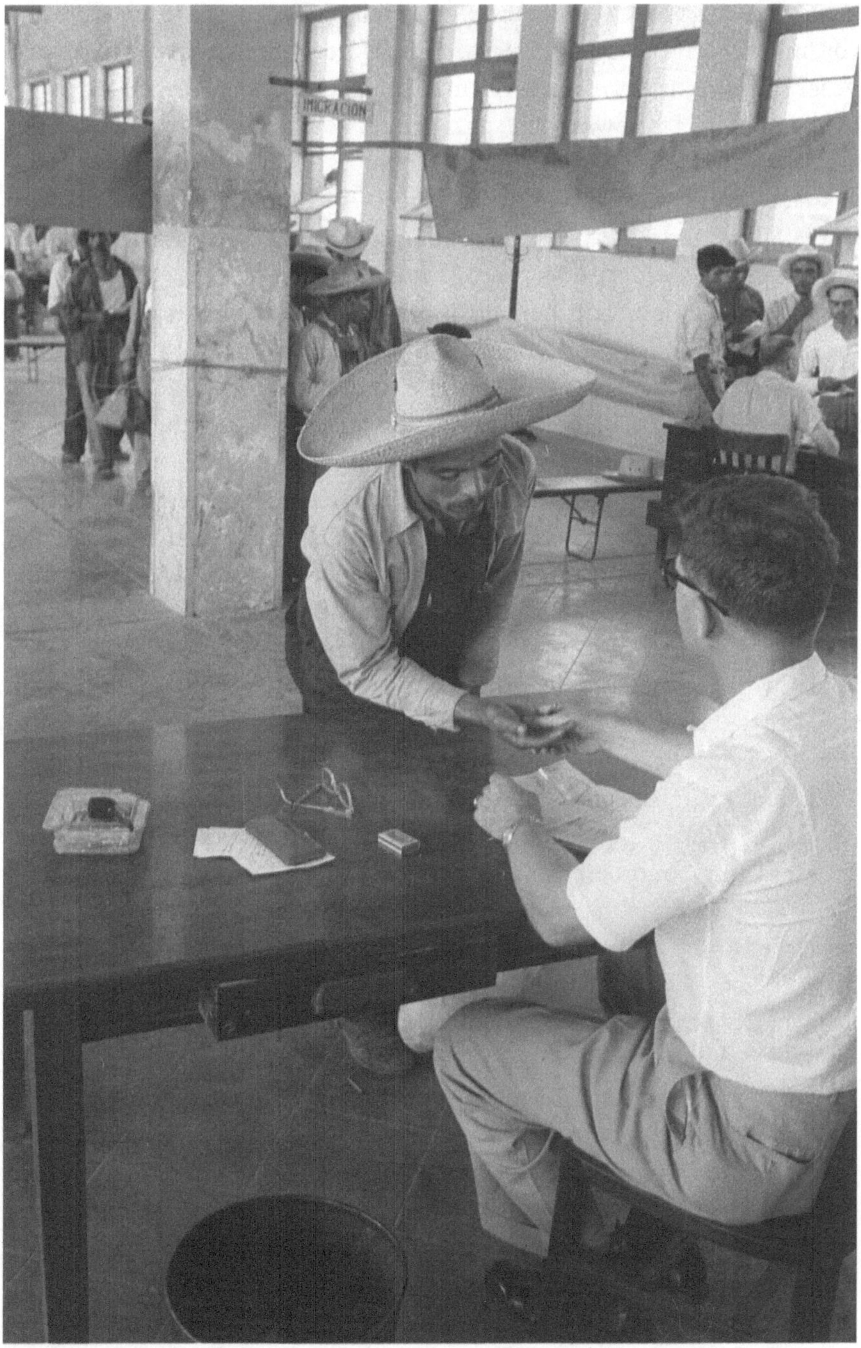

An official checks a bracero's hands for calluses at the Monterrey Processing Center, Mexico. Leonard Nadel Photographs and Scrapbooks, Archives Center, National Museum of American History, Smithsonian Institution.

Tri-City Airport every two hours. The result of this coordinated effort, according to Morris, was that "by Sunday night more than 5,000 brown-skinned American citizens will have arrived from their homeland, 2,180 miles away."[41] While Michigan's growers and sugar refinery operators were excited about the influx of a fresh group of migrant farmworkers, this enthusiasm was not shared by everybody. Dr. V. K. Volk, a Saginaw health officer, made it a point to racialize Puerto Rican migrants alongside ethnic Mexicans and African Americans. According to Morris, "Pointing out that half the patients in the huge Saginaw County Tuberculosis Hospital are Mexicans and Negroes brought here for field work, Dr. Volk expressed grave alarm." Volk rued the fact that, to his knowledge, the Puerto Rican migrants were not examined for tuberculosis (TB) before boarding their planes in San Juan. "I am gravely concerned about the whole experiment," expressed Volk.[42] Volk's unease about the arrival of Puerto Rican migrants is a complicated one. One consideration is that tuberculosis was relatively widespread in the 1940s and into the 1950s. Although the United States did not begin systematically tracking national TB incidence rates until 1953, many farmworkers did indeed die from this disease. Even into the 1940s, upwards of 55,000 people were dying annually from tuberculosis.[43] Still, Volk straddles a thin line by deciding to racialize the still-arriving Puerto Rican migrant farmworkers alongside Mexicans and African Americans. Irrespective of Volk's motives for grouping Puerto Ricans, Mexicans, and African Americans with one another, one of the issues faced by public health authorities revolved around the responsibility of caring for tubercular patients.

From a public health perspective, migratory workers that were US citizens presented a gray area of responsibility for local government officials and agricultural employers. As Dr. Leeder commented during his statement to the Truman Commission, "It is a problem that is on our own doorstep and it is only we that can solve it, I mean only our local, state, and Federal departments."[44] Whereas some Tejano families and individuals would drive their own family car or pickup truck from Texas to Michigan, many other Mexican American farmworkers were brought north in large groups by labor contractors.[45] As Dr. J. F. Thaden concluded in his 1940s study "Migratory Beet Workers in Michigan," the process of the recruiting and transportation of workers from Texas was the "most crude." Specifically, Thaden was describing the common trips north from Texas that lasted upwards of two to three days with few stops or rest breaks, and which were typically done on the back roads of state lines to avoid local labor and health authorities.[46] As these travel conditions were by no means safe or sanitary, it was no surprise that some Tejano workers would fall ill during the trip.

While there did appear to be some genuine concern about the transmission of tuberculosis and the public health impact it could have on local communities, the more influential factor appeared to be the financial costs that the state of Michigan was obligated to cover. As stated in a *San Antonio Express* article entered into the record at Oklahoma City's hearings for the Committee to Investigate the Interstate Migration of Destitute Citizens, "Since Michigan law requires that the State must provide hospital or other care for all persons with tuberculosis, Michigan established the clinic here [San Antonio, Texas] to prevent entry into the State of persons infected with tuberculosis or other contagious and infectious diseases."[47] The law referred to in the news article was Michigan's Tuberculosis and Hospital Sanitoriums Act 177 of 1925. Although the tuberculosis death toll was generally decreasing during the early 1940s, the communicable disease remained a problem in South Texas. From 1940 to 1943, the number of deaths nationwide resulting from tuberculosis decreased from 60,428 in 1940; to 59,251; 57,690; and 57,005; respectively. Yet, in South Texas, the Texas Tuberculosis Association estimated that the tuberculosis death rate for Mexican Americans was 209 per 100,000 people, 91 per 100,000 for African Americans, and 31 for Anglos. The state's tuberculosis association went so far as to express that the "concentration of Latin-American population in South Texas is responsible for that section's high death rate."[48] Furthermore, the incidence of tuberculosis that appeared in the Texas medical examinations for migrants seeking work in Michigan's beet fields was only increasing during this period.[49]

As mentioned in the previous chapter, a clean bill of health from the tuberculosis exam was required before a Tejano migrant worker could receive their official identification card that would then be provided to labor recruiters or employment agencies. In 1939, out of 4,271 prospective migrant workers tested in Texas, 1.89 percent were found to have pulmonary tuberculosis. With 5,753 workers tested in 1940 and 7,597 in 1941, 2.1 percent and 2.59 percent were diagnosed with TB, respectively.[50] Thus, with this longstanding migratory stream from Texas to Michigan and the inability of officials to offer appropriate health services to this group, questions remained about who was responsible for the health of migrant workers, evidenced in the testimony of A. B. Love, an agricultural economist at Michigan State, to the Truman Commission. At the hearings, Love acknowledged a position that other officials likely held, stating, "It is questionable as to whether or not all of the health facilities in Michigan should be spent on a migrant from Texas who is here for two months."[51] Love conveyed this gray area of medical care that Mexican American migrants existed within. They were not residing in the state where they held permanent residence, Texas, and they were also in a state—Michigan—where many were skeptical about providing care for transient individuals who would likely only be in the state for a few months.

Another element that factored into the racialization of migrant farmworkers was that the presence or absence of Latinas in the fields had the potential to generate tremendous debate. While some growers and local communities preferred the nuclear family structure that Mexican American families brought to Michigan, women working in the fields also defied some of the most conventional gender norms held during this period. The pathologizing of Mexican Americans as dirty or unsanitary was partially the result of the labor that Tejana women were performing outside of the household. Edgar Johnston, a professor of education at Wayne State University, expressed this position during his statement to the Truman Commission. When discussing dietary and health issues in the fields, Johnston states that "in two-thirds of the migrant families the mother was working regularly in the fields and there was not adequate home care in the preparation of the food."[52] According to this logic, by spending time working in the fields, Tejanas were neglecting their household duties, therefore resulting in an unkempt home and improperly prepared food. Johnston later goes on to describe a situation in Isabella County where eleven of the twenty wells that migrant families had access to were contaminated. By characterizing the migrant groups as hygienically deficient, blame could be placed on them, rather than the employer or local government for not providing workers with proper amenities. If Tejano families in Isabella County were indeed getting sick more frequently than the general population, it was more likely the result of the contaminated wells and poor housing conditions than inadequate food preparation.

These racialized medical tropes profoundly shaped the perceptions of Latinxs in midcentury Michigan. Throughout the Truman Commission hearings, numerous public health officials, medical doctors, and academics presented their understandings about Latinx migratory farmworkers. In doing so, these producers of policy and knowledge gave legitimacy to these racialized characterizations of Latinx migrants. When Reverend Norman Hughes, executive secretary of Bay City Council of Churches, gave his statement to the commission, he presented a direct example of how these perceptions shaped the hostility that the public would show toward Latinx migrants. Hughes recalls the attempts to create a childcare center for Tejano children so that they would not have to work in the fields, but local farmers who held attitudes of "indifference, apathy, or hostility" derailed these attempts.[53] This group of farmers went as far as forcing one minister out of town who tried to provide resources for migrants. According to Hughes, their reason for doing so was that "many of them [farmers/locals] assume every Texan [Tejano] family has syphilis. That is the common assumption."[54] To be clear, the issue of TB was a legitimate health concern among Mexican American migrant communities. In any case, the characterizations that European Americans in Michigan held of Latinx migrants as being diseased and unsanitary went far beyond public health anxieties about TB. It had very real consequences—social service providers denied resources to migrants, all levels of government ignored the inadequate work conditions within the agricultural industry, and locals rationalized their indifference, if not outright hostility, toward Latinx migrants.

Respectability, Mobility, and Gendered Agricultural Migrations

During their time in Michigan, one of the ways in which Mexicans, Mexican Americans, and Puerto Ricans were relationally assessed was via notions of respectability. During the hearings for the Truman Commission on Migratory Labor, S. L. Durham, chairman of the Michigan Migrant Ministry, glowingly recalled her experiences that summer with Puerto Rican migrants, which were contrasted in relation to past experiences with ethnic Mexicans. Durham stated to the Commission, "Usually when we ask the men [ethnic Mexicans] what studies they wish to take up when our groups come together each summer, they will say arithmetic, but these men [Puerto Ricans] did not say arithmetic. Do you know why they always say arithmetic? They always say they want to count what is coming to them and to be sure they get all that is coming to them. These men [Puerto Ricans] said they wanted to learn our language."[55] Durham then goes on to recount another anecdote where some of the Puerto Ricans cooked dinner for members of the Migrant Ministry to show how much "they try to get the people [Michigan locals] to feel they are one of them."[56] Ultimately, Durham is making the argument that, to her pleasure, Puerto Rican migrants were more interested in appealing to the local population, if not assimilating into it, than ethnic Mexicans. While Puerto Ricans desired to learn English so that they could communicate with members of the Migrant Ministry and the local community, the ethnic Mexican migrants were presented as only selfishly concerned with money. Related to that, whereas Puerto Ricans proactively sought to be part of the local community, ethnic Mexicans were not particularly inclined to do so.

During the Commission hearings, Durham was not alone in sharing these sentiments. Harold Gough, a sugar beet grower and president of the Crosswalk Sugar Beet Growers Association, presented a similar characterization. Gough states, "They [Puerto Ricans] were honest, clean sort of fellows, never any trouble, never had a merchant in the town complain about the Puerto Ricans."[57] Further to this point, Frank Morris, the *Detroit Times* staff writer, reported that despite the fact that the Puerto Rican migrants are being referred to as stoop workers, "few of them appear to deserve the name. Most of them are wearing sports jackets, slacks carefully pressed, and sport shirts opened at the neck."[58] While these assessments of Puerto Rican migrants may seem innocent enough, it was often done so with implicit, if not explicit, reference to the Mexican workers in the fields. While the Puerto Ricans may have arrived more "respectfully" or "cleanly" dressed than Mexicans and Mexican Americans, it was this same attire that left them unprepared for the turbulent Michigan temperatures and the rugged labor they were about to perform. The lingering cold became such a problem that the Puerto Rican government even had to appropriate some funds so that migrants in Michigan could purchase proper clothing.[59] Thus, ethnic Mexicans were labeled and characterized as dirty, rather than prepared. Whether it was their perceived interest in assimilation, their honesty, or more expensive clothes, a wide range of individuals—including growers, social organizations, and writers—developed essentialized differentiations between Puerto Rican and ethnic Mexican migrant workers in Michigan.

The intersections of race and gender were on full display when observers assessed the family arrangements of the Latinx migrant farmworkers. While the Bracero Program and Operation Farmlift only recruited male workers, Tejanos often came as family units—with wives, children, and other relatives joining the men. The presence of women in the fields had the potential to shift the hierarchical desirability of Mexicans, Mexican Americans, or Puerto Ricans. Furthermore, regardless of whether or not the wives of migrant workers were present in the fields, they were still held responsible for the cleanliness and health of the male workers. On the subject of his preference between "Spanish Mexican" or "Texas Mexican" (Tejano) workers, Harold Gough, president of the Crosswalk Sugar Beet Growers Association, decisively responded that he preferred Tejanos. Gough's reasoning was that "he has his wife with him and his family, and they are more contented, they are not worried about anyone they left being home sick, they do the cooking, and

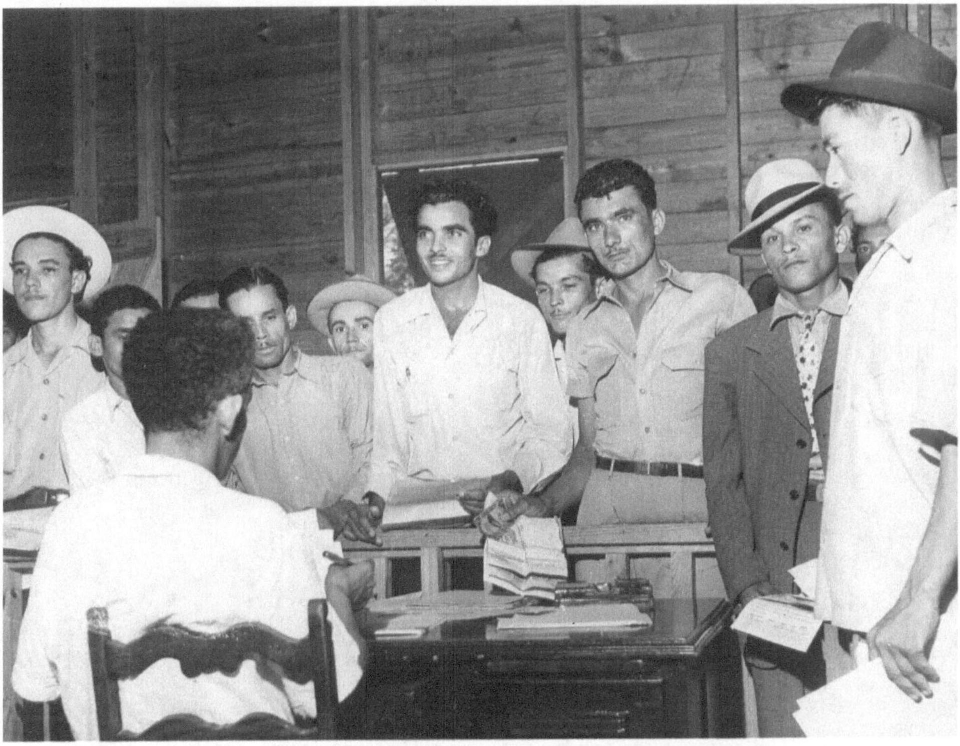

Rosskam, Louise. Salinas, Puerto Rico. July, 1948. At the airport. Agricultural workers ready to leave for the United States where they are going to work. *Archivo General de Puerto Rico, Instituto de Cultura Puertorriqueña Colección Departamento de Instrucción Pública, Fotografía Oficina de Información de Fortaleza / Gobierno de Puerto Rico.*

it is more of a complete arrangement."[60] He positions the Mexican American family work crews in stark contrast to the Mexican braceros. Gough describes the *solos,* or single Mexican men who migrated to the United States on their own, as individuals "who get in a penny ante game, they get a bottle of liquor and all of a sudden they get into a fight and they leave."[61] Without being so blunt, what Gough and other growers likely preferred about families was their ability to wield control over their constricted mobility.

For some growers in Michigan, they preferred Mexican American migrants because of the family considerations that they had to grapple with. Although there were different consequences, braceros could be better positioned to defy the measures of mobility control that growers placed on workers. For example, Gerardo Hernandez Pau was one such worker who deserted his contract in September 1948. Recruited for work in Tampico,

Tony Spina Collection: Migrant family in house. Undated. (spina_47217). Tony Spina Photographs, Walter P. Reuther Library, Archives of Labor and Urban Affairs, Wayne State University.

Tamaulipas, Pau and other braceros traveled by train to Detroit before dispersing to farms in the area. After months of substandard living conditions and broken wage promises, several braceros decided that they had suffered enough. Pau wrote, "Then my friends and I, seeing how bad the situation was, and having in mind the needs of our families in Mexico, to whom we could send no money, decided to come to Detroit and see Father Kern, who had previously assisted a friend of ours."[62] As the abandonment of a bracero contract immediately made them eligible for deportation, this decision was not made lightly. Thus, different sets of calculations and considerations had to go into that decision for family groups of Mexican American migrants versus those of Mexican braceros. As Genevieve Carpio argues in *Collisions at the Crossroads*, "The purpose behind attributing racial meaning to mobility has remained constant: it has served to foster white claims to Indigenous territories and to maintain control over diverse sources of labor in a multiracial region."[63] This was certainly the case for many Midwestern growers who associated a larger presence of Mexican American families in the fields with a more stable work force and harvesting season.

According to the assessment of Max Henderson, executive secretary of Michigan Field Crops, Inc., the reason for their tumultuous experience was that "he [the Puerto Rican migrant worker] did not have a woman in the family with him to do the cooking and to keep the place cleaned up, and the Puerto Ricans did not fit into the family-type housing that we had."[64] By placing the Mexican American family units in relation to the Puerto Rican single men who arrived for the 1950 harvest, women, or the lack thereof, were even used as a rationalization for some of the failures of Operation Farmlift. Furthermore, Henderson argued that because Mexican American families were typically together in the fields, they did not need to be paid every two weeks to remit back home. Rather, they could be paid less frequently or at the end of the season. On the other hand, the Puerto Rican migrants wanted their money with a regular frequency, so that they could remit back to their families on the island. Henderson contended that this aspect was "overlooked in the contract."[65] Henderson feigned obliviousness regarding the fact that the Puerto Rican men who traveled to the Midwest alone and desired to remit money back home might present a different set of expectations than migrant families who worked and lived together. Yet this claim is suspect since Mexican braceros had been abandoning MFCI contracts and leveling identical complaints for years.

Similar to Gerardo Hernandez Pau's plight, Eduardo Morales abandoned his bracero contract in 1948, the result of general mistreatment, a staggering amount of wage deductions, and an inability to send money back to Mexico. Beginning his journey in Progreso, Yucatán, it would take Morales twelve days of travel to reach Saginaw, Michigan. After logging over a month of nearly twelve-hour workdays, Morales netted only $20.91 following $42.02 of deductions. Frustrated by their time in the sugar beet fields, Morales hoped for a more gainful experience picking cucumbers. "I went to Blanchard, Mich. and started working eagerly, since I have a family to whom I could send not a single penny. . . . So I was forced to come to Detroit in order to get some help and not with the intention of violating the US law. On the contrary, I just want to be given a job which allows me to send some money to my family."[66] Henderson placed the blame for the Puerto Rican migrants' negative experiences in Michigan on them being a novel group of migrants to the area who were ill-prepared for the absence of women and the "family-type housing." Yet, these circumstances were no different than the ones that braceros encountered since the beginning of the program. Although Henderson scapegoated women and families as the reason for the tumultuous harvest season, the accounts of Puerto Rican workers, as well as Mexican workers in the years leading up to the Truman Commission, show that their grievances were directed toward the stunning amounts of deductions, the withholding of pay until the end of the harvest season, and the generally inhumane living conditions. For agriculturalists, the presence or absence of women and families accompanying male migrant workers was thus used for hierarchically organizing their preferences for different groups of Latinx agricultural workers.

As the statements of Pau and Morales document, migrant men also engaged with narratives of family, but did so with different intentions than those of the agriculturalists. For the migrant workers, the heteronormative family was used to legitimize the necessity of improved labor conditions. Some of the most harrowing stories to emerge from the Truman Commission hearings highlighted this aspect of the Puerto Rican agricultural experience in Michigan—Santos Cintron's story being one of them. Cintron told the Commission about leaving his wife and seven children in Puerto Rico to work in the Michigan fields. Because he was not able to send money back home, his wife had to resort to buying food on credit from the local store. Eventually, the storeowner ended her line of credit. While it is unclear what Cintron's family did for food and other necessities after that, other wives of migrant farmworkers had to resort to selling off their furniture to pay for basic subsistence.[67]

While these conditions led many Puerto Ricans to contest and challenge growers to pay them more frequently, these complaints also resulted in the gendered and racialized trope that characterized Puerto Rican men as weak, specifically in relation to ethnic Mexican farmworkers. As S. L. Durham, chairman of the Michigan Migrant Committee, commented, "As usual . . . the Spanish-speaking Texans had little complaint. They had been through all of it before. . . . It takes a lot of something that is very serious to make Mexican people complain."[68] On the other hand, Harold Gough, who otherwise spoke very positively about the Puerto Rican migrants, claimed "they would be crying about this, that and the other."[69] Whereas Mexicans and Mexican Americans were generalized as tough and durable, the complaints made by Puerto Rican men resulted in some branding them as weak, and, therefore, less masculine. This rhetorical distinction between the toughness of ethnic Mexicans and Puerto Ricans diminished the valid claims that the Puerto Rican migrants raised about labor conditions in Michigan. Alongside public health and US citizenship, gendered understandings of mobility and family competed to shape the way that agriculturalists created hierarchies regarding which Latinx migrant group was deemed most desirable.

"Puerto Ricans, American Citizens Just as Much as You or I": US Citizenship as a Contested Terrain for Labor Rights[70]

In 1950, Father Clement Kern established a three-person investigative group to uncover information regarding the working conditions of Michigan's most recent group of agricultural laborers, Puerto Rican migrants. Although it is unclear whether Father Kern's motives were to comparatively analyze the wages of Puerto Ricans and Mexican workers, the study that he and the committee conducted implicitly did so. After this committee investigated the conditions that Puerto Ricans encountered, it concluded, "The results of their time-studies of sugar beet acres proved what the Mexican consul had proved in 1945—that a single man in working the beet fields, could not make sixty cents an hour, but that he would do well to average twenty cents."[71] According to this investigation, in terms of wages, the Puerto Rican migrants that arrived in Michigan in 1950 were no better off than the Mexicans that had been in the fields for years.

Santos Cintron's emotional testimony during the President's Commission on Migratory Labor gained a significant amount of traction in both local and mainstream press sources. Following eight weeks of work in the fields, the grower employing Cintron notified him and other workers that there would be no more work. Expecting to have earned a total of $43.65 and demanding his payment, the MFCI notified him that he actually owed the company $9.69. As the *New York Times* described, Cintron "left a wife and seven children in Puerto Rico in June to come to Michigan to earn money for their support." Additionally, in an attempt to demonstrate that this was not a solitary incident, this article added that Cintron's experience "was typical of others."[72] Although many of the Puerto Rican workers contracted to work in Michigan had been told that they would not have to pay for the cost of transportation, most were charged at least $55 for the cost of airfare to the fields. Eduardo Morales, a contract worker from Yucatán, Mexico, decided to go to Michigan based on the promise that he would be able to make a decent living working in the fields. After a month and two days of working from seven in the morning to seven in the evening, he received a statement notifying him that $42.02 would be deducted from the $62.93 he thought he had earned, with most of the charges being for food.[73] Because many of the food and grocery stores were owned by some of the large agricultural companies, it was quite common for food to be exorbitantly overpriced. The tactics used by growers against both migrant groups was linked to their racialization as a single group of exploitable workers. Puerto Rican laborers were then subjected to the same deduction practices that had been in place for Mexican workers.

In May of 1948, the *Detroit Free Press* started reporting on the seasonal arrival of Mexicans to harvest Michigan's sugar beets. It reported, "Most of the laborers are natives of Texas. Some are from New Mexico. Nearly all are American citizens."[74] This was one of only a few articles that referenced the fact that a significant proportion of Mexican migrant workers were actually US citizens by this time. By 1948, there were nearly as many Mexicans with formal US citizenship working in the Michigan fields as there were Mexican nationals. According to Michigan's Farm Advisory Committee, there were 13,000 "Texas-Mexicans" and 16,000 "Mexican Nationals" who had migrated to work in the state's agricultural industry the previous year.[75] Two years later, the 5,000 airlifted Puerto Ricans would join the ethnic Mexican migrants in Michigan. Although nearly half of the Mexican laborers in Michigan's fields were US citizens at this point, they were afforded different opportunities than Puerto Ricans to use citizenship claims as a means for contesting abusive labor conditions. As Natalia Molina explains, "Consistently contrasted to blacks and Puerto Ricans based on citizenship status, Mexicans were cast as immigrants. . . . Because distinctions were rarely made between Mexicans and Mexican Americans, it left the impression that all Mexicans, including Mexican Americans, were immigrants."[76] This was best evidenced when the President's Commission on Migratory Labor made its visit to Saginaw, Michigan, which primarily focused on Puerto Rican laborers. This begs the question, why did the commission's hearings primarily focus on Puerto Rican workers when there was a much larger contingent of Mexican laborers in the same region?

Kern took advantage of this moment to bring attention to the dreadful labor conditions and the negligence of Michigan growers. For years before Puerto Rican migrants arrived in Michigan, Kern had attempted to make government officials aware of the conditions Mexican workers encountered in the fields. "The government holds wage hearings every January and not a single worker is represented," Kern declared. "When we step in, our testimony is pooh-poohed, because they say we don't know the good happy workers, and besides we're only do-gooders anyway."[77] Because ethnic Mexican migrant workers would typically return to Mexico, Texas, or disperse throughout Detroit following the harvest season, few, if any, migrants could testify at the wage hearings in January. For example, on January 4, 1949, the year before Puerto Rican migrants would arrive to Michigan, the *Detroit Free Press* ran a short article covering the hearings that would help set the wages and work standards for the upcoming season. Advocating on behalf of the migrant farmworkers at this hearing was a representative of the Consumers League of Michigan and Father Kern, who was identified in the article as a representative of the Mexican Field Workers Defense Committee. Whereas these two supporters of farmworkers pled for higher wages, improved housing conditions, and an investigation into the use of child labor, sugar beet growers and processors recommended that piecework rates be reduced and for the "bonus" to be increased for workers that stayed in the area until the harvest was completed. At the 1949 Detroit hearing, there was actually a migrant worker in attendance, but their presence was dismissed as relatively inconsequential. As the *Detroit Free Press* reported, "From the only actual beet field worker present, Tomas Ledesma, of 421 E. Jefferson, who does not speak English, the committee received only friendly smiles and a complete lack of comprehension."[78] Therefore, the Truman Commission on Migratory Labor was a rare opportunity for migrant workers to have their voices heard, as well as to have issues pertaining to their experiences in the Midwest represented more broadly.

Throughout the Commission on Migratory Labor's visit to Saginaw, there were frequent rhetorical references to the fact that Puerto Ricans possessed US citizenship. In their newspaper article appropriately titled "American Atrocities," Gordon Blake writes that the Puerto Rican migrants are "American citizens just as much as you or I." Blake continues, "This incident will forever remain a blot on the escutcheon of American justice and fair play. While we are fighting to make the world safe for democracy, America, it seems, is becoming less and less a safe place for Americans."[79] In a radio broadcast discussing the conditions of Puerto Ricans working in Michigan, Frank Edwards declared, "Those Puerto Ricans are American Citizens. Several in that group are veterans of World War II. Five of them married with families."[80] Some journalists thus invoked the citizenship status of Puerto Ricans to criticize the work conditions prevalent in Michigan's agricultural industry. In addition to elevating the citizenship status of Puerto Ricans, the radio segment also tied in their "patriotic" military service to the United States and heteronormative nuclear families as reasons for why the workers were deserving of restitution. In the media coverage of the Saginaw commission hearings, Puerto Rican guestworkers are consistently recognized as US citizens deserving of improved labor conditions. Yet very little of the same exposure was afforded to Michigan's ethnic Mexican migrants. This approach of invoking the citizenship of

Puerto Ricans as a means for articulating the necessity of improved working conditions was effective in the attention it brought to the rights of migrants, but it could exclude Mexican braceros and other ethnic Mexicans who were not citizens. Ultimately, Puerto Rican laborers did succeed in bringing attention to the agricultural work conditions in the Midwest and in demonstrating the necessity of broader migrant rights. Yet, this did not save them from some of the demeaning treatment that noncitizen migrant workers were subjected to.

One of the most explicit ways in which Michigan's Mexican and Puerto Rican contractual laborers were racialized as foreigners was via the regulation and monitoring of their bodies. Cindy Hahamovitch contends, "In the imagination of US officials, guestworkers were men of color whose movements had to be carefully monitored."[81] This was done through the use of identification numbers, which were assigned to both Mexican braceros and Puerto Ricans that were brought into Michigan during Operation Farmlift. For the braceros working in Michigan, workers had a card with their identification number and their name that they were instructed to always keep with them. For Puerto Rican laborers, any correspondence sent from the Puerto Rican government's Department of Labor that concerned a specific contract worker always included their identification number alongside their name. Although Mexican and Puerto Rican workers had some ability to subvert the surveillance efforts of growers and the state, these identification numbers were conceived as a mechanism for regulating and monitoring these "transient" workers.[82] In this realm, possessing US citizenship did not prevent Puerto Ricans from having their movements monitored and tracked.

Formal citizenship did not protect Puerto Rican migrant workers from the harsh work conditions of Michigan's agricultural industry or tracking that braceros were subjected to; it also could not fully prevent threats of deportation. The racialization of migrant labor equated Latinx farmworkers with noncitizenship, even for those born with US citizenship. A letter Father Kern received exposed the lack of knowledge about the citizenship status of Puerto Ricans and how migrant laborers were assumed to be noncitizens. Two months after the Truman Commission's hearings in Saginaw, the medical superintendent of Ypsilanti State Hospital wrote to Kern about one of their patients. The representative of the hospital matter-of-factly stated, "We are writing to inform you that our patient, Mr. Herminio Matias, will be deported to Puerto Rico on the morning of November 16th."[83] The next day, the medical superintendent sent a follow-up letter to Kern that "Herminio Matias was not deported on this date as had been planned. The patient refused to board the plane with the immigration official at the Willow Run Airport, and it was necessary to return him to this hospital."[84] This letter encapsulated the shaky ground that Puerto Ricans' US citizenship rested on, particularly for migrant workers. There were alarming consequences that could result from the presumed foreignness of Latinx migrant workers, regardless of citizenship status. In short, using US citizenship as a way of articulating the necessity of migrant rights was a precarious approach. While useful in garnering sympathetic media coverage support, its effectiveness in materially improving labor conditions for migrant workers was minimal.

Conclusion

At least initially, Mexicans, Mexican Americans, and Puerto Ricans were all sought by Midwestern agribusiness for their supposedly innate ability as agricultural workers. This racialized trope that Latinx migrants were better suited for stoop labor, particularly for harvesting sugar beets, subsumed the three Latinx groups into an indistinguishable whole. This racial logic underpinned growers' continued recruitment of temporary migrant workers to Michigan's fields. Yet, eventually, many in Michigan began to formulate hierarchies that were equally based on racialized sets of characterizations. While these constantly evolving hierarchies lacked any unifying or clear logical pattern, they demonstrated the fluidity and malleability of notions of race. Depending on the characterizations and classifications being used, the elevation of one group as "preferable" was often in relation to negative stereotypes of the other Latinx group. Thus, there was a fluctuating hierarchy of who was the preferred group of Latinx laborers.

Public health officials, academics, reformers, and politicians played a critical role in the dissemination of these characterizations to the broader public. These officials utilized understandings of respectability, gender, health, and mobility to legitimize their desires for different groups of Latinx migrant farmworkers. Influential figures lent credence to the racialized tropes concerning Mexicans, Mexican Americans, and Puerto Ricans in Michigan. The 1950 visit of the Truman Commission on Migratory Labor in Saginaw emerged as a platform where the shifting racialization of Latinxs would be on full display. At the same time, the arrival of the Truman Commission also provided an all-too-infrequent opportunity for Latinx farmworkers to publicly challenge the power and authority of Midwestern agribusiness. This defiance allowed Latinxs to criticize the harsh wage structure of agricultural labor, demand improved living conditions and healthcare, and, most importantly, articulate the necessity of more expansive migrant rights and protections.

CHAPTER THREE

A Migrant Public Sphere

Networks of Exposure and Institutional Interventions

On July 8, 1946, Francisco Espinosa and Uvaldo García crafted a letter that they would send to journalist Marcelino Mendoza in Detroit. Espinosa and García sought to ingratiate themselves with Mendoza by recognizing his "great patriotism" and all the services he had provided to other Mexican nationals in Detroit. Feeling disheartened from the lack of attention to the struggles of migrant agricultural workers in the region, the letter writers state that "it seems like God forgot about us and that the word of man has no value, because the abuses continued on and on, and hope was lost." They had left their families in Chihuahua, Mexico, along with thousands of others, sold their crops and animals, and went through the complex process of obtaining a *bracero* contract, all with the hopes of providing a better life for their family. These aspirations of upward mobility were crushed with the realization that even working ten hours a day would never result in them making the "minimum wages" stipulated in their contract. Employer-imposed deductions impeded workers from obtaining their expected pay. These deductions included pay for the cook in the camp, their coal, and the bus trips to the local store, all of which amounted to $1.50 per day of deductions for each worker. With these complaints in mind, but no Mexican consulate in the immediate vicinity, Espinosa and García decided to advocate for themselves to their employers.[1]

In return for their complaints, they earned the epithet "agitators." The growers sent Espinosa and García to work in different fields and isolated them from the rest of their labor crew. Finding these circumstances intolerable and afraid of going on a "blacklist" that might deny them a future bracero contract, they asked their employer to send them back to Mexico. Refusing this request, the growers informed the two braceros that they could not leave the fields without first being jailed, possibly for up to two months. Concluding that it was worth the risk, Espinosa and García wrote to Chicago's Mexican Consul and then made their way to Detroit. Although what happens next is slightly unclear, the two indicate that they transcribed the letter they wrote to the consul in Chicago and brought that to Detroit's consul, who then technically gave them permission to return to Chihuahua. Yet, he informed them that they still needed to return to the farm they were working on before they could go back to Mexico. "As you can imagine, Mr. Consul," wrote Espinosa and García, "how could we go back there if we only have four cents in our bag?"[2] As these braceros had already written to Chicago's consul and personally visited the one in Detroit, what did they seek to achieve by writing to Marcelino Mendoza? This chapter proposes that the answer to this question hinges on the concept of a "migrant public sphere."

In 1945, alongside William F. Foley, Mendoza began publishing a semimonthly Spanish-language newspaper titled *La Colonia*.[3] Ultimately, Espinosa and García hoped that this letter would help expose the ordeals faced by migrant agricultural workers in the Midwest. Before more thoroughly detailing their experiences in the fields, the two former braceros articulated their purpose and desired outcome from writing this letter, stating, "Please publish it [for] our compatriots, both workers and residents of this country, [to] realize the arbitrariness and abuses that have been committed."[4] As we see from this vignette, and as we will see from others, one of the most powerful methods available to migrants for contesting the power of growers and state officials is what I am terming the migrant public sphere.

I use the term "migrant public sphere" to describe the process by which Latinx migrants sustained a transnational circulation of information through their travels, correspondence, and the print press. Although various branches of the state—such as the US Department of Labor, the Mexican Consulate, and the Puerto Rican Department of Labor—frequently neglected worker grievances or misled the public about agricultural labor conditions, migrants utilized their personal experiences and historical memory to act as a counterbalance to official state narratives. Participating in the migrant public sphere helped forge a broader circulation of knowledge that allowed migrants to be more informed about what would await them in the Midwest's agricultural industries. At the same time that migrants propelled this public sphere with their expanding *networks of communication*, often times, they were seeking to disrupt *networks of movement* by discouraging prospective migrants from participating in temporary guestworker programs. There were indeed some measurable outcomes that resulted from the migrant public sphere. This could take the form of mobilizing and organizing Latinx workers in the fields with the intention of hindering or halting the daily operations, or it could consist of diplomatic interventions via consulates, bureaucratic agencies, and other legal recourses. Even if participating in the migrant public sphere produced irregular victories, migrants created an outlet for articulating their experiences.

In Mexico and Puerto Rico, literacy was on the rise. At the same time that labor migration was expanding via the Bracero Program and the Farm Labor Program, so were the literacy rates in both territories.[5] These intersecting state-sanctioned labor migration programs, as well as increasing levels of literacy, are the context for understanding the transnational public sphere that migrants would create through their travels, their correspondence, and their strategic use of the press. Migrants of course used other mediums outside of the written word to communicate, such as the telephone and radio, but newspapers and letter writing provide the clearest archival trail of the migrant public sphere. This chapter begins by briefly outlining a few of the central tenets of the public sphere, criticisms of it, and the continuing utility of this framework. This is followed by a conceptualization of the migrant public sphere, and an examination of how this approach shaped the ways that migrant farmworkers sought to improve their rights and conditions within the agricultural industry. The scope of this chapter, for the most part, underscores the networks forged by Mexican immigrants and Puerto Rican migrants. However, it is worth noting that this is not the full extent of the migrant public sphere.

Mexican Americans who settled in the Midwest also contributed to this public sphere by writing to the "*La Voz del Público*" ("The Voice of the Public") section of San Antonio, Texas's *La Prensa,* for example. Individuals like Telésforo Oviedo, sometimes on behalf of Saginaw's *La Unión Cívica Mexicana,* wrote letters addressed to Ignacio E. Lozano Jr., the son of *La Prensa*'s founder and eventual editor of Los Angeles' *La Opinión,* and Alonso S. Perales, a lawyer, diplomat, and Mexican American civil rights activist.[6] In these letters, Oviedo advertised *La Unión Cívica Mexicana*'s services for assisting immigrants with their paperwork, questioned the Bracero Program's role in displacing Mexican American farmworkers, and criticized the city government of Saginaw for not improving the facilities and services of the Mexican neighborhoods.[7] Other contributors, like Gabriel Torres writing in 1954 on behalf of the Migrant Workers Defense League, sought to persuade *La Prensa* readers *not* to come to Detroit and other Michigan cities. With the declining number of defense contracts and industrial production reaching its lowest level since 1945, according to Torres, prospective migrants would "avoid much suffering and headaches" if they were disabused of the idea that fortune and vast employment opportunities awaited them in Detroit.[8] Beyond newspapers like *La Prensa,* which served Spanish-language readers, there were also English-language county newspapers across South Texas that reveal a similar migrant public sphere in their "Spanish Section," "Latin

News," or some other similarly titled section. Although not the focus of the chapter, this is an area due for further examination.

Considering the Public Sphere and the Migrant Public Sphere

Social, political, and cultural theorists continue to debate the strengths, limitations, and parameters of what constitutes "the public sphere." First presented in *The Structural Transformation of the Public Sphere*, Jürgen Habermas states, "The bourgeois public sphere may be conceived above all as the sphere of private people come together as a public; they soon claimed the public sphere regulated from above against the public authorities themselves, to engage them in a debate over the general rules governing relations in the basically privatized but publicly relevant sphere of commodity exchange and social labour. The medium of this political confrontation was peculiar and without historical precedent: people's public use of their reason."[9] The public sphere consists of a public of private individuals using dialogue and reason to critique public authorities (such as the state, police, or courts). Public opinion, then, becomes a vehicle for conveying the needs of society to the state. According to Habermas, the public sphere was the result of twin historical processes: the gradual emergence of capitalist markets and the development of spaces of social life, media, and topics of discussion that encouraged rational-critical debate. Regarding the first process, emerging capitalist markets required reliable information to bolster the circulation of commodities, with literacy and print being an important component of this. The second process—based on reading circles, coffee houses, salons, and the print press—brought together private individuals who publicly used reason to critique government, science, or literature.[10]

Pablo Piccato, historian of Mexico, offers important insights concerning debates over the utility of "the public sphere" for scholars of civil society, culture, and politics. Piccato summates Habermas's conceptualization of the public sphere as a universally accessible space where individuals discussed topics of common interest with the assumption that reason was evenly distributed and that the opinions of private citizens would impact public opinion. Yet, as Piccato also mentions, the regular emergence of authoritarian regimes and the exclusion of some from full political participation indicates that the public sphere is tentative rather than a completed historical process. The framework for the public sphere that Habermas formulates in *The Structural Transformation of the Public Sphere* has certainly been susceptible to historical and theoretical criticism. These critiques range from historical and chronological imprecisions, a focus on European bourgeois elites, the class and gender exclusions, among other shortcomings. Regarding these criticisms, Piccato's assessment is that scholars have evaluated *The Structural Transformation* as a precise historical study, rather than as an outline for a broader theory. This chapter follows in that vein by assessing the public sphere as a productive approach for examining how migrant workers transformed private interests into public dialogue exchanged with others and how they utilized this approach to make their concerns known to state officials.

As private individuals forge a public sphere through communicative practices and public dialogue to address shared concerns, the private sphere and public sphere function as relational realms. Habermas argues that "the fully developed bourgeois public sphere was based on the fictitious identity of the two roles assumed by the privatized individuals who came together to form a public: the role of property owners and the role of human beings pure and simple."[11] In short, Pablo Piccato states, "For Habermas, public and private were mutually constitutive."[12] For Mexican, Mexican American, and Puerto Rican migrants, as well as the family members that remained behind, the public sphere and private sphere were not just closely associated, but they mutually reconstructed and reinforced the other. In this case, private families are writing across various borders and deforming notions of separations between private, community, and public spaces.

As scholars typically assess the public sphere within the context of specific nation-states, this chapter will demonstrate that migrants stretched the public sphere that they created across national, continental, and colonial borders. Migrants from the Texas-Mexico border, the interior of Mexico, and Puerto Rico circulated ideas and information through their travels, through local newspapers, and through other media networks that proved capable of extending the reach of this public sphere. For example, what are the implications of Mexican braceros building a migrant public sphere that challenges the authority of both Mexican and US state officials or institutions? Or, how should scholars consider the numerous Mexican nationals making claims upon representatives of the state, but who are situated in the United States, like the Mexican Consulate? Because of the Bracero Program's nature, specifically that it a was binational labor agreement, the complaint system of migrant laborers inextricably implicated the United States and Mexico. Also important to this discussion of a transnational migrant public sphere and its relationship to a specific nation-state, particularly for Mexican and Puerto Rican migrant workers, is how they challenged and subverted the authority of the state. As Piccato mentions, "While political parties and representative forms of government are important [to the public sphere], their impact becomes less consequential when their political legitimacy is contentious, and when people begin asking who speaks for them and why."[13] In the case of Latinx migrant agricultural workers in the Midwest, the public sphere they created was informed by questions surrounding whether government officials could adequately respond to their needs. In short, a migrant public sphere challenges us to consider how the typically "national" context of a public sphere is tested by migrants who are consistently traveling, writing, and disseminating information across national and territorial borders.

Major Spanish-language press sources, like *La Prensa*, frequently published articles about "El México de Afuera," or the communities of Mexicans spread throughout the United States. One reason for this is that, during this period, the Mexican and Puerto Rican governments were concerned about their constituents living and working in the contiguous United States, but were equally invested in controlling the perceptions and attitudes that others in the United States had of their constituents. Yet, migratory laborers also developed judgments about the places they lived and labored and were inspired to correct the narratives propagated by state officials. The transnational travels and correspondence of migratory farmworkers allowed them to recover some of the control over their situation that they were denied while working in the fields. Through migration, correspondence, and the press, Mexican and Puerto Rican migrants who had spent time in Michigan were able to create a public sphere centered on historical memory and their experiences there. By sharing their experiences with a broader public, migrant workers, to some extent, were able to control the narrative surrounding the agricultural conditions in Michigan. It is important to note that these networks of information were not necessarily intended to dissuade future migrants. Rather, this public sphere allowed potential migratory laborers to make the most informed decision possible. Some migrants still made the decision to migrate north, despite knowing the difficult conditions they would encounter. Thus, the migrant public sphere was the accumulated migratory experiences of Mexicans and Puerto Ricans in Michigan, which they then disseminated to a broader audience through letter writing, newspapers, and other forms of communication.

The Mexican Migrant Public Sphere and Consular Intervention

When Mexican migrant workers in Michigan encountered work and living conditions that were particularly dire, as seen in the last section, they would sometimes seek to organize among themselves to gain concessions from growers. Whether this meant writing to them or leaving the fields and visiting them directly, helpful bureaucrats could go a long way for migrant workers in need. As historian Julie Weise writes in *Corazón de Dixie*, "These men [braceros] believed that as full citizens in a modern nation, Mexico, they were due better wages and working and living conditions in the United States; they hoped and expected that Mexican consular representatives would use their political power to enforce superior conditions."[14] While the amount of support and assistance workers received from bureaucrats varied, these institutional figures factored significantly, both negatively and positively, into how farmworker concerns were addressed.

In a letter to Sarah Hepburn of Royal Oak, Michigan, Thomas Keehn, chairman of the National Citizens Council for Migrant Labor, addressed the lack of oversight and accountability regarding the conditions of migrant workers. Keehn wrote, "The only recourse Mexican workers will have is through their Consuls. . . . This amounts in effect to little or no protection, since no Federal or State agency is required to make inspections or to enforce the very vague terms of the contract."[15] Devoid of any protections from state or federal labor laws (i.e., worker's compensation, minimum wage, unemployment compensation, minimum housing standards, etc.) and with little other recourse, braceros in Michigan, and elsewhere in the United States, were heavily reliant on the assistance of their local Mexican consul. As Weise contends, an "activist consul" could help Mexican braceros recover lost wages, improve work/living conditions, and secure other fringe benefits. Yet, while consular assistance could improve the quality of life for braceros, they still existed on the margins of society.[16] The amount of support and initiative provided by a consul toward intervening in bracero-related cases varied drastically on the consul. There was no standardized or universal reaction by consul representatives to the complaints raised by Mexican nationals. During the mid-1950s, the attentiveness of Detroit's consul to bracero concerns, at times, bordered on apathy. So much so that, during this period, some incidents in Michigan required the intervention of Mexican consuls in Texas.

During the summer of 1953, the state of Michigan was increasingly earning a reputation for having exceptionally poor working conditions for migrant workers. One of the likely reasons for the perilous conditions and for why the Mexicans intensified their organizing efforts during this same summer, was because of the lack of institutional support that braceros were receiving from the Mexican consul in Detroit. On June 18, 1953, Raúl Michel, the Mexican consul for El Paso, Texas, began to write a series of letters to Omar Josefé, the Mexican consul for Detroit, Michigan. These letters detail a stream of braceros that had already crossed the Mexico-Texas border, traveled to Michigan to work for Michigan Field Crops, Inc., and who now ended up back in El Paso.[17]

The first arrivals were five braceros from three different work crews. Two of the braceros that were part of the same crew, Tomás Rodríguez and Ricardo Escobedo, ended up having their contracts canceled after a disagreement regarding their rate of pay. While they were originally informed that they would earn a piecework rate, with which they could individually earn more money the more efficiently they worked, they were ultimately paid according to the volume of produce picked by their entire crew of twenty-five laborers, and then the earnings were divided equally among the crew. Rodríguez and Escobedo were incensed because they felt they had put more effort into the work than the rest of the crew. Furthermore, they alleged that the rest of the laborers were consciously working slower in a form of protest against the employer. The employer then withheld work from the two disgruntled braceros for a week, after which they returned to the fields with the rest of the crew, without the permission of the employer. Rodríguez and Escobedo had only been working for two hours before they had their contracts canceled, were detained by police, and then returned to El Paso. This case reveals an interesting characteristic of these particular employers/growers, which may have been a shared attitude among growers on a broader scale. In this instance, a labor disruption in the form of a slowdown was more tractable and tolerable than vocally displeased workers. Rodríguez and Escobedo not only claimed to have been working more diligently than the rest of the crew, but they also informed the employer of the purposefully lackadaisical pace of the other workers; and yet their contracts were canceled. The employers found the vocally disruptive braceros to be more of a threat and direct challenge to their preferred field practices and, therefore, determined they had to be removed from the camp. While Rodríguez and Escobedo were neither the first or last braceros to have contracts canceled over minor complaints or disputes, the regularity with which braceros were returning to El Paso and other parts of Texas from Michigan was alarming for agencies within the Mexican government.[18]

What prompted Consul Michel to begin this correspondence with Josefé was that following the first group of five workers, which Rodríguez and Escobedo were a part of, another fourteen workers returned with canceled contracts by the MFCI, and sixteen more were arriving soon. When it came to labor disputes and contract cancellations, Josefé's track record, particularly in 1953, demonstrated his tendency to side with growers and the US Department of Labor and against Mexican braceros. With that being said, Josefé was not a completely unconcerned institutional figure. In October of 1952, the year before this stream of mass contract cancellations, Josefé was quite involved with trying to recover unpaid wages that were denied to thirteen undocumented non-bracero Mexican workers.[19] The context and representations of these cases ultimately shaped the amount of support that Mexican laborers could expect to receive. In the case of the workers who were denied earned wages, Josefé was emboldened to declare to the acting district director of the INS that these practices were "not only inhuman but above all, antidemocratic."[20] Despite the fact that they were undocumented, they were characterized as "good" workers, which can symbolize a range of qualities from honesty, to hardworking, to obedience, and so on. Josefé explains that this group dedicated themselves to twelve-hour workdays and even accepted a lower rate of pay in exchange for an end-of-season bonus from the grower, which was a verbal agreement. Thus, it was the Mexican workers who were diligent and loyal, and the growers abused their trust and broke their word of honor by not paying out the bonuses. However, in the case of Rodríguez and Escobedo, despite all indications otherwise, they were branded as "bad" workers. These two were coded as disruptive, for vocally complaining directly to the growers, and disobedient, for returning to the fields against the instructions of the growers.

These examples demonstrate that representations of workers were not only based on their actual work productivity, but they were also the result of personality and character traits, which could be manipulated by different actors for different purposes. As the Mexican Consul inherently functioned as a nationalist institution, it was exceedingly concerned with the image of its nationals to the broader US public. At least during the early periods of the program, braceros were often referred to as representatives of a US-Mexico Good Neighbor Policy.[21] Thus, in order to manage and control the image of braceros and other Mexican workers, consuls were heavily invested in notions of respectability, which could determine who was deserving and undeserving of their assistance. The workers most deserving of assistance were those that were compliant and normative, even if it meant tolerating abuse. As one newspaper article reported, "True, in many cases they were exploited. That will hamper our Good Neighbor Policy for years to come. But this is not true everywhere. In some communities they were gratefully welcomed as neighbors and allies and became, unconsciously, amateur ambassadors, taking back with them our friendship and gratitude."[22] Although it was an "unfortunate" consequence of being a migratory laborer, it was the workers' obligation to withstand the abuses they received from growers. Whereas Rodríguez and Escobedo found the system of pay to be intolerable, the thirteen Mexican noncontractual workers were worthy of consular support for their ability to endure twelve-hour workdays for a lower-than-normal rate of pay.

For Mexican immigrants navigating the institutional landscape that the consul was entrenched in, it was difficult for them to predict where they could expect to find support. While the Mexican Consul was an institution that had legitimate legal power, support for migrant workers was still dependent on a final decision from specific individuals. During the early to mid-1950s in Detroit, Michigan, this person was Omar Josefé. While braceros during the 1953 summer did not find Josefé to be very receptive to their concerns, El Paso's Consul Raúl Michel became very troubled with the situation in Michigan. After a total of thirty-five Mexican workers contracted by the MFCI had arrived in, or were on their way, to El Paso, Michel found the contract cancellations to be in violation of the 1951 Migratory Labor Agreement, with Josefé being partially responsible for lack of oversight. While Michel claims that Josefé signed off on the firings of the first five workers, for the rest of the workers, there did not appear to be any evidence to show that Josefé conducted any interviews or authorized the contract cancellations. In short, the MFCI and United States Employment Service (USES) canceled the contracts unilaterally, which was not permissible. In an impassioned call to action, Michel wrote to Josefé, "It is evident, therefore, that the working conditions in that region are extremely bad, and if we add to the complicity of the Representatives of the USES in allowing and helping these anomalies, the situation is even more serious."[23] Michel then continued by pleading for Josefé to make his "protest more expansive."

This letter, and the incident more broadly, reveal significant aspects about Michigan agriculture, the bracero experience, and institutional support for migrant workers. Consul Michel was stationed on the US side of the Ciudad Juárez-El Paso border. As this was one of the principal sites for braceros and other Mexicans to enter the United States, and return to Mexico, he was an authority on Mexican migrant work conditions throughout the country. Michel and the El Paso Consulate interacted with thousands of braceros from throughout the United States who had either completed their contracts, left on their own before completion, or had contracts canceled. Thus, Michel's assessment that "It is evident . . . that the working condition in that region are extremely bad" is a critical condemnation of Michigan's agricultural industry. Michel was trying to intervene in a way that would assist braceros that had already been contracted to Michigan, as well as prevent an issue that would continue to fall on the hands of Mexican consuls across the Texas-Mexico border for years.[24]

Later that summer, in August of 1953, Omar Josefé was at the center of facilitating information between the US Department of Labor's Regional Office in Cleveland, Ohio, and the *Secretaría de Relaciones Exteriores* in Mexico City, Mexico. This correspondence addressed the firing of four Mexican braceros working at the Food City Pickle Co. in Battle Creek, Michigan.[25] Another four men would later suffer the same fate as the first group. According to the official investigation by the US Department of Labor's Regional Office, the growers initiated the process that eventually resulted in the firing, jailing, and deportation proceedings of the workers because "[they] were causing unrest, dissatisfaction and a general slowdown among a group of 130 workers under contract to him."[26] According to the Department of Labor's report, the four workers began their organizing efforts almost immediately when they arrived in the fields. This continued for two weeks before growers threatened them with termination of their contract and deportation if they did not pick up the pace. While in-field labor disruptions and threats of deportation for noncomplying braceros were not uncommon, the details of this incident exhibit the lengths that migrant laborers in Michigan went to in order to enact change in the fields.[27]

Pedro Miranda Gómez and José Hernández were identified as the main leaders of this group of braceros, as well as the source of the "disruptions" occurring in the fields. The actions of these two labor leaders demonstrate the deep desire that they had to organize braceros and other migrant workers in the state of Michigan. As the Department of Labor's investigation into this incident proceeded, it was discovered that Gómez and Hernández were going on their third straight summer of leading strikes, slowdowns, and sit-downs in the Michigan fields. These included a 1951 strike in Fremont, a 1952 strike in Lakeview, and this year's 1953 incident in Battle Creek, Michigan. Gómez was described as being "especially proud of the fact that he is a 'leader of men' and that he has formed strikes in other areas before." Hernández's expression of pride came in the form of carrying "clippings from Mexican newspapers indicating that he led strikes in Michigan for the past two years."[28] Through their actions and their statements, these two men made it clear that their sole purpose in migrating north to Michigan was to organize workers. This was a sustained effort over the course of at least three summers to influence power dynamics in the fields.

An important aspect of this episode is the level of planning involved with this strike, which indicates that this was not a spontaneous occurrence, but was a calculated disruption. This is not to dismiss slowdowns, sit-downs, and more impromptu strikes. Rather, this incident shows braceros and other migrant workers were not against organized labor. As evidenced with this case, some attempted, and then attempted again, to organize Mexican workers in Michigan. It also demonstrates the ambitiousness of organizing braceros. Braceros, "wetbacks," and other workers without US citizenship were considered to be a detriment and damaging to the mainstream farmworkers movement of the 1960s. Furthermore, the penalty for dissent by braceros in the fields was detention and deportation. Thus, the farmworkers leading the strike understood the repercussions of their actions, and also understood the uphill struggle to organize workers unprotected by state, labor, and immigration laws. Finally, while there were certainly large segments of the migratory population that were illiterate or partially literate, others were able to utilize their literacy to make legal claims based on the 1951 Migrant Labor Agreement. A focus on these aspects of the event provides for a markedly different perspective on migrant labor and the preparation some workers undertook to organize themselves.

A characteristic of their approach with this strike was the staggering of separate waves of defiance. After about two weeks of work slowdowns and several meetings with Joe DeRuiter, owner and manager of Food City Pickle, Gómez and three other workers were pulled from the fields and informed that their contracts were being terminated. Afterward, the remaining 126 workers came into the living camp from the fields. At this point, Gómez "got up and made a long and impassioned speech to his fellow workers inciting them to refuse work and in general, creating a disturbance in the dormitory."[29] DeRuiter then insisted upon calling Immigration and Naturalization Service to remove the four workers. Although this incident had seemingly concluded, the remaining workers still refused to return to work. It was then determined that Hernández and three other braceros were leading the further refusal to work. With the likelihood that Gómez and his three other partners would be removed from the camp, there was a secondary group in place led by Hernández. Thus, there was a deliberate strategy to prolong the strike as long as possible by having a contingency plan.

On August 21, 1953, Pedro Miranda Gómez, the detained and eventually deported strike leader, penned a letter to Omar Josefé, Detroit's Mexican

Consul. Gómez wrote that he had been selected as the collective spokesperson and representative for the group of eight workers fired from Food City Pickle. Gómez wrote this letter while out on parole during the deportation proceedings to express their displeasure with the consul's role, or lack thereof, in this incident. Demonstrating his legal and contractual acumen, Gómez wrote, "You did not participate in a joint investigation of our case as provided by in Article 30, Section (b) of the Migrant Labor Agreement, as Amended, and we therefore demand that you forward this notice of objection, without delay, to the representative of our government in Washington, DC, so that a final determination of the alleged violation of our work contract may be made."[30] Gómez applied this clause for two reasons. First, Davenport's report for the Department of Labor argued that the grounds for termination were based on two articles of the labor agreement, which the workers dismissed. These stated that laborers must take "corrective action" to resolve worker-employer related issues and that workers "'perform all agricultural work required of him with proper application, care and diligence.'"[31] While the growers are the ones subjectively determining "proper application" and "diligence," Gómez is not necessarily objecting to that point. Rather, he is arguing that regardless of whether those articles were defied, he and the other workers were denied their right to a comprehensive joint investigation by the Department of Labor and the Mexican Consulate. Second, Gómez is charging Josefé with not being involved in the investigation and, therefore, neglecting his responsibility to the Mexican braceros. According to Davenport, Josefé did indeed agree to the termination of their contracts, but this was done over the phone and without a physical visit to the fields to investigate the workers' claims. This letter exhibits how Gómez, and the workers he represented, were prepared to engage with the limited legal protections provided for in the 1951 Migratory Labor Agreement, that he possessed a comprehensive and applicable knowledge of the work contract, and that the Mexican government was not above criticism and accountability.

The 1953 incident at Food City Pickle also exposes the intersections of Michigan's agricultural industry, the Department of Labor, and the Immigration and Naturalization Service. Moreover, these institutional connections did not go unrecognized by the workers themselves. On August 12, Gabriel Torres and Emery Biro completed a comprehensive investigation including identifications of each of the terminated braceros, the complaints of the arrested, interviews with workers, an interview of Davenport, and they also offered their own conclusions regarding the situation. It is unclear who these men represented, whether they were investigating on behalf of another party, or if they occupied some other position altogether. What is evident from their letter, though, is their criticism of the involved government agencies. The authors of this letter state, "He [Davenport] showed the workers that he was interested only in carrying out the will of the owner who wanted the men fired. . . . The men felt that they would find at least impartial treatment by the US representative, but on the contrary they found only a servant of the pickle company."[32] With the findings that Davenport had terminated the workers' contracts at the request of DeRuiter, owner and manager of Food City Pickle, and without hearing the workers' side of the story, the actions of the Department of Labor were evidence enough to demonstrate that they were acting as an extension of the growers.

With the involvement of so many different government agencies (INS, Border Patrol, Department of Labor, and the Mexican Consul) that frequently dismissed migrant worker complaints, these migrants were sensibly concerned with whether or not anyone had their interest in mind. In the report's conclusion, Torres and Biro reflect on the reasons for why the eight workers were fired. They write, "Because they are Mexicans apparently they have no recourse against an employer who does not 'like them.' . . . The real reason seems to be that the men were good representatives of the 130 fellow workers and since they were out-spoken and sought their rights, they were jailed."[33] The reality for immigrant farmworkers on temporary contracts was that a grower could relatively easily cancel their contract, thus immediately turning them into undocumented and deportable migrants. Furthermore, this was particularly true for those who were active in organizing their fellow workers. Growers were well aware of this leverage that they had on migrant workers, and they used it as a disciplining force. As Torres and Biro state, "The resistance was broken" once the eight workers were removed from the camp for deportation.

The termination of a bracero contract was the only action necessary to make a Mexican contract worker liable for deportation. While the power to terminate a contract was held by representatives of the Department of Labor, the Immigration and Naturalization Service executed deportations. Thus, once we consider who is capable of performing contractual terminations and deportations, the entanglement between these agencies/departments and agricultural growers becomes more evident. Another important characteristic of the bracero and undocumented experience in Michigan is their presence within the regulatory web of Border Patrol agents stationed at the "other border." In this particular case, Detroit's INS office sent Border Patrol inspectors from Port Huron, Michigan, which is separated by a bridge from Point Edward, Ontario.[34] Thus, while the fired workers had already been forced to endure inspections along the US-Mexico border, they now found themselves being policed by agents operating in the US-Canada borderlands.

This case offers a glimpse into transnational labor organizing that had its origins 1,634 miles away from the Food City Pickle Co. in Battle Creek, Michigan. The coordination of this labor unrest began in Monterrey, Nuevo León. Gómez and Hernández were community leaders in Nuevo León and had a significant amount of influence on the distribution of bracero contracts at the local level. According to other workers that were interviewed for the official investigation, the strike leaders were capable of causing "considerable trouble next year when it came to recontracting time in Mexico . . . [because] their acceptance or rejection at the reception center in Monterrey depended upon the recommendation of Gómez and Hernández."[35] While the Department of Labor's account of this incident suggests that other workers only went along because they were threatened, other accounts of the situation at Food City Pickle indicate that that assessment is far too simplistic.

What can be gathered, though, from the above statements is how the execution of the binational Bracero Program was vitally dependent on transnational local developments. One question that needs to be resolved is: How were Gómez and Hernández capable of receiving a bracero contract in Michigan year after year, despite being recognized as strike leaders and labor organizers? The last sentence of the official investigation report states, "In the opinion of the writer, these two men are not agricultural workers, they have cost the American government and their representative employers an untold amount of money and it is hoped that they can be restricted from importation into the United States under agricultural contract again."[36] One explanation for this is the amount of influence they held at the local level. As community leaders in Monterrey, a location with a reception center for prospective braceros, they had some level of decision-making power that could dictate who did and did not receive contracts. Thus, they likely had the ability to select themselves as contract recipients or instruct someone to select them, which allowed for their yearly migration to Michigan. While the planning of the strike and obtainment of bracero contracts occurred in Monterrey, Nuevo León, the impact of these preparations was felt in Battle Creek, Michigan's pickle fields.

Generating $75,000,000 per year and accounting for around 30 percent of the entire crop harvested in the United States, the cucumber pickle is a staple of Michigan's agricultural industry.[37] If the crop is allowed to grow too large, it becomes less useful for pickling and processing.[38] Thus, it is necessary to pick them at precisely the right time. As Carl Davenport wrote in the Department of Labor's report, "Pickles have to be taken off the vines as they come of proper size, if they are not removed at that time, they grow too large to have much commercial value, thus creating substantial loss to the company concerned."[39] In total, the strike stopped work at Food City Pickle for two days, which, in combination with the timing of the strike, cost the company thousands of dollars of product. Realistically, the actions of the strikers here did not dismantle the Bracero Program or vitally disrupt it as a whole, but they do demonstrate how the program operated on an everyday level. Despite the negotiated binational agreements between the United States and Mexico, the vetting process for dispersing contracts, the actual contracts that Mexican nationals signed, and any other bureaucratic or institutional measure put in place by either government to ensure that this program was executed effectively, this program could still be fundamentally shaped at the local level by everyday migrant laborers. In this instance, where braceros from Northern Mexico conceived of a plan to lead a strike and then carried it out in Southwest Michigan, migrant workers demonstrated their capabilities of having a ruinous impact on a company's harvest season.

The case of the 1953 Food City Pickle strike in Battle Creek, Michigan, exhibits the desire and resilience that some migrant Mexican labor leaders had for organizing workers in the state. With individuals like Gómez and Hernández traveling from Nuevo León to Michigan for three consecutive summers, braceros in Michigan demonstrated an aptitude for organizing other migrant workers. This was displayed not only through actual strategy used during the strikes and slowdowns, but it also included legalistic and contractual knowledge of the binational labor agreement that brought them to the United States. Yet, this case also reveals the web of power structures in place to discipline workers who deviated from the demands of the growers. From the Department of Labor and INS, who acted in accordance with Michigan growers, to the Mexican Consul, who was complicit in this incident, there were a variety of government agencies who, knowingly or not, preserved power relations in the fields. Last, this case shows how the Bracero Program functioned both at the local and transnational level. From leveraging community power in Monterrey, Nuevo León, to secure bracero contracts, to carrying out a strike that would cost Food City Pickle thousands of dollars of lost crops in Michigan, this binational labor agreement was profoundly shaped by ordinary people in little known locations. While bureaucrats in Washington, DC, and Mexico City shaped the terms of the Bracero

Program, migrant laborers in places like Battle Creek, Michigan, determined the outcomes of the program.

The most popular and accessible way of contributing to the migrant public sphere was through Spanish-language newspapers. The promise of a migrant public sphere of information was at its best when news outlets and agricultural workers worked in unison. Founded in 1913 by Ignacio E. Lozano, *La Prensa* for many years reached more Spanish-language readers than any other newspaper in the United States. It had a readership that spanned across Mexico, and the US *La Prensa* covered the Mexican Revolution and the state of Mexican politics more broadly; detailed the conditions of Mexicans living in the United States; provided information about global developments, such as the latest entrance of nations into World War I; and even more obscure items, like the publications for sale at Lozano's bookstore.[40] Differentiating *La Prensa* from earlier Spanish-language newspapers, Daniel Morales writes, "One aspect, however, stood out: it sought to create a real and imagined community around Mexican identity, a community that was both deeply tied to nationalism and that existed outside of the nation itself."[41] Ultimately, one of *La Prensa*'s main objectives was to keep Spanish-language readers in the United States informed on current events in Mexico, and to keep people in Mexico informed on the experiences of their family and friends across the border.

During the 1956 harvest season, *La Prensa* sought letters, complaints, and other correspondence from braceros. On August 25, they published an article stating, "The apathy of the Mexican Consular authorities in Detroit, Michigan, in disregarding the complaints of our bracero compatriots . . . has been manifested in a letter sent to our newspaper, which is the fruit of *La Prensa*'s campaign near the bracero reception centers in Hidalgo and Eagle Pass, Texas, when giving away [free] copies of this newspaper to the contracted braceros, we ask them, in a flyer, among other things, to report the abuses committed against them."[42] This article and the accompanying letter include each of what I argue are the three main pillars of the migrant public sphere: to feel like their voice is being heard, to communicate to a broader audience (whether it be individuals, like partners or relatives, or to the press, such as newspapers and radio), and to prompt action, particularly from government officials. Not only was *La Prensa* receptive to letters and other correspondence from migrants, but as shown here, it was actively encouraging it.

The letter being highlighted in the newspaper was written by a bracero whose name *La Prensa* chose to withhold. This worker was contracted to

Swanson Farms in Ravenna, Michigan, and wrote about the injustices he and the hundreds of other braceros there experienced. He alleges that the owner declined to follow the contract, paid the workers "arbitrarily," practiced discriminatory acts, and only gave some of the contracted laborers actual work. He reported that although they were supposed to receive 75 cents an hour, many failed to even earn 2 dollars a day. Yet, the most severe criticism from the newspaper and the letter writer was saved for Detroit's Mexican Consulate. *La Prensa*'s article concludes, "The matter is now in the hands of the Secretary of Foreign Affairs of the Government of Mexico, so that a thorough investigation is carried out and the justice to which our compatriots are entitled is given, punishing as appropriate, the company and calling the necessary attention, as it should be, to the Mexico office in Detroit, Michigan so that, no matter how small the complaint, the corresponding investigation will be carried out, as have other Consular Representatives in the Southeastern Region of the United States of America." Ending the article on this note exhibits several things: First, at the very least, that the publicity surrounding conditions in Michigan made its way up Mexico's institutional hierarchy; second, that workers and the press were going to jointly hold the consul and other representatives of the Mexican government accountable for their responsibilities; and third, that future migrants would be aware of agricultural work conditions in Michigan and might be better served by consuls in Texas, or somewhere else besides Detroit's consulate.[43]

The last quote from the unnamed bracero's letter states that, with the cooperation of *La Prensa*, "I will not rest in denouncing the arbitrariness [of wages and work time] of the company until it is corrected, in other words, [until the company is] put on a blacklist."[44] Recalling the 1957 situation where hundreds of braceros contracted for the MFCI returned to Eagle Pass, Texas, it was articles and correspondence like these that provided agricultural workers with the information to best handle particular situations. The streams of migrants who left the Michigan fields during the mid-1950s did not arbitrarily end up at the consulate in Eagle Pass or Hidalgo. Rather, these were sites that they knew would be more receptive to their complaints. The workers who wrote to newspapers and other press sources were strategic and intentional with their goals. As the bracero letter writer stated, his specific objectives were twofold: to work cooperatively with *La Prensa* in exposing the work conditions in Michigan and to have Swanson Farms banned from contracting future workers. Letters and/or communication and broader information outlets created and sustained the migrant public sphere. This letter and article simultaneously inform an expansive readership about agricultural work in Michigan and appeal for an appropriate response to worker grievances. Migrant farmworkers understood the power of a broad audience and used it skillfully to transmit important information transnationally.

Eventually, in September of 1957, Mexico's *Secretaría de Relaciones Exteriores* sought for Michigan Field Crops, Inc. to be placed on a list of companies and organizations that were unacceptable for future braceros.[45] One of the main reasons why the problem of contract cancellations in Michigan multiplied over the course of the 1950s was because of the lack of institutional oversight by the Mexican Consulate in Detroit. As the power of growers over braceros and other migrant workers went unchecked by the US Employment Service, Department of Labor, other federal and state agencies, and, at times, the Mexican Consulate, the inaction of consuls was tantamount to complicity.

A Puerto Rican Migrant Public Sphere

"We are in the obligation to reciprocate with highest phrases, this treatment the state has had for its visitors. The honor that you have given to the Puerto Rican groups will be a symbol of more fraternity between the United States and Puerto Rico."[46] This was part of a July 1950 letter sent to the *Detroit Free Press*. Written by Saturno Quinones, who along with three other signatories called themselves the Committee of Publicity, this group of migrants was part of "Operation Farmlift." This group of letter writers were engaging in a broader dialogue about the treatment of Puerto Rican farmworkers on Michigan farms, whether the program had thus far been successful, and, ultimately, the future of the program in Michigan. While growers were often quick to sing the praises of Puerto Rican migrants as upstanding guestworkers, migrants and other observers were not always as quick to return the favor toward the farmers.[47]

As William Dorvillier, a correspondent for Puerto Rico's *El Mundo* and later a founder of *The San Juan Star*, reported, at the Truman Commission hearings, there was hardly a bad word said about the work ethic or conduct of the migrant workers. As for whether Puerto Rico should ever participate in the program again, Dorvillier had this to say, "Puerto Rican farmworkers should never return to Michigan sugar beet fields without an ironclad contract guaranteeing decent living conditions and reasonable income."[48] Given this context, the tone and content of the letter to the *Detroit Free Press* from the Committee of Publicity is curious. "We, the Puerto Rican, never forgets a good deed," continues the letter, "Puerto Rico has contributed its sons in

Morales, Luis. *Gobernador Muñoz Marín estrecha la mano a Regalada Rodríguez de Cordero en una pobre casa del barrio Jurutungo. Ella es la esposa de uno de los obreros de Michigan. Archivo Fotográfico del Periódico El Mundo de la Universidad de Puerto Rico.*

two wars to defend democracy. We four are all veterans of those wars. The American people may be sure of our cooperation in this new conflict as we did in the other two wars—fighting under the same flag and same God."[49] The letter writers are never fully transparent about their intentions for it. The committee could have been attempting to present Puerto Ricans as "model minorities," which Gina M. Pérez's *The Near Northwest Side Story* examines. What appears to be more straightforward is that this letter to the state's preeminent newspaper conveyed gratefulness, patriotism, and the Good Neighbor-esque language of fraternity at a time when it was questionable whether the Farm Labor Program would have a future with Michigan agribusiness.[50] The following decade, when the FLP was at another critical juncture, Puerto Rican farmworkers would rely on this tradition of the migrant public sphere.

Toward the end of June 1964, the Commonwealth of Puerto Rico entered into a contract with I. Miller Pickles, Inc. of Edmore, Michigan, to supply them with a number of agricultural workers. These workers were part of Puerto Rico's Farm Labor Program, under the Department of Labor's Migration Division. Two hundred and sixty migrant workers signed contracts that stipulated a wage of $1 per hour over the course of 13 weeks, with a minimum of 160 hours of work per four-week period. Problems arose on September 5, one month into the contract, when all operations of the employer were stopped, and this was exacerbated on September 8 when Isaac Miller filed for bankruptcy. Prospective workers flew by plane from Puerto Rico to Michigan expecting to make hundreds of dollars on a contract guaranteeing three months of secure labor. Yet, after working for a month without receiving a paycheck, they were informed that Miller Pickles filed for bankruptcy and the plant manager lacked authorization to pay them. *El Mundo* followed the developing matter, reporting, "The workers tried to riot on Sunday when they learned of the factory closure and the non-payment of their wages and transportation expenses, but the intervention of political officials and religious representatives prevented serious incidents."[51] After becoming aware of the growing unrest, Edmore's mayor, Charles Mox, contacted W. Willard Wirtz, US secretary of labor; Orville Freeman, US secretary of agriculture; and Puerto Rico's Department of Labor. Frank Zorilla, secretary of labor of the Commonwealth of Puerto Rico, then instructed Joseph Monserrat, director of the Migration Division, to travel to Michigan. Once there, Monserrat arranged for the migrant workers to return to Puerto Rico while officials gathered details. The workers' agitation captured the attention of local and national officials, but it would take more than that to resolve this situation. Puerto Rican workers necessitated the continued institutional and legal assistance of government representatives to not only recover their unpaid wages, but also the wages they had not yet worked but were guaranteed in their contracts.[52]

On September 22, 1965, more than a year after Miller Pickles filed for bankruptcy, Judge Edward Benson returned a decision in Michigan's Western District Court as to whether Puerto Rican farmworkers would be compensated for their unfulfilled contracts. Exactly a month after the declaration of bankruptcy, Zorilla filed a claim against I. Miller Pickles for the amount of $90,875.95 as compensation for the lost wages of the contract laborers. The arguments made by Zorilla and his team of lawyers grappled with the National Bankruptcy Act. It was generally uncontested that the 260 Puerto Rican workers were collectively due $14,719.30 as a priority claim for the "wages earned" from August 23 through September 9. What was disputed, though, was the interpretation by Puerto Rico's secretary of labor that the phrase "wages earned" in the Bankruptcy Act also included "wages guaranteed by a contract of employment but not representing compensation for actual work performed."[53] In short, the Puerto Rican legal team was making the claim that the migrant workers were also entitled to the wages that they did not get a chance to earn, but which were "guaranteed hours" according to their contract.

Judge Benson ultimately ruled that the Puerto Rican agricultural workers would only be entitled to a priority wage claim of $14,719.30. The balance of the claim, $76,159.65, was determined to be a "general non-priority unsecured claim," meaning Miller Pickles was not liable to pay the workers for the remainder of the contract that went unworked. As a reminder of the omnipresent colonial relationship between the United States and the Commonwealth of Puerto Rico, federal taxes reduced the priority wage claim for the agricultural workers by $2,855.55.[54] Thus, at this point, their compensation for enduring this ordeal still amounted to hundreds of dollars less than they had anticipated making for the duration of the contract. Furthermore, as with most bureaucratic processes, this lawsuit continued to drag along. On January 16, 1968, Lydia Torres Gonzalez, attorney for the secretary of labor of the Commonwealth of Puerto Rico, wrote a Petition for Review to Judge Benson requesting that Miller Pickles be ordered to pay the full amount originally ordered in the priority wage claim. Gonzalez's argument was that the original priority wage claims already included tax deductions and that they were exempt from the withholding of income tax because none of the workers earned more $600 during their time in the United States. This meant that three and a half years after the workers' contract was broken and two and a half years after the Commonwealth of Puerto Rico filed the lawsuit, workers had still not received compensation or a resolution for this situation. Because institutional intervention was undoubtedly the only avenue for recuperating the lost wages, it forced the Puerto Rican workers into a legal and institutional landscape that had, thus far, not produced any tangible results.[55]

Toward the end of August 1968, *El Mundo* reported that Puerto Rico's secretary of labor, Alfredo Nazario, finally began to distribute the proceeds of the bankruptcy case to the workers. In the end, Puerto Rico's Department of Labor secured a sum of $18,719.30 for the migrant farmworkers—the original $14,719.30, plus an additional $4,000 indemnity bond from Aetna Casualty and Surety Company for the failure of I. Miller Pickles to carry out the terms of the work contract. At the Santiago Iglesias Room of the Department of Labor office in San Juan, a group of thirty-five claimants and relatives representing the group gathered to receive their payments. Before handing out the checks, Nazario proclaimed, "We can be proud that our country [Puerto Rico] has a Department of Labor that . . . takes great care in protecting workers, no matter where they are."[56] While this statement was certainly intended for the migrant workers and their families that were adversely affected by Miller Pickles' bankruptcy and contract cancellations, it also sought to send a clear message to US employers. Nazario's comments reflected the Puerto Rican Department of Labor's increasingly assertive efforts to better protect the rights of contract workers and penalize employers that sought to bypass formal labor contracts. In 1967, a year before the Miller Pickles settlement, the *New York Times* reported, "The Puerto Rican Department of Labor has intensified a campaign to protect the nearly 40,000 men who work from spring to fall on United States fruit, vegetable and tobacco farms."[57] The result of this heightened effort was the arrest of ten employers, or their labor intermediaries, who were recruiting Puerto Rican migrant workers in violation of Commonwealth Law 87.[58]

During the spring of 1967, Puerto Rican authorities arrested the employers and labor contractors at the San Juan International Airport. In addition to prohibiting employers or recruiters from hiring workers or facilitating transportation to the US mainland without prior authorization from the Puerto Rican Department of Labor, Commonwealth Law 87 also required a fixed wage, a minimum amount of work hours, description of work and living conditions, and insurance. The Department of Labor's continued pursuit of the Miller Pickles settlement was part and parcel with its effort to require and enforce labor laws that would protect Puerto Rican migrant workers. More than four years after arriving in Michigan, Pedro Lin, of Guayama, received the first check from Nazario. For Lin and the 259 other migrant workers, the long-overdue restitution for this legal battle amounted to a check for $74.49. At least in this instance, the workers did eventually receive the modest settlement owed to them. Still, navigating the bureaucratic and legal landscape was tedious, time-consuming, and frequently unfulfilling.[59]

With 1964 being the last year of the Bracero Program, the Puerto Rican Department of Labor considered the summer of 1965 to be an important one for their Farm Labor Program. In 1965, the Farm Labor Program attempted a "pilot program" in Michigan called the Lake Erie Operation. The Puerto Rican officials tried to account for as many variables as possible in an attempt to make the Lake Erie Operation a successor to the Bracero Program in Michigan.[60] This included a contractual agreement between the growers or growers' organizations and the migrant workers, thorough camp ground inspections by representatives of the Puerto Rican government, preventative measures to ensure Puerto Rican workers did not abandon contract, and stipulations that would appease growers. While the Department of Labor took these precautions to ensure the successful execution of this program within the contiguous United States, an unanticipated factor that they had to reckon with was "Michigan's Image in Puerto Rico."

During the mid-1960s, Guadalupe Ruiz was known as the "troubleshooter" or "compliance man" in the Michigan fields. In terms of the regional bureaucracy for Puerto Rico's agricultural program, Luis Machado was the Midwest Region Director of the Department of Labor's Migration Division; Raul Vega was the Michigan Representative for Farm Labor Program/Migration Division; and Guadalupe Ruiz was the one who worked directly with growers and Puerto Rican farmworkers. Ruiz would investigate complaints, handle situations among workers, and move disgruntled workers to other farms. In a 1965 letter from Ruiz to Machado concerning "Michigan's Image in Puerto Rico," Ruiz writes, "It took a lot of time to fight the image of Michigan in Puerto Rico as a result of two previous disasters in that state. One more than 15 years ago in which 5000 workers suffered serious consequences; and another last year with the 'Miller Pickle' in which 200 workers have not yet collected their salaries."[61] As this letter attests, Puerto Ricans on the island maintained a long-lasting historical memory regarding the agricultural work in Michigan. Whether it was the tragic plane crash before the start of the 1950 season where twenty-seven Puerto Ricans died, the 5,000 Puerto Ricans who suffered through an unexpectedly turbulent experience during that same harvest season, or the hundreds of former workers who waited years for compensation from their bankrupt ex-employer; Puerto Ricans had an enduring understanding about this particular state.

While it is tempting to concentrate on these spectacular and dramatic episodes as the sole cause of Michigan's image, a migrant public sphere established through everyday experiences, written correspondence, and the press, were equally important influences. The lawsuit resulting from the Miller Pickle bankruptcy surely triggered memories of the historical shock stemming from that first large-scale migration of Puerto Ricans to Michigan nearly fifteen years prior. Yet, part of why this incident was so easily retrievable from the memory banks of Puerto Ricans was because of the routine and regular reminders of what could be expected from Michigan's agricultural industry. During the 1965 harvest season, Puerto Rican officials on the archipelago received a series of complaints from the family members of workers who migrated to the Michigan fields. Matilde Fernandez, an orientation coordinator in Puerto Rico for the Farm Labor Program, began investigating a case of workers who were illegally recruited from Manatí. Through conducting interviews in the neighborhoods of Campo Alegre and Cantera in Manatí, Fernandez found concerned family members of two workers who, without notice, left the Michigan fields. These family members provided written letters alleging mistreatment and lack of available work. William Santana corresponded with his father, and Ricardo Sierra wrote to his wife and mother. While Santana and Sierra's initial complaints to family members were actually enough to have an official from the Puerto Rican government visit the fields to investigate, the two workers denied their complaints out of fear of retribution and retaliation against them and the other workers of the camp. In order to escape the camp, they pretended to go into town for shopping, leaving all their belongings behind, and eventually making it to Chicago and New York. These types of stories circulated on a weekly basis throughout the island and sustained the negative image of Michigan. These experiences were communicated to family and friends verbally and in written correspondence, which then, as this case shows, became broader neighborhood and public knowledge. While Santana and Sierra only sought to directly convey their hardships in Michigan to their immediate family members, some Puerto Rican migrants had grander objectives.[62]

Representatives of the Puerto Rican government in the Midwest were earnestly trying to make the 1965 Lake Erie Operation a successful one. For growers, they were doing everything possible to quickly resolve issues that arose in the fields, trying to prevent migrant workers from skipping contracts, and encouraging the growers to participate in this program for the upcoming summers. For workers, the Midwest's Migration Division was trying to hold growers accountable to the contracts they signed, visiting the labor camps regularly, and urging migrants to be "good" workers. In an August progress report regarding Aunt Jane's Foods in Dearborn, Michigan, Guadalupe Ruiz wrote to Anthony Vega, "[Management/growers] are satisfied with the production and are earnestly trying to make a go of this experiment. . . . Be ready to give any assistance required and to try to improve relations among the workers themselves."[63] Throughout each of the field reports concerning Aunt Jane's Foods, Ruiz consistently emphasized several things: that growers were satisfied with the production, that Puerto Rican officials needed to keep growers interested in the program, and that they should ensure "the best possible selection of men" for future work contracts.[64]

When it came to representing the program to growers, workers, and the broader public, Puerto Rico's Migration Division and Department of Labor were invested in spinning the Lake Erie Operation as a successful one. Ruiz contentedly reported to Vega that out of 101 workers contracted to work on the camp of Aunt Jane's Foods, none "skipped" out on their contracts. This is a number that the Puerto Rican government could provide to future growers and migrant workers in order to ease any concerns, of either party, about participating in this program. By this account, everyone involved was satisfied. Yet, this is a misrepresentation of the facts. While zero workers "skipped," or abandoned the camp without notice, Ruiz reports that there were nine workers who did not technically "finish their contract"; two who enlisted in the Army, two who were unable to work due to previous injury, three from sickness, one because of an emergency back in Puerto Rico, and one out of "mutual agreement" with the company. Additionally, though, there were twenty workers who "were not working out very well" and the company convinced them to ask to be sent home early. Somehow, these workers were still considered to have "completed their contract." In total, more than a quarter of the workers left Aunt Jane's Foods early. This clear misrepresentation of what was happening in the fields by Puerto Rican officials is one of the reasons why workers felt the need to regain control of the narrative surrounding the migrant experience in Michigan.[65]

On September 3, 1965, Anthony Vega received a letter, which was later passed onto Ruiz for investigation, from the Humacao District Office in Puerto Rico about a letter sent from agricultural workers in Michigan to WMDD radio station in Fajardo, Puerto Rico.[66] Enrique Ayala, the worker who wrote in to WMDD radio, began the letter, "My dear friend Alvira," then asked this person to get permission to air the names of the signatories of this letter during the morning news. Ayala continues, "Since we have arrived here, we have been suffering. They promised us one thing at the Department of Labor [Puerto Rico's Department of Labor/FLP representatives] and they have not complied here. . . . The Department of Labor here [US Department of Labor], or the one who intervenes, works with the farmers, talks with them, and then tells us that everything is fine."[67] This letter expresses a starkly different account of the Lake Erie Project than the one that government representatives conveyed.

From the quality of food at the camp, to the lack of work hours being provided, Ayala and the sixteen other signatories felt that the growers, the US Department of Labor, and their own government representatives had failed to uphold their ends of the agreement. Beyond that, though, what likely drove them to write this letter to the radio station was that they felt unheard. The two agencies responsible for protecting their contracts were seen as either closely tied to the growers, in the case of the US Department of Labor, or promoting a more optimistic narrative, in the case of their own government. Not only did this group want to share their experience, but they also wanted to do so to an expansive audience. They aspired to have it reach hundreds and, maybe, thousands of Puerto Ricans who were listening to the morning news. While some agricultural workers contributed to the migrant public sphere so that future workers could make a more informed decision about migrating, others just wanted to be heard. They realized there was a prevailing and more desirable narrative than the reality they were experiencing. The migrant public sphere formed through travels, letters, and various press sources acted as a counterbalance to the more dominant narratives, one where migrants felt they could correct misinformation and disseminate it to a broader audience.

Conclusion

Whether it was through networks of exposure, the incidences of labor organizing, or the assorted institutional interventions by the Mexican and Puerto Rican governments, the creation of a migrant public sphere centered the experiences of the agricultural workers who spent time in Michigan's agricultural industry. Through a variety of communication methods—including letters written by workers, radio, and newspapers—Mexican and Puerto Rican laborers developed a public sphere that sought to challenge the dominant narratives surrounding the migratory experience in Michigan. Through various forms of communication, methods of collective organizing, and institutional interventions by government officials, the migrant public sphere transcended the United States' territorial and contiguous borders. When considering the legitimacy of the migrant public sphere, there could be questions and counterarguments regarding the possibility that migrants were not intentionally contributing to a broader network of information. First, this chapter has refuted the prevalence of that by documenting how frequently migrants went to great lengths to make sure that their written documentations of their experiences reached individuals or media outlets that could further disseminate their accounts. When individuals like Francisco Espinosa and Uvaldo García sought out Marcelino B. Mendoza to publish their letter in *La Colonia* or Enrique Ayala wrote to WMDD radio station in Fajardo, Puerto Rico, they were purposefully contacting media outlets that might be receptive or sympathetic to their problems, and which possessed the capability to present this information more widely. Second, although the intentions of migrants are important to account for, regardless of whether they contributed to this public sphere out of self-interest, out of frustration, or because of a desire to contribute to a collaborative dialogue about agricultural labor conditions in Michigan, the result was largely the same: a more complete body of information about their experiences in the Midwest, which could influence the decisions of future migrants and potentially improve conditions in the fields and camps for other migrants.

Noticeably absent from this chapter is a focus on Mexican American migrants who made up a significant portion of the seasonal migratory body. Mexican Americans certainly contributed to the migrant public sphere through Spanish- and English-language newspapers, as well as through other mediums. Although outside of the scope of this chapter, an analysis of how Mexican Americans utilized the migrant public sphere would deepen our understanding of this concept. A significant emphasis of this chapter is how the transnational public sphere could motivate bureaucratic intervention. For Mexican braceros, they could seek out their local consulate, while Puerto Ricans could reach out to representatives of the Migration Division or the Farm Labor Program. While the Mexican Consulate or Puerto Rico's Migration Division frequently only provided limited solutions to these troubles, at a minimum, they created a record of the complaints. If a central realm of the public sphere is the ability to challenge public officials, the critiques by Mexican and Puerto Rican migrants of their government representatives constituted a major motivating factor.

CHAPTER FOUR

Beyond a One-Hit Wonder

Question Mark and the Mysterians, Interstate Music Networks, and a Latinx Cultural Infrastructure

Lillie Gonzalez and her husband, Jose (or Joe) "El Pato" Gonzalez, were prominent figures in the Saginaw-Bay City, Michigan, Latinx community. More than just husband and wife, Lillie and Joe Gonzalez were also business partners—the couple partially owned two record labels, managed artists in both Michigan and Texas, and owned *El Pato* grocery store in Saginaw. The first time that Question Mark and the Mysterians, a group of Mexican American teenagers, auditioned for Lillie Gonzalez, they had no original compositions, so she turned them away. Six months later, the band returned with "96 Tears." In a 1981 Sunday edition of the *Detroit Free Press*, John Smyntek, assistant entertainment editor for the paper, conducted a brief interview with music critic Dave Marsh. Marsh, a Detroit-born writer, is the prolific author of dozens of books, edited volumes, and the former associate editor for *Rolling Stone* magazine.[1] In this interview, titled "Is Rock Music Dead?," Smyntek asked Marsh a series of questions concerning the state of rock 'n' roll, Detroit's position as a rock city, and the best music records to come out of the Motor City. Surrounded on this list by the likes of Stevie Wonder, Bob Seger, Marvin Gaye, Aretha Franklin, The Temptations, and others, the eighth-ranked song on Marsh's list was Question Mark and the Mysterians' hit song "96 Tears."

Question Mark and the Mysterians spent fifteen weeks on the *Billboard* charts and "96 Tears" peaked at No. 1 on October 29, 1966. Although the band are remembered as a "one-hit wonder" or only among "garage-rock cultists," this band had a more profound impact than they are given credit for. When placing the band within the context of interstate migration from the Texas-Mexico borderlands to the Midwest's fields, the Latinx cultural infrastructure, as I am calling it, and the afterlife of "96 Tears," it becomes clear how much more there is to the Mysterians' history. Moreover, the Mysterians are emblematic of the harvest route that led to the development of communities in mid-to-large Midwest cities. While the Mexican American members of this band were actually from all around the Tri-Cities of Saginaw, Bay City, and Midland, musical and cultural productions out of Michigan often became credited with emanating out of Detroit.[2] At the core of the harvest route were the range of experiences that migrant farmworkers encountered in agricultural settings before they set down permanent roots in cities or semi-urban areas.

This chapter charts the trajectory of Question Mark and the Mysterians and their hit song "96 Tears." The early members of the band were Mexican American teenagers, who were the children of migrant farmworkers that eventually settled in Michigan. The Mysterians' *Billboard* Hot 100 #1 record was the result of the intersections between the Mexican American music industry, agricultural labor, and the post-World War II migration of Latinxs to the Midwest. By historicizing the first "punk rock" band, a thorough examination of Question Mark and the Mysterians demonstrates the influence that Latinx Midwesterners had in shaping US popular culture. Notably, the impact was intergenerational, as artists and bands in the following decades would continue to cover "96 Tears" and adapt the irresistible organ riff. When examining the history of Mexican, Mexican American, and Puerto Rican migrant farmworkers in the Midwest, it is evident that labor extraction and exploitation shaped their experiences. Even in the face of this, the fields served as a cultural site where a different kind of production was possible.[3]

The Harvest Route, Question Mark and the Mysterians, and Punk Rock Music

Before Dave Marsh provided his list of the best songs to come out of Detroit, before he would become the prolific and influential music critic, he was writing articles for *CREEM* magazine. In the May 1971 edition of the monthly publication, Marsh introduced the term "punk rock" after going to a Question Mark and the Mysterians concert and writing about them.[4] Five years prior, Question Mark and the Mysterians were at the height of their musical success.

Before "96 Tears" would sell over one million records and propel Question Mark and the Mysterians to brief musical stardom, the band was comprised of aspiring musicians with backgrounds in various genres and with different levels of musical instruction. Regarding the familial backgrounds and origins of the band, there is some uncertainty and potential misinformation surrounding the birthplace of the members of the Mysterians. Forming in 1961, the newly created group was an instrumental band consisting of Bobby Balderrama, Larry Borjas, and Robert Martinez. Shortly thereafter, since the band needed a singer, Rudy Martinez, who became known as Question Mark, joined to form Question Mark and the Mysterians. In 1996, writing for Toronto's *The Globe and Mail,* Alan Nester reports that Question Mark was born in Mexico in 1945 and that the other band members "were expatriate Mexicans who somehow found themselves in the Central Michigan area."[5] While Question Mark is notorious for alleging that he was born on Mars and Robert Martinez would not reveal his birthplace, it is likely that all the members—including Frank Lugo, Eddie Serrato, and Frank Rodriguez—were Mexican Americans born in Texas. Nester presents the convergence of this band as an almost coincidental occurrence that "somehow" brought these band members together in Central Michigan. Rather, Question Mark and the Mysterians emerged within the context of two intersecting sociocultural processes: the migration of Latinx agricultural workers to the Tri-Cities and the vibrant music scene developing out of the same area.

Bobby Balderrama, one of the three founding members of the band, was born in O'Donnell, Texas, the product of a musical family. The most comprehensive review of the emergence of Question Mark and the Mysterians, the pinnacle of their success, the years immediately following, and their eventual reuniting comes from the website Michigan Rock and Roll Legends (MRRL). As described in the site's mission statement, "The most important migration in terms of music came from the agricultural South in the United States. . . . The people who came to live and work in these municipalities brought a variety of musical styles including Blues, Country, Gospel, Folk, and Latin. These were blended with R&B, Jazz, and Pop into a kind of cross-cultural musical stew that evolved into a very distinct style of Rock and Roll found in Michigan."[6] The MRRL's entry on Question Mark and the Mysterians provides a brief profile on each of the main members of the group, including a characterization of some of the formative musical influences on Balderrama whose father, brother, and cousin were all musicians. While his father played the guitar, accordion, violin, and harmonica, according to Balderrama, it was his cousin who influenced his music most. Balderrama recalls, "Cousin Henry had an album out down in San Antonio and watching him was really great. I learned to play chords from him."[7] While Balderrama's cousin showed him how to play the guitar, it was in the fields where he learned about rock 'n' roll music.[8]

Regarding their settlement in Central Michigan, Question Mark and the Mysterians were the result of what I term the "harvest route." The harvest route encompasses the migratory experiences in agricultural settings that occur before permanent settlement in cities or industrial settings. Encounters in the fields could prove formative to the social, cultural, and political development of Latinxs before they even reached "urban" destinations. The core members of Question Mark and the Mysterians achieved various levels of education and possessed assorted musical backgrounds by the time they joined the band, and their parents found permanent employment in different industries, but there was one constant that connected them to the Saginaw Valley area: that the band members and their families had come from backgrounds as migrant agricultural workers. Thus, when examining the creation and evolution of Latinx communities in small cities like Saginaw and Lorain, Ohio, or much larger urban centers, like Chicago or Detroit, scholars must consider the experiences that migrants encountered before they permanently settled in these areas. In a similar, although not completely comparable, sense, scholars of twentieth-century African American history have demonstrated how the first and second Great Migration shaped the development of music and cultural production. In *Race Music*, Guthrie Ramsey writes, "The blues muse from the 'agrarian South' trekked northward at midcentury migration, and performers mixed and matched with other styles from the 'urban North.' These activities created a field of new and varied rhetoric that laid the foundation for numerous developments of the next half century of cultural production in the United States and the world."[9] While some Latinx migrants made the direct trip from their place of origin to their desired Midwestern destination, others had to take more circuitous routes, which could involve several years of seasonal migration before their permanent settlement.

Migrant agricultural work throughout the Midwest and Michigan's urban-industrial neighborhoods produced many such bands and musicians. Despite the harsh labor conditions and the grueling circumstances of migratory life, the mobility of Latinx farmworkers to and throughout the Midwest generated new cultural productions. Much like the Mysterians, the career of Freddy Fender (Baldemar Huerta), a *Tejano* and country artist from South Texas, further exemplifies how the Midwestern harvest route can shape a sound. In a feature on Fender, the Country Music Hall of Fame highlighted the string of accomplishments in the mid-1970s that catapulted the artist to commercial success. In 1974, Fender released *Before the Last Teardrop Falls*, which the Recording Industry Association of America (RIAA) certified as "Gold" (500,000 units sold) in under a year. In 1975, the title track of the album rose to #1 on the *Billboard* Hot 100, as it also did on the country and pop charts. According to the Texas State Historical Association, Fender produced the first bilingual song to make the country charts. Fender's 1975 commercial achievement was followed by a series of award nominations and notable victories. From the Country Music Association, Fender won in the Single of the Year category, and was a nominee for Album of the Year and Male Vocalist of the Year. The Academy of Country Music named Fender the Most Promising Male Vocalist, and nominated the singer for Album of the Year, Single Record of the Year, and Song of the Year. Between 1975 and 1977, Fender landed seven songs on the *Billboard* Hot 100 chart, four songs that hit #1 on the country charts, and eleven Top 20 country songs. While Fender's commercial achievements and longevity far surpassed that of Question Mark and the Mysterians, the musical expressions of both Fender and the Mysterians were profoundly shaped by migratory labor and the harvest route, which informed their artistic and sonic identities.[10]

Born Baldemar Huerta in 1937 just northwest of the border between Brownsville, Texas, and Matamoros, Tamaulipas, Fender was the son of migrant farmworkers. In an interview for the National Council of La Raza's *Agenda* newsletter, Fender described his introduction to music. "I migrated very early," stated Fender. "In 1947 I was already working on the harvests in Michigan and Ohio. I was 10 or 11 and already playing guitar and singing songs." Fender's time as a child migrant worker in the Midwest was formative—and it is no coincidence that 1947 was also the first year that Fender started singing—but his time there was not the only influential stop along the harvest route. Fender also underscored his time in Arkansas picking cotton and the mischievous adventures that broadened his musical horizons. Fender recalled, "I would go to the black nightclubs, when I was supposed to be buying groceries, and I would slip into the black nightclubs and listen to a lot of blues on the jukebox."[11] *Wasted Days and Wasted Nights*, a biography of the late singer written by his daughter, Tammy Lorraine Huerta-Fender, is filled with details relating to the musician's upbringing, his earlier stage names (*Eddie con los Shades* and *El Bebop Kid*), his struggles with drugs, and an abundance of other accounts that shaped the musician's eventual rise to stardom. Huerta-Fender similarly emphasized the time her father spent in the Midwest, as well as the influence of blues and gospel music. In the biography, Huerta-Fender captured the impression that this period of exposure left on her father, writing, "Season after season, harvest after harvest, and the different melodies that echoed across the fields ingrained themselves into Balde's veins. He soaked in hillbilly and soulful music. As a young musician, this was perhaps the most developmentally rich time of Balde's musical career."[12] For Fender and the members of Question Mark and the Mysterians, this time following the harvest route introduced them to different instruments and a world of new genres that were previously unknown to them. Overall, their music was molded by the experiences of migratory labor.

In an interview conducted a decade after the peak of the Mysterians' success, Balderrama recalls the band and his family's humble beginnings. Balderrama states, "You have to understand, all of us from the Mysterians were born in Texas. My parents were migrant workers. My parents are good people and they never had nothing. In Texas, we lived in shacks with dirt floors, didn't have a home."[13] The Mysterians were the Mexican American children of migrant farmworkers. Like the hundreds of thousands of Tejanos, Mexicans, and Puerto Ricans that would come before and after the Mysterians, the fields and orchards of Michigan offered seasonal work for migrant families and men who came on their own. While most accounts of the Mysterians focus solely on the role of agricultural labor in bringing the members and their families to the Saginaw Valley, those experiences also shaped the development and transmission of their music.[14] Francisco Lugo joined the Mysterians when he was nineteen years old, and he attests that the fields and rural areas were a space where musical technique was honed.[15] For Balderrama, he became familiar with rock music when he was in the fields picking strawberries and another farmworker was playing the guitar.[16] As these two examples demonstrate, the fields were not only a space of labor, but also a cultural site. It was a location where migrants practiced and performed familiar forms of music, as well as became introduced to new musical genres.

Alongside Balderrama, who played the guitar, the other original members were Larry Borjas on the bass and Robert Martinez on the drums. As Balderrama remembers, "We were playing [in] teen clubs and stuff. And we didn't sing, we was all too shy to sing."[17] Following this period of only playing instrumentals, they recognized the need for having a vocalist, which resulted in the addition of their eccentric singer Question Mark. Initially, each member received a letter or symbol for their stage and band name. Balderrama was "X," Robert Martinez "Y," Borjas "Z," and Rudy Martinez "?"—but Question Mark would be the only member to stick to their name and persona. Recognizable for the black sunglasses that he always wore and his assertion that he was from Mars, Question Mark was the performative center of attention for the band. The name of the band that stuck, Question Mark and the Mysterians, came from a Japanese science fiction film.[18] According to the

New York Times, this 1957 color film, "The Mysterians," "has to do with a huge, globular fortress that plops to earth 'from the fifth planet' (wherever that is), envelops a group of glamour girls and is finally destroyed by a brave young Galahad."[19] It was out of this context—as the Mexican American children of migrant farmworkers, practicing in garages and basements, and deriving their name from a Japanese film—from which Question Mark and the Mysterians arose and began to find success during the mid-1960s.

Before "96 Tears" surged to the top of the *Billboard* charts, the band was performing locally and making a name for themselves in the Central Michigan area. One of the Mysterians' most frequent locations to play at would be the Mt. Holly Ski Resort, which was only sixteen miles from Flint and fifty miles from Saginaw. As reporters characterized them, in 1967 at Mt. Holly, Question Mark and the Mysterians were "practically the house band."[20] Some even reported that up to 2,000 fans would show up for Mysterians concerts at Mt. Holly. Through teen clubs and other venues like Mt. Holly, the original members of the Mysterians slowly began to generate a local following. Just as the band was coordinating their first recording sessions, they lost two of their founding members.[21]

Despite their role in the creation of the band and cultivating its early sound, Robert Martinez and Larry Borjas unfortunately missed out on the height of the Mysterians' fame. In 1966, the same year that the Mysterians recorded "96 Tears," Martinez was drafted into service for the Vietnam War. As Martinez recalls, "Our band had a really good thing going, but I had no choice. It was fate, and I missed everything from that point on." Once drafted, Borjas joined Martinez under the "buddy system" because "he knew his number was coming." Thus, within a short period of time, Question Mark and the Mysterians lost their drummer and bassist. Only after being stationed in Frankfurt, Germany, and returning to the United States for a two-week break did Borjas find out about the success of "96 Tears." Although Martinez was proud of the band's national success, he was absent for all of it. In relation to the other band members, Martinez had a very different memory of this period—as he states, "They had their moment, but it came and went. I have different feelings because I didn't experience the crowds and the bright lights."[22] While Martinez and Borjas may be overlooked because they were not present during the height of the band's success, they are very much a part of Question Mark and the Mysterians' legacy.

With the departure of two of the band's members, it was necessary to find new musicians. Explaining how the Mysterians replaced their departing band members, Question Mark recalls, "'But then, in March, Robert and Larry went into the service, so we didn't have a drummer or a bass player. Well, not for long, Robert got us Eddie and Larry got us Frank. Those two had been doing mostly Mexican music, so things really changed!'"[23] Eddie Serrato would become the new drummer and Frank Rodriguez the new bassist. As Serrato explains, he was born in Encinal, Texas, and was far more familiar with *conjunto* and Mexican music. In the late 1940s, Serrato's family settled in Saginaw when his father found a stable job at the Grey Iron Plant. At only fourteen years old, Serrato began playing drums for Conjunto Negrete and recalled playing at local auditoriums and dance halls that became popular for the Mexican bands they hosted. This time spent with Conjunto Negrete gave Serrato an opportunity to connect with other bands outside of Michigan. As he explains, "I got to know a lot of bands that used to come from Texas." Whether it was from formerly living in Texas, performing there, or establishing contacts there, members of the band frequently referred to their connections to the state. As will become more evident further on in this section, these connections to Tejano music and the industry would be an important part of Question Mark and the Mysterians' success.[24]

Alongside Serrato, Frank Lugo filled the band's other void. Lugo was one of twelve children in his family and was born in Weslaco, Texas. As they were a migratory family, the Lugos ended up in Vassar, Michigan, only twenty miles east of Saginaw. Describing how he learned to play music, Lugo states, "In the country it was kind of boring, what else is a kid to do, so I practiced and practiced. I am a self-taught musician." Out of convenience, the Lugos eventually re-settled in "the big town"—Saginaw. According to the 1970 Census, the state of Michigan contained several urban areas that were significantly more populated than Saginaw. Detroit, the state's most populous city, had 1,511,482 inhabitants. Additionally, other smaller urban areas like Grand Rapids and Flint had populations of 197,649 and 193,317, respectively. With a population of 91,849, Saginaw still represented a sizable urban community.[25] While Detroit is the most recognizable location in the state, notions of what constitutes urban space and "the city" are constructed relationally. Saginaw only possessed about six percent of Detroit's population, but in comparison to Vassar, where the Lugo family originally settled, Saginaw was "the big town." Thus, the experiences of some Mysterians highlight the importance of spatial scale and what constitutes the "urban" environment.[26]

The final member of the Mysterians was Frank Rodriguez—whose father worked at the Saginaw Steering Gear Plant. Sonically, one of the most identifiable components of "96 Tears" is the organ riff that pulsates throughout the song. This part of the song's composition can be credited to Rodriguez.

In 1966, Rodriguez joined Question Mark and the Mysterians as the band was going through its reorganization. *The Guardian* describes this period for the band and the influence that Rodriguez had on their sound: "Neighborhood keyboard wiz Frankie Rodriguez was called in for organ duty during the changing of the guard, adding a new dimension to their sound, and as luck (or the People of the Future) would have it, Little Frankie's impromptu four-fingered intro on what was to be their first recording would come to define the signature Mysterians sound."[27] Out of all of the Mysterians, Rodriguez was the most traditionally taught musician. Only thirteen years old at the time he joined the band, Rodriguez had already been playing the piano for eight years. More specifically, he was a trained classical musician. Although there are debates about whether it was a Vox or Farfisa organ used on "96 Tears," there is little confusion about the influence that Rodriguez's contribution would have on future musicians who borrowed and recreated the trademark riff of the Mysterians' song. Following the departures of Martinez and Borjas for the military, replacing them with Lugo and Serrato, and then adding Frank Rodriguez, the band was ready to record.[28]

In an interview with *The Guardian*, Question Mark provided his genealogy of the song's lyrics. Before his introduction to the other members of the band in 1962, Question Mark recalled his desire to learn how to play an instrument so that he could compose music for the lyrics he had. After connecting with a piano teacher who wanted him to begin with scales and other introductory material, Question Mark found himself too eager for this type of instruction. During this lesson, and with the instructor now just playing the piano, Question Mark states, "I sang, 'Too many teardrops for one heart to be crying' and 96 Tears came right out."[29] Fast-forward four years and Question Mark and the Mysterians had reconstructed a full band, and with a recording date arranged by Lillie Gonzalez, the band met at Frank Rodriguez's house in Bay City to prepare. In a separate interview, Question Mark cites this practice session as the "magical moment" where "96 Tears" fully materialized. With thirteen-year-old Frank Rodriguez on the keyboards, Question Mark became absorbed with the notes produced—"It wasn't so much what he was playing, but the sound was driving me crazy! I was saying to myself 'Where did I hear this?' . . . Then 'Little Frank' played it again and it entered my head. I knew I had heard that sound; it was from an old man playing the piano when I was singing lyrics a few years earlier."[30] Bobby Balderrama recalls this moment similarly: he had just finished playing some guitar chords, Rodriguez was "real dominant with the keyboards," and Question Mark was singing lyrics he wrote years before.[31] The next time that

Rodriguez played the riff, Question Mark remembered the chorus that would eventually echo throughout "96 Tears."

For the Mysterians' recording session that would ultimately lead to "96 Tears" and "Midnight Hour," Lillie Gonzalez booked the band at Art and Mildred Schiell's Bay City recording studio. Art Schiell, who was also a beauty salon owner, ran this small business between 1956 and 1969. From wedding recordings, orchestras, and eventually local rock musicians, Schiell's business card advertised, "We record Everything."[32] Describing the studio where the Mysterians' debut would be recorded, Question Mark states, "They had storm windows, no acoustics, no headphones, no separation—and so it wasn't like anything we had envisioned as a recording studio."[33] While Question Mark recalls the simplicity of this arrangement, the makeshift space was relatively well-equipped and the session only cost the band $50. From there, Pa-Go-Go label pressed between 750 and 780 copies of the single, "96 Tears" made its way to different radio stations, and the song's popularity grew exponentially.[34] The song began to gain traction on the Saginaw-Bay City station, then expanded to Flint, then Detroit, and then to Windsor, Canada's CLKW. Describing the 1960s music scene, James Thompson in his article "Detroit's Play-It-Extra-Loud Rock 'n' Roll Scene," explains, "This was a time when radio stations would still play local releases, when a hometown punk combo's crudely recorded single might be aired next to the latest releases by The Rolling Stones."[35]

This was the context within which the Mysterians found their early success and transformed a song recorded in a makeshift studio into a No. 1 hit—where the local popularity of "96 Tears" could be parlayed into a nationally recognized anthem. Bobby Balderrama conveyed this sentiment by recognizing Saginaw DJs Bob Dyer and Dick Fabian for their initial promotion and support, which helped the Mysterians gain exposure. As Balderrama expressed, "They just wanted to see a band from the local area do good."[36] Yet, despite the local fan base that the Mysterians were cultivating and their commercially thriving hit single, the band still encountered combative radio stations and concert venues.

According to Yolanda Gonzalez, daughter of Lillie and Jose, because Question Mark and the Mysterians were young Mexican Americans, some radio stations and teen clubs were reluctant or even refused to play their music or book the band for performances. Reflecting generally on these types of incidents, Balderrama states, "For all the negativity that came at us after our hit song, or before. All the people that were prejudiced—you know, they didn't want us to play there. I don't let that bother me. I just look at them as not very wise."[37] Although the band members' interviews and newspaper articles about the band speak frequently about their backgrounds as the children of Mexican American migrant workers or being the first *Mexicano* band to have a record sell a million copies, there is remarkably little scrutiny about how this part of their identity may have created difficulties in navigating the music industry. Through fleeting anecdotes and acknowledgment of discrimination, it does appear that this presented, at the very least, a small impediment to the band's access to radio play and performance venues. Just as Balderrama broadly recalled the "negativity" the band experienced before and after "96 Tears," Yolanda Gonzalez specifically cited one such incident. She states, "Daniel's Den refused to hire them. That was the big place there in Saginaw. There was a couple of places that wouldn't hire them because they were Hispanic."[38] There are several possible explanations for the notable absence of any nuanced discussion about the challenges their ethnic background posed to their early prospects. As Balderrama's earlier comment suggests, band members were aware of the discrimination but chose to minimize the implications of it. Another part of the equation is the role of Detroit's Motown Records in transforming the local and national music industry. Motown, with its array of Black singers, songwriters, and producers, was "at the forefront of sweeping challenges to the record industry's long-standing practices of racial segregation."[39] Their presence within the recording industry possibly created more for a Mexican American band with popular appeal. Finally, the Mysterians had the support of Lillie and Joe Gonzalez, well-regarded members of Saginaw's Latinx community. This couple had community, commercial, and political weight, which they did not hesitate to utilize.

More prohibitive than venues preventing the band from performing were the radio stations that refused to play "96 Tears." Contradicting Balderrama's recollection of disc jockeys supporting the band's music, Question Mark remembered more resistance from radio hosts, stating that Bob Dyer refused to play the song and Bob Dell threw their record in the trash.[40] Yolanda Gonzalez recalled one such incident where a radio host refused to play the band's music because they were Mexican American. Given Lillie Gonzalez's political engagements and as manager of the band, she was well-equipped to address these types of incidents. Lillie engaged in a wide spectrum of political activities: in January 1952, Lillie and Jose founded the Club Latino-Americano; she sought a position on the Saginaw City Council; and Michigan Governor George Romney appointed her as a member of the Governor's Commission on Migratory Labor.[41] According to Yolanda, Lillie cautioned the radio host, declaring, "This is discrimination, you're not playing it because they're Mexican. . . . If you want I'll call Romney right now. I happen to be a Commissioner of his." Through this confrontation, Lillie advocated for the band by asserting her political affiliations. Prepared for the DJ to capitulate under the pressure, Lillie and the Mysterians organized their friends and family to call in once the radio station played "96 Tears." This included parents, siblings, cousins, neighbors, and fans.[42] Question Mark similarly cited the inventive methods the band used to request their song, which ranged from mailing in postcard song requests, sending handwritten and typed requests, and phoning in.[43] Even when faced with resistant radio stations and concert halls, members of the band and their supporters circumvented these efforts and continued to circulate their music to a broader audience.

The band's major break arrived when "96 Tears" made its way to Windsor's CLKW. As CLKW possessed 50,000 watts of radio broadcast power, the station cast a wide geographic net—it reached Detroit, the Midwest, and, after midnight, Eastern radio stations.[44] With "96 Tears" becoming CLKW's most requested song in the station's history for a while, and in combination with the station's broadcast reach, the record surged to the No. 1 song in the country. While "96 Tears" spent fifteen weeks on the *Billboard* charts, on October 29, 1966, Question Mark and Mysterians' song spent one whole week as the No. 1 song in the country. In total, 1.2 million copies of "96 Tears" sold during this period.[45] As the song became too popular for Pa-Go-Go records to handle the record distribution, Cameo-Parkway swept in and signed a deal to handle the national distribution. Members of the band took pride in the fact that they achieved their initial success without the influence of major record companies. Balderrama explains, "Most bands make it big by having a major label supporting them, we didn't do it that way."[46] Cameo-Parkway's influence propelled Question Mark and the Mysterians to new levels of fame.

The Mysterians began touring nationally, making exponentially more money for their performances, and, eventually, appearing on *American Bandstand*. With "96 Tears" emerging as a radio fixture and the increased promotion from their distribution deal with Cameo-Parkway, the daily lives of band members changed dramatically. Describing the almost instantaneous fame of the band, Frank Lugo states, "All of a sudden I was signing autographs and getting paid money for something I enjoyed. We were on T.V., and radio and I was popular—it was a wonderful feeling."[47] During this brief period, the band went from making $200 a night, to $1,500. Increasingly, the Mysterians were performing more frequently outside of the Saginaw-Bay City area. For one, the band was too expensive for the local venues to book them.

Photo of Question Mark and the Mysterians, ca. 1970. Photo by Michael Ochs Archives/Getty Images.

Second, a few days after the Detroit Riot of 1967, Saginaw had its own. Mayor Henry G. Marsh, Saginaw's first African American mayor, denied entrance of the civil rights group United Power to a meeting on the state of the city's racial dynamics. Like many other cities in the country, Saginaw erupted during the year's "Hot Summer."[48] During this period, Question Mark and the Mysterians frequently performed alongside a range of different performers: from popular music groups, such as Sonny and Cher and The Beach Boys, to Tejano artists, like Sunny and the Sunliners and Freddy Fender. Arguably the height of this stardom was the band's appearance on *American Bandstand*, where they performed and Dick Clark briefly interviewed them.[49]

Question Mark and the Mysterians were never able to duplicate the success of their hit song. Moreover, touring and performing over the next few years took a toll on the band members. Frank Lugo explains, "I had enough for awhile [*sic*]. Being on the road that long will take a lot out of you."[50] Beyond fatigue from constant traveling and performing, the band encountered several other obstacles to replicating the success of their national hit. For one, Cameo-Parkway faced significant financial difficulties and disbanded in September 1967, less than a year after the Mysterians achieved their No. 1 success.[51] Second, although the circumstances are not totally clear, the Mysterians signed over their rights to "96 Tears," thus they were not able to collect royalties from it. Recalling the moment that this happened in record executive Neil Bogart's office, Balderrama states, "and then he [Bogart] starts talking how he wants us to sign some protection; he said it would protect our rights to get our royalties, or whatever. We all believed him, even? [Question Mark] did. So I signed it. We all signed it. And then a week later we all got a call that we had all just given all our rights away."[52] Because of the deal that the Mysterians signed with Bogart, who was the twenty-three-year-old vice president and sales manager for Cameo-Parkway, the band never received any royalties from their hit song.[53] And third, were minor legal problems. On April 2, 1968, police arrested Question Mark, or Rudy Martinez, and another individual on glue-sniffing charges.[54] Collectively, these conditions made it difficult for the Mysterians to match the success of "96 Tears."

Possibly their most recognizable contribution to the United States' modern music industry is their label as the first "punk-rock" band. Music critic Dave Marsh is credited with creating the phrase after attending one of the band's concerts. After watching a 1971 Mysterians performance in Flint, Michigan, Marsh returned to the *CREEM* magazine offices in Detroit and wrote, "Needless to say, it was impossible, even after two nights running of Tina Turner, to miss such a landmark explosion of punk-rock"—thus introducing a phrase that would evolve into an entire subgenre of rock 'n' roll.[55] In an interview recorded with Marlon Bishop, senior editor for the *Latino USA* podcast, Marsh recalls the affective impression that the Mysterians' performance left on him and the creative process that resulted in his now-famous phrase. He states, "It was crazed and it was beautiful . . . it was angry and maybe even a little vengeful. . . . He [Question Mark] had an edge to him on stage that not many performers in the mid-60s had and just a wild-man back there."[56] While Question Mark and the Mysterians' music may sound distant from contemporary punk rock artists, there were still parallel elements. As Marsh alludes to, the Mysterians possessed a rare stage presence for bands of that period. Music critic James Thompson characterized the band as a combination of "James Brown-style showmanship with the melodic Tex-Mex sounds."[57] Eddie Serrato recalled sets that only lasted two minutes because of fans rushing the stage or one instance where a fan climbed an eight-foot stage and made her way up to Bobby Balderrama—much of which he also credits to Question Mark.[58] The way that the "96 Tears" and "Midnight Hour" single coalesced is akin to bands that are more closely aligned with the genre. From their embryonic practice sessions playing instrumentals in garages and basements, to the medley of musical backgrounds that the band members came from, and the makeshift studio where the recording took place—there were many elements of this progression that are comparable to some of the punk rock bands that would emerge in the following years.

Pejoratively referred to as a "one-hit wonder," Question Mark and the Mysterians actually placed several songs on the US *Billboard* Hot 100 Charts. Less than two months after "96 Tears" made it to No.1, "I Need Somebody" peaked at No. 22 and remained on the charts for ten weeks. In April 1967 "Can't Get Enough Of You, Baby" peaked at No. 56 and stayed on the charts for six weeks. Then, two months after that, "Girl (You Captivate Me)" spent two weeks on the Hot 100 chart, peaking at No. 98.[59] Beyond the domestic success that "96 Tears" achieved, the song also made an appearance on the United Kingdom's *Billboard* charts—peaking at No. 37 and spending four weeks on the charts.[60] Perhaps Question Mark and the Mysterians' greatest chart- or ranking-related achievement is their place on *Rolling Stone*'s "definitive list of the 500 greatest songs of all time." At No. 213 on the list, this ranking exists as further validation of "96 Tears" importance. Furthermore, the chief curator of the Rock and Roll Hall of Fame also selected "96 Tears" as one of the 500 most influential songs that shaped rock music.[61] While these lists and rankings are not necessarily a conclusive reflection of a musician's legacy, Question Mark and the Mysterians' standing on these rankings does indicate the lasting impression that "96 Tears" left on American music.

Yet, the legacy of Question Mark and the Mysterians extends far beyond just charting multiple songs during this two-year stretch and their spot on *Rolling Stone* magazine's all-time song list. Through other artists covering the song, "96 Tears" took on a life of its own. Gabriel Solis defines a cover as "a new recording or performance of an older song that exists in the memories of musicians and audiences because of a strong, previous recorded version, and for which authority and authenticity are understood to be shared by the original performer and the covering performer."[62] Whether the musicians were from soul, Tejano, or rock 'n' roll backgrounds, every few years since the release of "96 Tears," artists from different genres have introduced or reintroduced this anthem to wide-ranging fan bases. For example, in 1967, only one year following the release of "96 Tears," Aretha Franklin and Big Maybelle individually recorded more soulful covers of the song. Through concerts or on studio recordings, artists ranging from Bruce Springsteen, Iggy Pop, David Byrne, Garland Jeffreys, Texas Tornados, and Joe 'King' Carrasco—to just name a few—have produced nuanced interpretations and versions of this song. It is through these covers that the music of Question Mark and the Mysterians has not only endured, but has potentially expanded to even broader audiences.

In a similar vein to Question Mark and the Mysterians, the legacy of another Latinx Michigan artist testifies to the ways that many casual listeners in the United States have overlooked, forgotten, or perhaps never even realized the impact of their music. A 2013 article by *The Associated Press* describes Sixto Rodríguez as "the greatest protest singer and songwriter that most people never heard of."[63] Labeled a "ghetto [Bob] Dylan," Rodríguez was born in 1942 in Detroit to working-class parents who immigrated from Mexico in the 1920s.[64] Fusing folk, rock, soul, and blues music, Rodríguez released *Cold Fact* in 1970 and *Coming From Reality* in 1971, both of which met with limited commercial success. Although Rodríguez failed to generate significant sales in the United States, his music found an audience in Australia and South Africa. Rodríguez lived a modest life in Detroit during the 1970s and 1980s, which included doing construction work, going to Wayne State University to receive a BA in philosophy, and even running for local government positions. Largely unbeknownst to Rodríguez, his albums were part of the soundtrack to the anti-apartheid struggle in South Africa. While Rodríguez did tour in Australia in 1979 and 1981, it was not until 1997 that his daughter, Eva Alice Rodríguez, learned about his South African fame after coming across an online forum dedicated to her father. Rodríguez's cult status was cemented by the Oscar-winning 2012 documentary *Searching for Sugar Man*, which follows two South African fans' search for the mysterious musician. Although a complete narration of Rodríguez's story is beyond the scope of this chapter, he is a figure that must be mentioned in any discussion of the Midwest's Latinx music scene.[65]

In a review of Boston punk band DMZ's debut studio album, columnist Mike Duffy writes, "The kingpin in DMZ is Mono Mann, lead singer, writer of the group's sonic blast songs and manipulator of a wonderfully sleazy Question Mark and the Mysterians-style organ."[66] As infectious as the chorus of "96 Tears" is, the organ riff echoing throughout is arguably the most memorable musical component. Played by then-thirteen-year-old Frank Rodriguez, this Farfisa or Vox organ would serve as inspiration for future music compositions. Question Mark and the Mysterians became associated with this specific sound—a cultural reference point whenever other musicians incorporated a similar keyboard or organ sound. "The Lines most often resembled other bands that make prominent use of the Farfisa organ, an instrument that defined the sound of one of the eminent progenitors of '60s punk rock, Question Mark and the Mysterians," writes Wayne Robins in his characterization of The Lines, a new wave band from England.[67] In one instance, a music critic even identified similarities between "96 Tears" and Philip Glass's opera, "The Photographer."[68] And on other occasions, newspaper columns referenced the Mysterians to opine on the quality of the Cincinnati Reds' outfield.[69] In short, the impact of the Mysterians was broad: from contributing to new subgenres of rock music, to curating a distinctive sound, and even becoming a popular culture reference. Off the strength of "96 Tears," Question Mark and the Mysterians became associated and recognized as innovators of this organ-driven sound in punk rock and new wave music. As some critics would realize, though, any analysis of the band's musical origins also necessitates accounting for the Tejano and Mexican American music that influenced the Mysterians' sound.

Latinx Interstate Music Networks

Members of Question Mark and the Mysterians present different recollections of some of the details as to the recording of "96 Tears," the promotion of the song, and the mainstream distribution of it. Reports differ on whether the Mysterians recorded "96 Tears" in March or April of 1966; whether the Pa-Go-Go or Bego label first distributed their record; and on the setting of the recording: a living room, an outdoor patio, or a studio that was an addition to the house. Yet, for the most part, there is a general consistency about this period's development for the band. On either March or April 14, 1966, the Mysterians recorded their hit song, but the band actually auditioned the calendar year prior. Question Mark recalls, "'We had an audition with Lillian Gonzalez, who had a record label. Her husband owned *El Pato* grocery store in Saginaw. We played for her and she said we weren't ready to be recorded. This was 1965 and we were jammin' and wanted to be recorded.'"[70]

Yolanda Gonzalez cites a parallel trajectory, appending that there were a few local groups trying to audition with Pa-Go-Go, the subsidiary record company of Bego. At first, when Question Mark and the Mysterians auditioned for Lillie, they had no original compositions, so she turned them away. Six months later, the band returned with "96 Tears." Lillie loved the song, even though Jose was unconvinced. Lillie's excitement about the song triumphed over his skepticism. According to Yolanda, "It wasn't hard for my mom to twist my dad's arms."[71] The Mysterians' relationship with Lillie Gonzalez was not only instrumental to the success of the band, but it was also part of a more expansive network of Tejano music in the Midwest.

In a 50th Anniversary of "96 Tears" edition of *Mi Gente Magazine*, Eddie Serrato described the various involvements of the Gonzalezes in the Michigan and Texas area, and how Lillie came to be the manager of the Mysterians. Serrato, former drummer for the band, states, "[Jose and Lillie] used to sell a lot of records of the bands from Texas, out of their grocery store at 5th and Carroll. They also promoted these bands by bringing them to Michigan. The Gonzalez's had a lot of pull in town and I guess that's how they came into the Mysterians' picture."[72] Lillie Gonzalez, perhaps better known for her chain of *El Pato* restaurants that she owned throughout the Rio Grande Valley, was, alongside her husband, also an influential figure in the Southwest and Midwest's regional music industry.[73] Before the name *El Pato* would adorn buildings throughout South Texas and serve a variety of Mexican dishes, the same name would be used to create a *tienda*, or shop, at 1201 Carroll Street in Saginaw. *El Pato*'s main store opened its doors after Jose saved up enough money working in Detroit and moved north to Saginaw.[74] It functioned as a versatile store for the growing Latinx community—it was a *panadería* (Mexican bakery) and *tortillería* (made fresh tortillas), and it sold *tamales, masa, barbacoa,* and other food staples that one might have a difficult time finding at the other local grocery stores. Eventually, Lillie and Jose Gonzalez even began selling music records at *El Pato*, a decision that would gradually propel the family into the music industry.[75]

As Yolanda Gonzalez would recount, her parents' earliest involvement in the music arena was the creation of a Spanish-language broadcast on a local radio station. With Salvador Luna as the DJ, this program aired Saturday mornings and advertised itself as the "Mexican Hour" and the "Latin American Program."[76] Their commitment to facilitating the circulation of music in Michigan expanded one summer when a woman, who was a migrant fieldworker, asked if she could bring a record player to *El Pato*. While playing conjunto and Tejano music on this record player, other Latinx shoppers inquired about whether they sold that kind of music there or where they could find it. This led Lillie Gonzalez to begin traveling to Chicago so that she could purchase records from a vendor there and bring them back to Saginaw, which she did, and which resulted in a small "record department" in *El Pato*. This resulted in seasonal migrant workers and permanent Latinx residents lamenting the absence of dances and concerts in the area. Jose Gonzalez opened a secondary business, Star Distributorship, which provided Mexican food products to stores in Michigan, Indiana, Illinois, Wisconsin, and Ohio. As a result, he was familiar with connecting Latinxs to goods and services that were still scarce in the agricultural areas or mid-sized urban environments of the Midwest. Lillie and Jose subsequently sought out conjunto bands from Texas, largely from the Rio Grande Valley, and contracted them to play throughout the Midwest. To make these trips more worthwhile, Jose would contract these bands for other dances in Illinois, Indiana, and Wisconsin, thus facilitating a brief Midwestern tour for these conjunto bands from Texas. One of the bands that the Gonzalezes would bring north was Conjunto Bernal.[77]

Brothers Eloy and Paulino Bernal formed Conjunto Bernal along with a third member, Rubén Perez. As Yolanda Gonzalez recalls, "Their trio just had beautiful voices." Perez's inclusion was quite consequential. Anthropologist and ethnomusicologist Manuel Peña cites the trio's song "Mi Único Camino" as the first time a conjunto included three-part harmonies.[78] Furthermore, Eddie Serrato, drummer for the Mysterians who had his musical start with Conjunto Negrete, referred to Paulino Bernal as "probably one of the greatest Conjunto artists there ever was."[79] During one of their trips to Michigan, the Gonzalezes asked the Bernals why they were not recording more of their music. Eloy and Paulino replied that record labels in Texas preferred more popular dance music, as opposed to the type of songs Conjunto Bernal played. When Jose Gonzalez questioned them on what it would take for them to record their music, Paulino responded by advocating for their own independent label. This relationship between Bernal and the Gonzalezes led to the founding of Bego Records around 1963, a name based on the beginning of the surnames Bernal and Gonzalez. Bego Records, which was the first record label the Bernals and Gonzalezes founded, focused specifically on conjunto and Tejano music. Based out of McAllen, Texas, Bego Records ultimately released music from some of the most notable *Norteño* and conjunto bands of this period, and of future eras.

In *The Texas-Mexican Conjunto*, Manuel Peña describes the central components and development of conjunto music. Beginning in the 1920s, Peña argues that Norteño and conjunto, to the Tejanos, achieved a recognizable style after World War II. With the accordion and the *bajo sexto* (sixth bass) at the center of the ensemble, the other instruments went through several adjustments. First, there was the incorporation of the *tololoche,* which musicians would eventually substitute for the electric bass, and second, drum sets were adopted.[80] Summarizing the technical skill and influence of Paulino Bernal, Peña concludes, "Bernal had taken the various stylistic strands that had been coalescing around a uniquely fashioned Tejano accordion ensemble, perfected them, and achieved a synthesis that marked the apex of conjunto music's evolution."[81] For various reasons, during and after World War II, major record labels discontinued the recording and sale of conjunto and Tejano music in the United States. Yet, this disinvestment mobilized Latinx businesspeople to create their own small-scale recording companies, with two of the earliest and most influential labels being Falcón Records and Ideal Records.[82] The creation of Bego Records is at the junction of these two developments: first, the growth of Norteño and conjunto music in the Southwest; and, second, the emergence of Latinx-owned record labels that replaced the mainstream record labels.

A third development that contributed to the formation of Bego and Pa-Go-Go was a more regionally specific one, which was that many locations across the Midwest lacked a cultural infrastructure sufficiently equipped to provide the attractions desired by Latinx migrants. As evidenced by Lillie Gonzalez's trip to Chicago to find conjunto records, larger cities were more likely to have accessible cultural and entertainment resources. The Gonzalezes were not the only Latinxs in Michigan during this period, or before, who sought to promote dances and to contract musicians for performances, but they were part of a growing network of individuals in Michigan and the Midwest who sought to cultivate a popular culture scene in mid-sized or semi-urban cities. The introducing of radio programs, the selling of records, and the booking of musicians for dances were critical contributions toward sustaining and expanding a cultural landscape adapted toward the needs of Latinxs in Michigan.

Saginaw's *Gladiador* publication advertised itself as "*Periódico Quincenal Independiente al Servicio del Pueblo Latino Americano,*" or, roughly, "Biweekly Independent Newspaper Serving the Latin American People."[83] While this newspaper certainly catered to Saginaw's Latinxs, it also provided reporting for locations outside of the city. Rosendo Alaniz was *Gladiador*'s representative in Alma, Michigan, and relayed information concerning Alma and the surrounding areas.[84] An article from their July 24, 1964 edition congratulated

Jose and Lillie Gonzalez's signing of popular conjunto musician Tony De La Rosa to an "exclusive artist" contract with Bego Records. Along with celebrating the signing of De La Rosa, *Gladiador* also recognized the remarkable catalog of artists already contracted to the Bego label, including Ruben Vela and Paulino Bernal. The Texas Conjunto Music Hall of Fame would induct all three of these artists—Vela in 2003, and Bernal and De La Rosa in 2006.[85] Though not mentioned in the *Gladiador* article, Los Relámpagos Del Norte were another ascending band recording on Bego during this period.

The duo Los Relámpagos Del Norte released their record *Ya No Llores* on Bego in 1964. An advertisement in the *Latin Times* promoted the band's first performance in East Chicago, Indiana, for August 27, 1966. Urging readers not to miss the grand debut of Los Relámpagos Del Norte, the *Latin Times* endorsed the duo as the most prominent conjunto of the moment and the pride of Bego Records.[86] A few months later, Los Relámpagos Del Norte traveled to Detroit and performed alongside Lola Beltran and Jose Alfredo Jimenez at the Stratford Theatre, just a few miles west of the Corktown neighborhood, widely recognized as the *colonia* where recent Latinx migrants settled.[87] The band was comprised of Cornelio Reyna and Ramón Ayala, with Ayala developing into one of the most iconic and prolific Norteño musicians ever. According to ethnomusicologists Manuel Peña and Catherine Ragland, Paulino Bernal came across Ayala and Reyna performing on the streets of Reynosa, Tamaulipas, right across the border from McAllen, Texas, where Bego Records listed their official address. As Ragland notes in *Música Norteña*, the Bernal brothers were conscious that their success was partially a result of their eminence among recent Mexican immigrants. Perhaps for this reason, in seeking talent for Bego Records, Paulino Bernal crossed from McAllen to Reynosa, where he encountered Ayala and Reyna.[88] With musical acts such as Ruben Vela, Tony De La Rosa, Conjunto Bernal, and Los Relámpagos Del Norte, Bego Records possessed a lineup of artists whose musical ingenuity would define and transform the genre of conjunto music.

Pa-Go-Go Records, which was a subsidiary of Bego, released music by a broader array of artists—from musicians in English and Spanish, and across a variety of musical genres.[89] The name "Pa-Go-Go" records, the label that signed Question Mark and the Mysterians, stood for the three founders of the label: Paulino Bernal (Pa), Rudy Tee Gonzales (Go), and Jose and Lillie Gonzalez (Go).[90] Based out of San Antonio, Texas, Pa-Go-Go used Rudy Tee Gonzales's address on the front of their records. In an interview for the documentary *As I Walk through the Valley*, Yolanda Gonzalez describes an ongoing conversation that occurred between Rudy Gonzales and Jose and Lillie

Gonzalez, stating, "Rudy started talking to them [Jose and Lillie] that some of the groups are wanting to go over to the English field, but it was pretty hard here in Texas for anybody to cross over." Through the signing of musicians across Michigan and Texas, and those who performed in English or Spanish, Pa-Go-Go did functionally achieve a crossover record label.[91]

Rudy Tee Gonzales was a musician in his own right, whose band, Rudy and the Reno Bops, combined elements of traditional Mexican music with soul, R&B, and rock 'n' roll. Rudy Gonzales acknowledges this desire to combine musical elements when he refers to his emulation of James Brown's dance moves. Akin to Jose and Lillie's relationship with Paulino Bernal, they were in contact with Rudy Gonzales because his band was performing throughout Michigan. Despite Pa-Go-Go listing their address in San Antonio, several of the artists on the label were from Michigan—including Question Mark and the Mysterians, Sir David & His Knights, and Count and the Colony. Furthermore, during Pa-Go-Go's brief existence, they struck an even balance of record releases, with eight in English and eight in Spanish. Matching the linguistic diversity of artists on the label were the genres they were performing, ranging from rock to rancheras and polkas. Thus, when considering the relationship between Bego and Pa-Go-Go and the reason why all parties involved would want to launch a second record company, the objective of creating a "crossover" label is the distinctive divergence. No record released on Pa-Go-Go would eclipse the commercial success of the Mysterians' "96 Tears" single, but this early effort toward engineering a music label with crossover appeal was a significant one.[92]

A purpose of this chapter is to understand the profound impact that Latinxs from Michigan had across various genres of music. Thus, when assessing the role of Bego Records within conjunto music, I emphasize the role of Lillie and Jose Gonzalez. This is not to overstate the role of the Gonzalezes and diminish Paulino Bernal's involvement. As in the case of Los Relámpagos Del Norte, Bernal possessed a unique ear for musical talent, as well as the deeper connections to the Tejano music industry. Equally important though, the Gonzalezes financed Bego and were experienced in managing other parts of the business operation—including the record contracts, selling products, and navigating the transportation networks between and throughout the Southwest and the Midwest. None of this material intends to suggest that these conjunto bands and artists would not have found success elsewhere, had Bego not signed them. Nor does it infer that these artists were not already well-known in their own right. Rather, what I seek to highlight is this expansive network of Latinx entertainment and cultural production—one that extended from the Rio Grande Valley of the Texas-Mexico borderlands to Detroit and the nearby Michigan-Canada border.

Conclusion

The early band members of Question Mark and the Mysterians were Mexican American teenagers who were also the children of former migrant agricultural workers that eventually settled in Michigan's Greater Tri-Cities region. The Mysterians' No. 1 song, "96 Tears," was the result of the intersections between the Tejano music industry and the post-World War II migration of Latinxs to the Midwest. Historicizing this band, and the Pa-Go-Go and Bego record labels, emphasizes the formation of transnational and interstate networks, demonstrates the cultural influence of Latinxs nationally, and unsettles distinctions between urban and rural spaces. The accomplishments and impact of Question Mark and the Mysterians and their 1966 anthem, "96 Tears," shaped the US musical landscape in a variety of ways, including creating a No. 1 single, inspiring covers of their song by some of the most well-known artists of this period and after, as the first "punk rock" band and being partially responsible for the introduction of a new phrase into the musical lexicon, and engineering an organ riff that other musicians would imitate and adapt.

In the case of Lillian and Jose Gonzalez, who managed Question Mark and the Mysterians as they rose to fame and who distributed the original release of their "96 Tears" single, they were contributors to the expansion of Latinx entertainment and commercialism in the postwar Midwest. As Lillie and Jose Gonzalez were involved in Star Distributorship, *El Pato* grocery store, and the promotion of dances and concerts across the Midwest, they were in a unique position to facilitate interstate music networks from Michigan to the Southwest. Beyond leaving an impact through the cultural form, there was also this larger cultural infrastructure developing. The range of ventures—food distribution, entertainment, and retail—indicates their contribution to a broader Latinx cultural infrastructure in the region. Furthermore, Yolanda Gonzalez described that after the passing of Jose and then Lillie, she examined the detailed financial records kept by her mother. According to Yolanda, her parents loaned out upwards of $250,000—money that went to customers, employees, conjunto bands, and others. This too is a significant component of the social, cultural, and economic sustainability of local Latinx communities. For those who may have lacked adequate access to financial institutions, loans would surely assist in nurturing a burgeoning community, particularly for those who were recent migrants.

Largely, the band members and their families were participating in the process of exiting the migratory stream and settling in locations where they might find permanent work. Many achieved the ultimate goal of moving from the fields to the factories. While migration and agricultural labor were surely arduous processes, it is also important to recognize how migrants made the most of these circumstances—to the point where it could be generative. The music of Question Mark and the Mysterians was the product of migration and the encounters with other Latinxs along the way. Some Latinx migrant families, like the Balderramas, the Borjas, and the Martinezes, were able to exit the migratory stream and begin to live a more stable life in the Midwest. Yet, for other migrant farmworkers and their families, it remained necessary for them to continue following the harvest route throughout the region. In the process, the organizing efforts of migrant farmworkers reached new heights and made the heartland the center of the farmworker justice movement.

CHAPTER FIVE

Migrant Rights, Migrant Justice

The Farm Labor Organizing Committee and the Making of a Midwest Movement, 1967–1991

Introduction

In August 1979, leaders and members of the Farm Labor Organizing Committee (FLOC) gathered for the fledgling union's first convention. At Frank and Joe's Ballroom in Holgate, Ohio, César Chávez, then president of the United Farm Workers (UFW) and a nationally recognized labor activist, spoke to a crowd of around 400 supporters. During the address, on behalf of himself and the UFW, Chávez endorsed the strike and consumer boycott that FLOC was conducting against Campbell Soup Co. and Libby, McNeill & Libby, Inc. At this assembly were seventy-three farmworker delegates, who re-elected Baldemar Velásquez as president and Ray Santiago as secretary-treasurer of the organization. While Chávez's presence at FLOC's first constitutional convention and his declared support for the union may have snatched the headlines for local newspapers that got wind of the event, there were other significant items and positions that emerged out of this gathering.[1]

The resolutions that the delegates approved were aimed at a range of labor and political issues. In terms of the resolutions directly related to FLOC's unionizing efforts, delegates decided to continue their tomato strike and consumer boycott of Libby and Campbell, and to maintain FLOC's health, legal, and fundraising programs. The strike demands included an hourly wage, an increase in the piece-work rate, health care benefits, and a guaranteed minimum of work hours per week. The scope of the resolutions passed also extended to the realm of national-level politics, with FLOC declaring its opposition to nuclear power, the revival of the Selective Service draft, and the deportation of undocumented immigrants.[2] At the same time that FLOC held their inaugural constitutional convention, the budding organization's members were already considering how they could expand their unionizing efforts beyond their base in Northern Ohio. Organizers set their sights on Southern Michigan's tomato industry.[3]

Jose Garza—a former farmworker, son of *Tejano* migrants, and now a Wayne County mental health emergency phone referral operator—was part of a small FLOC support committee looking to make strides organizing Latinx farmworkers and supporters in Michigan. Describing the difficult road ahead, Garza stated, "'It's going to take awhile, and it could even take years to organize Michigan farmworkers . . . I see it as a protracted struggle.'"[4] César Chávez echoed a similar sentiment a few months after FLOC's inaugural convention. Chávez was in Michigan to promote the UFW's boycott against Red Coach iceberg lettuce. "'Until there's farmworker collective bargaining legislation, by state statute or federal law, it's going to be difficult to do much more than hold our own in California,'" stated the UFW president.[5] This visit drew the ire of Berrien County's Farm Bureau president, Alan Prillwitz, who saw Chávez's campaigning as a desperate attempt to save a "'dying organization.'" In Prillwitz's opinion, the only states where the UFW had generated significant traction was in California and Arizona. Accordingly, this visit was part of a larger initiative to reinvigorate the UFW by making inroads into parts of the country where few had previously been made, like Michigan, Ohio, and Florida. Allegedly, even though Chávez previously visited Berrien and Van Buren County (Southwestern Michigan), no labor organizing had actually taken place yet in either of the neighboring counties.[6]

César Chávez, Jose Garza, and Alan Prillwitz each spoke about the past and future of unionizing Midwestern migrant farmworkers. While each of them represented different organizations with distinct intentions, they appeared to share a similar forecast about the prospects of organizing ethnic Mexican and Latinx agricultural workers: it was a distant objective at best, and improbable at worst. When Chávez visited Michigan in 1979, the labor leader predicted that FLOC was still around three to four years away—in addition to the year that they had already been striking in Ohio—from marshalling enough public support and applying sufficient labor pressure for corporations like Campbell's Soup Co. to recognize and bargain with the union.[7] Ultimately, it would take even longer than that. On February 18 and 19, 1986, the Farm Labor Organizing Committee signed their first collective bargaining agreement (CBA). The contract was between FLOC, Campbell's, their pickle subsidiary Vlasic Foods, and twenty-eight of their tomato and pickle growers in Ohio and Michigan. This innovative three-way agreement linked the interests of the three main parties involved in Midwestern agribusiness: farmworkers, growers, and corporations.[8]

As a result of this CBA, nearly 800 farmworkers would now be able to work under a union contract. Among other guarantees, FLOC farmworkers would now receive higher wages, health insurance, a paid holiday that would occur near Labor Day, and the right to be a member of the union without fear of retribution or harassment. Baldemar Velásquez, FLOC president, began the CBA booklet by addressing the members of the organization. Velásquez triumphally wrote, "Dear Sisters & Brothers: As many of you know, FLOC has been fighting for the rights of farmworkers for nearly 20 years, and we have struggled for 7 years to get a contract with Campbell Soup. We are proud to say that the contract is now a reality!"[9] In addition to these benefits that all members would gain, those who had participated in FLOC's earliest labor actions would receive additional compensation for their struggle *hasta la victoria*. Each of the families that went on strike against Campbell's in 1978 would receive up to $2,000 for their lost wages and prolonged sacrifices on behalf of the union. As Velásquez concluded in the CBA's introduction, "This is only our first contract. Our struggle for complete justice and dignity is not over yet. There are many things still to be done, and many workers who still don't enjoy the benefits of a contract."[10] On both accounts—that this was only FLOC's first contract and that there were still more Latinx farmworkers that would be interested in union recognition—Velásquez was correct.

The year after FLOC entered into their collective bargaining agreement with Campbell Soup Co., Heinz was the next major corporation that followed suit and signed a three-way contract with the expanding union. This new agreement absorbed twenty-seven farms and an additional 700 workers into FLOC's fold. The flourishing organization continued this momentum in the following years as they renegotiated contracts with Campbell, Vlasic, and Heinz, while also ratifying new agreements with Aunt Jane's and Green Bay Foods—the other two major pickle companies in Northwest Ohio and Southeast Michigan. Thus, within six years, FLOC had negotiated and agreed to contracts with all major pickle companies in Ohio.[11] As FLOC was founded in 1967, it took the union twenty-five years of organizing to achieve this level of recognition and success.

During this drawn-out period, there was a steep learning curve as Velásquez, and other early members of the union, considered how to best confront Midwestern agribusiness. It was during the first ten years that organizers shifted their attention away from growers and redirected it toward the corporations that held the power and resources to raise the pay of migrant farmworkers and offer improved benefits. This chapter begins by charting the origins and trajectory of FLOC. Following that, it will concentrate on a particularly powerful moment in the union's history: the boycott of Campbell Soup Co. and the nearly six-hundred-mile march from Toledo,

Ohio, to the Camden, New Jersey, headquarters of the corporation. In the preface to W. K. Barger and Ernesto M. Reza's *The Farm Labor Movement in the Midwest,* Velásquez wrote, "For the most part, the thread that has woven staff, members, and supporters together into effective action has been the church. . . . FLOC must continue to encourage the involvement of the Church among staff, members, and supporters alike and seek the next step that God has called us to take together."[12] Velásquez's statement here intertwined the role of churches, labor unions, consumers, and supporters. This part of the chapter examines how FLOC cultivated a moral authority, which, alongside the support of influential religious organizations, helped propel the union's successful boycott of Campbell Soup.

Throughout FLOC's boycott of Campbell, news coverage of the lengthy struggle regularly referred to the union in relation to their more established contemporary—the UFW. *The Herald-Palladium,* a local newspaper distributed in Southwest Michigan, reported, "The FLOC is a sister union of Cesar Chavez's United Farmworkers union in California."[13] For several reasons, this association of FLOC with the UFW was valuable and appropriate. FLOC maintained a fruitful relationship with Chávez. From Chávez addressing the crowd at FLOC's inaugural constitutional convention in 1979, to Chávez joining FLOC members for the final stretch of the march to Campbell headquarters in 1983, and finally to Chávez speaking in Lansing, Michigan, for the 1990 Midwest Hispanic Unity Conference—the UFW president was a consistent and visible supporter of FLOC.[14] With an unmistakable president in Baldemar Velásquez, the utilization of sensational labor actions, and as the United States' two most successful unions of agricultural workers during this period, there was a strong resemblance between FLOC and the UFW. Yet, it would be a mistake to excessively emphasize the parallels between these farmworker unions. Despite the appeal of likening the two organizations, there were indeed significant distinctions between them.

This chapter argues that the history of the farmworker movement in the United States appears radically different when the United Farm Workers are decentered and further attention is reoriented toward the Farm Labor Organizing Committee. While the UFW and Chávez were an immensely valuable source of support for FLOC, it would be a mistake to characterize the organization as merely an extension of the UFW. The periodization of the farmworker struggle must be rewritten when FLOC is elevated to a position of prominence within this economic, political, and social movement. By the late 1970s, the UFW was in a state of decline—a current that would only continue in the 1980s as the union was weakened by a reactionary political environment and neoliberal economic developments, as well as internal disagreements, the loss of leadership, and the depletion of union contracts. However, it was precisely during that period that FLOC began to establish a foothold in the Midwest and secure the first three-way contracts between the farmworker organization, growers, and the corporate food giants. FLOC's organizing strategies, coalition building, and eventual contracts run counter to the dominant narrative of union suppression and decline during the 1970s and 1980s.

The history of FLOC, much like the history of the Midwest within the fields of Mexican American and Latinx history, has remained peripheral despite its extensive contributions as a labor union and social justice movement. As *Latinx Encounters* considers how agricultural workers in the Midwest redefined migrant power, justice, and rights throughout the course of the twentieth century, we need not look any further than FLOC.

The Farmworker Movement

In the FLOC president's report to the union membership at the organization's fifth constitutional convention in 1991, Baldemar Velásquez stated, "First, let me congratulate all of you for making FLOC the only other significant union of farmworkers in the country today. The other union, of course, is the United Farm Workers, in California, led by our brother and our leader Cesar Chavez."[15]

As Velásquez suggests, it was common knowledge to FLOC members, and feasibly the broader American public, that the "other" union was the United Farm Workers. As members of FLOC likely found the association with UFW inescapable, this chapter would be providing a fragmentary account of the US farmworker justice movement without contextualizing the UFW's influence on it. Historian Matt Garcia's *From the Jaws of Victory* thoroughly assesses the spectacular rise and stinging decline of the famed labor union. As Garcia details, César Chávez coordinated the National Farm Workers Association's (NFWA) first official meeting in 1962. While delegates selected officers for their governing structure at this meeting, it would not take long for Chávez to reorganize the leadership. In 1964, Chávez took over as president, Gilbert Padilla went from board member to vice president, Dolores Huerta was brought into the organizational fold as a co-vice president, and Tony Orendain remained in his original position as secretary-treasurer.[16]

Prior to the formation of the NFWA, the American Federation of Labor–Congress of Industrial Organizations (AFL-CIO) chartered the

Agricultural Workers Organizing Committee (AWOC) in 1960, with initial organizing efforts necessarily taking place prior to that. These unionization efforts were led by Norman Smith, Al Green, Clyde Knowles, and Larry Itliong. As a Filipino labor contractor with radical political views, Itliong was well-positioned to help build a strong California union of migrant Filipino farmworkers. Along with Itliong, Philip Vera Cruz, Ben Gines, Peter Velasco, and Andy Imutan were crucial to AWOC's recruitment and organizing among Filipinos. While AWOC and the NFWA had differing philosophies for the most effective organizing strategies, they were still largely working along parallel tracks, with AWOC having success among Filipino workers and NFWA with Mexican farmworkers. During this period, Huerta was an important intermediary between the two upstart unions. Eventually, these parallel paths reached a crossroads on September 8, 1965, when Itliong yanked Filipino workers from nine Delano vineyards. The Delano grape strike had now begun.[17]

This decision to strike, though, came as a surprise to Chávez and forced him into a decision he was reluctant to make at this point in time. Despite the shock, about a week later, on September 16, Mexican Independence Day, Chávez convened a meeting at Our Lady of Guadalupe church in Delano. While the NFWA membership was overwhelmingly ready to join the strike that exact moment, Chávez waited a few days before officially calling the strike. In addition to the nine vineyards that AWOC was already striking at, the NFWA began to picket ten more.[18] As the fates of these two unions were now intertwined, they now had to take their organizational relationship to the next level. Garcia describes how, "Early on, differences in resources brought the two closer together. The NFWA had not accumulated a strike fund or a permanent home, whereas AWOC had AFL-CIO money and Filipino Hall."[19] While there still existed some tensions that needed to be addressed between them, in August 1966, AWOC and NFWA agreed to a merger, becoming the United Farm Workers Organizing Committee. Furthermore, it was resolved that Chávez, *not* Itliong, would be the union's president.[20]

During this first year of the grape strike, another tactic moved from the periphery to the center of the movement—the boycott. Thus, the strike, the boycott, and marches were the UFW's core strategies. Chávez, Huerta, and the UFW attracted the support of a wide array of interest groups across the country. Richard Griswold del Castillo details how "the UFW attracted hundreds of volunteers from urban universities, religious organizations, and labor unions. Chavez's alliance with organized labor and his use of mass mobilizing techniques, such as a dramatic farm workers march on Sacramento in 1966, made the grape strike and boycott part of a growing protest movement in the United States."[21]

While the UFW is most associated with organizing in California, they were also active in states like Texas and Arizona. More importantly, the success of the UFW as a labor union and social justice movement necessitated a national, and even international, commitment to enforcing the grape boycott. By 1970, these efforts had paid off. All twenty-six Delano growers signed a historic agreement with the UFW, ending the Delano grape strike—a prolonged struggle that lasted for five years.[22] As the *Detroit Free Press* exclaimed, "The first successful national boycott in US labor history belonged to Chavez."[23] While this marked the end of this particular episode in the UFW's history, there would be more upcoming challenges for the UFW throughout the 1970s.

During the fall of 1970, the International Brotherhood of Teamsters had already begun attempts to sidestep the UFW and expand their number of contracts. In 1970, when the UFW signed its contracts with the grape growers, lettuce growers preempted the entrance of the UFW into their fields and began to sign with the Teamsters. In 1972, the Teamsters held onto their lettuce contracts while enticing grape growers to sign contracts with them. Garcia argued that in this case "the Teamsters' actions illustrate one of the major ironies of agricultural unionism in California: the union that proves it can organize farm workers invites more, not less competition from competing unions."[24] As the Teamsters signed what Chávez called "sweetheart deals" with California grape and lettuce growers, the Teamsters' pursuit of union contracts and desire to erode the influence of the UFW immersed farmworkers into a violent, even fatal, and financially costly conflict. With Chávez visiting the "city of unions" in 1974, the *Detroit Free Press* described the battle that the UFW and Teamsters were embroiled in: "Disturbed by the image of its 'goon squads' harassing UFW strikers, the Teamsters have launched a $100,000-a-month campaign to win the hearts and minds of the field workers away from Chavez, and to convince shoppers that a label bearing Teamster doublehorse emblem makes grapes and lettuce just as palatable as does the UFW's black eagles."[25] As the UFW continued their struggle against California's grower-Teamster alliance, Chávez's campaigning and visits to Michigan, and the Midwest more broadly, were important signifiers of the union's need for steady support from the United Auto Workers (UAW) and the AFL-CIO.

Chávez and the UFW wrestled to maintain the support of the boycott from sectors of society—consumers, activists, students, religious groups, and organized labor. While these efforts were occurring and, rightfully, grabbing the headlines, a much smaller, Midwest-based organization was planting the seeds for their own union. Early on, Chávez, perhaps arrogantly or naïvely, assumed that unionizing migrant farmworkers in the Midwest would not be a tall order. In 1971, Chávez was a speaker for the seventh constitutional convention of the Michigan state AFL-CIO. Chávez spoke to an audience of 1,200 at the convention, and the UFW secured the support of the state AFL-CIO's 300,000-person membership. Here, Chávez committed the UFW to union organizing drives in twenty states across the country, including Michigan. "'We want to pay back the debts for your help. . . . We want to join with you to bring about a better life for the migratory workers in Michigan,'" stated Chávez. In his interview with *The Packer*, a long-standing publication reporting on news in the fruit and vegetable industry, Chávez declared, "Michigan is not going to be a difficult state for us to organize. There are some beautiful unions here with much power.'"[26] While Chávez and the UFW had certainly been the beneficiaries of varying degrees of support from the UAW and the AFL-CIO—which did oscillate over time—Chávez's confidence in the support that Midwestern organized labor would provide to farmworkers was misplaced.[27] Andrew J. Hazelton's *Labor's Outcasts* examines the broader relationship between the AFL and CIO and farmworker unionization efforts. Hazelton, who is largely focused on the period between the New Deal and the end of the Bracero Program, writes, "In the postwar period, national labor leaders with the AFL and CIO decided against devoting resources to farmworkers. . . . What could the labor movement do with workers beyond the reach of federal and state administrative procedures that national unions used daily?"[28] Chávez had clearly underestimated how difficult of a task this would be and eight years later, at FLOC's first constitutional convention, admitted that there remained significant hurdles.

The Origins of the Farm Labor Organizing Committee

Baldemar Velásquez was born in Pharr, Texas, a small city right across the border from Reynosa, Tamaulipas, in 1947. Baldemar was one of Cresencio Velásquez and Vicenta Castillo's nine children. The story of Baldemar and his family is characteristic of many of the Mexican American migrant families that eventually made their way to the Midwest. His father, Crescencio, was born in Driscoll, Texas, and entered the migrant stream out of necessity at a young age. Baldemar's mother, Vicenta, was born in Pharr, the location where her parents settled after fleeing the tumult of the Mexican

Revolution in 1910. Like the thousands of other ethnic Mexicans who traveled north for the harvest season during the post-World War II period, the Velásquez-Crescencio family drove in a converted-truck that was covered with a canvas tarp. Beginning in the Rio Grande Valley, the family picked their way through the cotton fields in Texas, followed by tomatoes in Ohio, and finally cucumbers in Michigan.[29]

For Mexican American migrant families, once children reached their fourth or fifth birthday, it was time for them to help out in some way. Whether bringing water to their working family members, carrying empty baskets to haul more produce, or assisting with caring for even younger kids, migrant children had to contribute as soon as they were old enough to. "'I remember once my baby sister had whooping cough . . . I didn't know what to do. I patted her on the back, and somehow she got her breath,'" recalled Baldemar when thinking about the immense pressure of this responsibility.[30] Typically, the goal of migrant families that followed the crops from Texas to the Midwest was to earn enough money during the summer months to sustain the family through the winter after they returned to Texas. Yet sometimes, the inconsistencies of the harvest season left families short of earning enough to complete the circular migration. This was the case for the Velásquez-Crescencio family, who settled out of the migrant stream in Gilboa, Ohio, after being unable to earn enough to return to South Texas.[31]

While the early years in Ohio were not easy for the family, historian Dionicio Nodín Valdés notes that Baldemar Velásquez was fortunate enough to attend college, with those years being formative to his pursuit of justice for migrant farmworkers. In addition to attending college during the Civil Rights Movement of the 1960s, Velásquez "also learned about César Chávez and the efforts of the United Farmworkers in California."[32] As FLOC's December 1972 newsletter recounted, "In 1967, Baldemar Velasquez, an ex-migrant and student at Bluffton College, stirred by the organizing of Cesar Chavez and the success of UFWOC, began organizing migrant workers and other low income people in Northwestern Ohio."[33] Thus, in 1967, one year after AWOC and the NFWA merged into the UFW, Baldemar began to form FLOC with his father and a small cadre of farmworkers. During these early years, FLOC's efforts were centered on Midwestern growers, who hired, paid, and oversaw the Mexican American farmworkers. FLOC's first labor action was initiated during the 1968 harvest, when the organization sought negotiation meetings with Lucas County growers. As the county growers refused to recognize FLOC as legitimate representatives of their employees, the negotiations proved to be futile, and FLOC decided to strike.[34]

Portrait of Baldemar Velásquez. Courtesy of the Toledo Lucas County Public Library and Baldemar Velásquez.

While police and growers harassed and attempted to intimidate the striking workers, the growers were ultimately unprepared for this rather spontaneous labor action. The possibility of this strike damaging the season's tomato harvest was enough for the thirty-three growers to concede to FLOC and the striking workers.[35] This swift victory earned FLOC the right to organize on the thirty-three growers' farms, provided a higher wage for the farmworkers, and prevented growers from firing or harassing workers for union activity. Unfortunately for FLOC and the workers they represented, this was a fleeting moment of success. Whether temporarily switching crops or using connections to local press to demonize the organizing of farmworkers, over the next few summer harvests, Northwestern Ohio tomato growers refined their methods for stifling FLOC's efforts.[36]

During the 1969–1970 harvests, only eleven new contracts were signed, while many of the original ones were lost. As Barger and Reza contend, one of the legitimate grievances that growers had with the organizing was the fact that they had limited control over the wages and living conditions they were able to provide for the migrant farmworkers. "They [growers] claimed that their own ability to provide wages, housing, and other benefits were governed by the prices paid by the large food-processing corporations," state Barger and Reza.[37] Correctly, Midwestern growers argued that their ability to improve wages or living conditions for the workers was largely dictated by corporations like Campbell Soup Co., Libby, and Heinz. These corporations made determinations about the volume of produce required for the upcoming year, sold their own seedlings to growers, and entered into contractual agreements whereby the grower committed to selling the entire harvest back to only that food-processing company. As the Midwestern growers were largely at the mercy of the corporate food processors, farmers were increasingly arguing that they were being squeezed. Eventually, as FLOC organizers subscribed to this argument, they dramatically shifted their labor organizing strategies. In short, with the food corporations wielding significant control over the Midwestern agricultural industry, the wages that growers could offer to migrant farmworkers were tied to the prices that corporations offered the growers for their product.[38]

Between 1970 and 1976, FLOC was in a state of flux as they reorganized and reconsidered the organization's best path forward. As Valdés describes, "By 1970 FLOC turned from unionization to civil rights and community issues, and for the next four years the union function was largely neglected."[39] Following that momentary season of success where FLOC secured and then lost a number of contracts with growers, they began to engage in broader community organizing. FLOC oriented their efforts around larger civil rights issues, such as challenging the discrimination faced by migrant farmworkers, creating a gas and food cooperative, creating a legal aid clinic, and filing lawsuits against growers. With the legal clinic serving twenty-seven members within its first two months of being operational, there was clearly a need for these services.[40]

It was important that FLOC did not completely withdraw from organizing after they were unable to more forcefully capitalize off of the early contracts they secured. At a 1971 meeting, FLOC members made an ideological commitment to creating a campaign that could eventually take on the food processors. They realized that their small organization could still be capable of challenging local growers, but in order to even think about taking on the likes of Campbell, Heinz, or Libby, they would need to build a real organization with the capacity to mobilize enough people to show up for rallies, picket worksites, and contribute dues.[41] Thus, during this period, FLOC continued publishing their newsletter, maintaining support among already existing membership, building coalitions with supportive organizations and institutions, and developing deeper inroads with local Ohio communities. For example, they organized events that included rallies, games, and activities for the children of supporters who were referred to as "future *Flocistas,*" and performances by FLOC's "*Pobres de la Tierra*" *teatro*.[42] Their December 1972 newsletter attested to this commitment, with their concluding paragraph asserting, "Today FLOC continues to respond to the need to organize, and to initiate and participate in activities aimed at eliminating the causes of poverty. Having gained from its experience in terms of information, insight, and understanding, FLOC moves foreward [*sic*] as a union of people, from various walks of life, committed to the realization of this ultimate goal."[43] In short, it was during these years that FLOC matured in their understanding of how to effectively attain improved rights for migrant farmworkers and financially sustain this movement.

Even if this liminal period was not one where FLOC exclusively focused on unionizing farmworkers, it was an ideologically significant one. As the *South Side Express* described this period, "FLOC tried several methods of organizing these workers. . . . Although the [food and gas] coops [*sic*] provided a useful service, FLOC found that they did not unionize workers. . . . Instead of dissipating its energies in providing services, FLOC began to concentrate on organizing and research."[44] While FLOC still saw utility in providing these services, organizers eventually concluded that by offering these services to migrant workers, they were absolving corporate agribusiness from paying higher wages. In short, there would not be as large a need for food and gas cooperatives or other forms of assistance if processing companies would pay farmworkers a living wage.

The organization realized the power that corporate food processors held over both farmworkers and growers in the Midwest and recognized the necessity of locating fresh sources of financial support. In August 1973, FLOC's newsletter reported on a trip that nine of the organization's members took to New York City. This visit served two purposes. First, it reestablished contact with past funding sources and expanded their network of locating possible benefactors, with the visit resulting in FLOC submitting applications to multiple foundations for assistance in funding their Rural Urban Institute for Intercultural Documentation and Development. Second, this trip to New York gave FLOC members a chance to continue assessing and critiquing the unbalanced power structure that dictated the Midwest's agricultural industry. As the newsletter stated, "The trip provided some of the new staff members the opportunity to present the FLOC program and its relationship to Ohio's unique agri-industrial situation."[45] While this reporting suggests that the connection between farmworkers, growers, and processing companies was particular to Ohio, as FLOC's organizing efforts expanded and as their awareness of how the Midwest's agricultural industry operated, it would become clear that this was actually a regional structure.

In late August 1976, FLOC was thrust back into action as they supported a strike at Morgan Packing Company, a tomato processing plant in Warren, Indiana. Although this was certainly not a company operating on the same scale as Campbell, Libby, or Heinz, this was still an opportunity for FLOC to engage a food-processing company and put into action some of the lessons they had learned since the time of their last successful strike. Alongside Benito Lopez of the United Mexican American Services (UMAS), FLOC and frustrated workers engaged in a tense struggle against John Morgan Jr. of Morgan Packing and local authorities. Lopez possessed years of experience as an organizer in Indiana, participating in actions like a 1971 march for migrant farmworker rights that started in Marion and ended at the governor's mansion in Indianapolis. In a similar fashion to FLOC's successful 1968 strike, the Morgan Packing labor protest was initiated rather spontaneously.[46]

The strike began after labor contractors employed by Morgan recruited eighty workers from Texas and promised them employment at the Warren cannery (Morgan Packing Co. owned four tomato processing plants, with one of them being in Warren). When the migrant workers arrived in Warren, officials at Morgan refused to hire them, leaving most of the ethnic Mexican migrants unemployed for over a month. In some cases, if the migrant was fortunate enough, they might be hired for a few hours each day to clean up the processing facility. While Morgan contended that labor recruiters brought more workers than the company requested, the practice of over-recruiting Mexican migrants as a reserve labor force in case there was insufficient local labor for the harvest season was a fairly common one for employers.[47]

When it was becoming clear that the migrants from Texas—who had likely still been staying at Morgan's worker camps—were becoming agitated, John Morgan and representatives of the packing company sought to mitigate the growing unrest with deceitful promises of full employment for all of them. On August 24, after it was obvious to the migrants that Morgan would not be delivering on those assurances, the workers staged a preliminary walk-out and called for a complete shutdown of the Warren plant until all the workers' demands were met. Velásquez, who was representing FLOC and acting as spokesperson for the migrants in Warren, stated that the central demands of the striking workers were that all heads of families be hired to work in the cannery, that they be guaranteed a minimum employment of ten hours a day, and that they receive a written contract for the next year. Within two days, striking workers set up a barricade at the gate of the plant's entrance. With tomato field workers, who also lived in the camp with the cannery workers, joining the cause, the strike force grew to over 200 people at the height of the tomato harvest. As Morgan struggled to extinguish the workers' militancy, they turned toward the legal system as a possible solution.[48]

Following a temporary restraining order issued by the Huntington Circuit Court, the protestors took down the barricade. Yet, by August 30, just four days after the initial barricade went up, the barricade was restored after the court-mandated talks failed to produce sufficient progress and the restraining order expired. The conflict came to a climax on Friday, September 3, after a federal district judge ruled in favor of Morgan's petition for an injunction. Although Judge Jesse Eschbach said that Morgan's treatment of the migrant workers was a "'national disgrace,'" this federal court order authorized US Marshalls to remove the barricades.[49] *Nuestra Lucha* described what ensued: "Although Morgan constantly ordered the help of law enforcement officials, it took a federal court order and 50 arrests to dismantle the barricade. In all, there were 63 total arrested, and the strike leader Velasquez was twice arrested for various illegal, contempt of court and criminal trespass charges."[50] Although other outlets reported that the number of protestors arrested was 46, the fact of the matter was that the US Marshalls made a significant number of arrests. Fortunately for all parties involved, Morgan, FLOC, and the striking workers came to a compromise that would end the stalemate.[51]

Four days after authorities arrested the striking workers, the migrants voted to end the strike after receiving several key concessions from Morgan. Progress in the negotiations came after FLOC filed a complaint about Morgan's recruiting and hiring practices, which secured these representatives of the workers a hearing in front of the Indiana Civil Rights Commission. With mounds of tomatoes continuing to pile up as the strike halted operations at the Warren processing plant, Morgan capitulated. The terms that FLOC and Morgan agreed to were immediate, full employment for all workers that were promised jobs; a minimum of ten hours of employment per day with optional overtime hours; itemized pay stubs that showed all deductions; a discontinuation of the ten-cent hourly deduction that went to labor contractors and crew leaders; upgraded living quarters; a grievance procedure overseen by the Indiana Civil Rights Commission; and a raise in the piecework rate of the tomato farmworkers that saw their pay go from twenty cents per thirty-three pound hamper to twenty-four cents per hamper. The striking workers were also more inclined to take the deal with Morgan after Judge Eschbach passed down lenient sentences for those arrested for striking and defying the restraining order. The adults detained pled no contest to the charges of contempt of court and were sentenced to thirty days probation. Furthermore, the minors were released immediately with no further repercussions.[52]

As a result of the settled strike, the migrant workers, with the support of FLOC and UMAS, had secured forty-seven new positions from Morgan Packing Co.—thirty-four at the Warren processing plant and the rest at a cannery in downstate Indiana. The conflict with Morgan reinvigorated FLOC as they turned their sights toward even larger food processors. Indicative of FLOC's renewed sense of purpose in the aftermath of their successful challenge against Morgan, the week after the strike was settled, the *Fort Wayne Journal-Gazette* reported that FLOC was sending their thirteen organizers into Northwest Ohio's tomato and cucumber fields to recruit new union members and to try to secure contracts for the 1977 harvest season. Reflecting on the role that this incident would have on the trajectory of FLOC, Velásquez observed, "'It [the Morgan Packing Co. strike] was a major event in that it tested our negotiating and mobilizing ability. It also gave us a taste of the forthcoming fight with the Campbell Soup Company.'"[53]

Cream of Exploitation: The Campbell Soup Boycott and Mobilizing a Moral Authority

In July 1977, *Nuestra Lucha* relayed a significant announcement that was indicative of FLOC's growing influence. From Keene, California, César Chávez and the United Farm Workers' executive board announced to the press that they would be formally endorsing FLOC. The announcement read, "The United Farm Workers of America recognizes and supports the struggle of the Farm Labor Organizing Committee to win dignity and justice for farmworkers in the Midwest. We share common goals and a common commitment to liberating farmworkers from discrimination and exploitation that impoverishes so many of our people in this rich land."[54] This endorsement from the preeminent farmworker union in the country came as an encouraging sign of the momentum that FLOC was continuing to generate in the Midwest. One year after their successful support of the migrant workers in Warren, Indiana, FLOC members were on the cusp of celebrating the tenth anniversary of the organization's existence.

During that decade, FLOC matured from a small group that consisted of part-time staff to a year-round organization that was capable of providing a range of services and was supported by dues-paying members. A decennial celebration was an opportunity ripe for reflection about the organization's accomplishments as well as missteps, but it was also an opening for leaders and members to consider what they wanted to achieve in the upcoming years. With regard to the former, Velásquez stated, "'For a long time my people had a battle going with the growers but we did not realize they are unable to give us the things we want and the responsibility falls on the canneries.'"[55] In terms of the latter, *Nuestra Lucha* bluntly declared, "The present organizing campaign involves critical decisions on an all-out confrontation with the tomato industry."[56] In order to prepare for this formidable challenge, FLOC began developing a three-year plan that could achieve collective bargaining agreements between farmworkers and the corporations that relied on produce from the Midwest.[57]

One of FLOC's first steps in this three-year effort was to begin a dialogue with growers and the canneries, even though the organization was aware that this would likely be an unsuccessful approach. In 1978, FLOC mailed out nearly 500 letters of invitation to local agricultural industry employers—442 to Ohio growers and fifty-five to canneries—for a joint meeting to be convened in Bowling Green, Ohio, on July 27. Whether it was because they disliked the prospect of migrant farmworkers having union representation or because they were opposed to positioning themselves against powerful corporations, out of those invitees, only 16 growers attended and zero corporate representatives, which was expected. At this meeting, Velásquez made it clear that if an agreement could not be reached between the Midwestern tomato canneries, growers, and migrant workers, then FLOC would be forced to initiate a strike. One of the purposes of this meeting was to align the interests of growers and migrant workers, and to reassure the growers that it would be the responsibility of the canneries to cover the additional costs for the workers' improved wages and benefits. In addition to bargaining recognition, FLOC demanded certain conditions for the pickers and crew leaders.[58]

For the farmworkers, the demands included a $0.35 piecework rate per 33-pound hamper (up from $0.24 per hamper), a minimum hourly wage of $3.25 that would go into effect if the piecework rate did not yield $3.25 for the hour, a guaranteed 28 hours of work every two weeks, medical coverage, and a designated custodian to maintain the camps. For crew leaders, demands included higher rates of pay for loading the produce, supervising the work crews, and hauling. "If what we are doing sounds outlandish or somewhat radical, it is only because the tomato industry and the public has become accustomed to literally a peonage system to harvest its tomato crop," said Velásquez at the July 27 Bowling Green meeting.[59] These demands were to be presented to nine canneries in Ohio, and if they were not met, FLOC leaders were adamant that the tomatoes would be left on the vines to rot. As FLOC expected that the canneries would not engage with them, a meeting was scheduled for the following month in Leipsic, Ohio, where organizers expected to hold a strike vote. If FLOC doubted that the canneries would yield to the demands for pickers and crew leaders or recognize the organization as legitimate representatives of the region's farmworkers, they were confident that a strike authorization would be financially costly to the tomato processors. The previous year, Ohio produced 417,000 tons of tomatoes valued at $27.5 million. With the state growing over 20,000 acres of tomatoes each year, it was the second-largest producer of tomatoes in the country, albeit far behind California as the top producer. With the peak harvest period approaching, over six hundred farmworkers gathered in Leipsic to decide whether to strike.[60]

On August 20 at the Leipsic meeting, FLOC members voted to authorize the strike and called for a nationwide strike of Libby and Campbell products. While this marked an end to the organization's attempt at creating an amicable dialogue between the farmworkers, growers, and the corporate food processors, this was only the beginning of what would prove to be an eight-year struggle to secure three-way contracts with Campbell and Libby. Following the vote in Leipsic, nearly 2,000 farmworkers struck the tomato fields of Northwest Ohio. Although there were sympathetic growers who were willing to immediately recognize the union and offer the modest wage increases, FLOC refused to sign any contracts that did not also involve the canneries who purchased the crops from the growers. With the height of the tomato harvest only lasting around three weeks, FLOC organizers were already thinking about how to maintain a strike for the next summer, as well as considering other avenues for building support and hurting the profits of the corporations.[61]

One method in particular—a national consumer boycott—had proven to be a fiercely successful approach for the United Farm Workers in recent years. *Nuestra Lucha* acknowledged the utility of this strategy, writing: "Although strikes will continue to be a major tool against the canneries next summer, only through a hard and probably long struggle will FLOC be able to win this fight. FLOC is now calling on its friends throughout the country to help organize boycott communities and to help raise funds to support this continuing struggle."[62]

Predictably, representatives of Libby and Campbell were displeased with the prospect of a national boycott. The corporate stance was that the farmworkers were employees of the growers, thus the processors should not be involved in this conflict. As Alexis Shantz, spokesperson for Libby, McNeill & Libby Inc., stated, "'A threatened FLOC boycott of Libby products would be another attempt by that organization to embroil a neutral employer in a primary labor dispute with tomato growers.'"[63] This was a perspective echoed by Campbell Soup, whose spokesperson said the company would not bargain with FLOC because the union did not represent any of Campbell's workers. This was *the* most common refrain corporate food processors used to deflect responsibility. FLOC did not technically represent Campbell or Libby's workers but did represent many of the farmworkers who harvested the tomatoes for these companies' products, which is why the organization would not settle for anything less than three-way bargaining and contracts between farmworkers, growers, and corporations.[64]

The following summer, in 1979, FLOC held their first constitutional convention in Holgate, Ohio. This gathering was held to set organizational policies, and to elect officers and a Board of Directors for the union. *Nuestra Lucha* advertised that "this convention marks the first time in the history of the Midwest that farmworkers have come together on such a scale to unite their voices in protest of such conditions under which they have been forced to live and work."[65] Whether through letters, donations, endorsements, or withheld consumption, farmworkers, organized labor, and consumers backed FLOC and their first convention in a range of ways. In a letter to Campbell's division of Consumer Affairs, Nancy J. Davis, then an assistant professor of sociology at Indiana University, defiantly conveyed their support for FLOC, writing, "I am writing to inform you of my boycott of all Campbell's products until your corporation stops exploiting farmworkers in the tomato fields of Ohio and agrees to sign a contract with the Farm Labor Organizing Committee (FLOC) expressive to that intent."[66] While each of these aforementioned groups of stakeholders were cornerstones of FLOC's organizing efforts, there was one other segment that provided crucial financial and social support for the Midwestern farmworkers' movement.

Major religious groups wrote in and voiced their encouragement for FLOC's first constitutional convention, including the Office of Minority Affairs for the Presbyterian Church in the United States, the United Methodist Church, the National Conference of Hispanic Bishops, and the National Assembly of Religious Women, just to name a few.[67] The 1979 constitutional gathering was a monumental event for the growing Midwestern farmworker movement and as the harvest seasons came and went, FLOC created a stronger foothold in Ohio and forged deeper inroads among Michigan and Indiana's migrant farmworkers. Despite the progress in organizing workers, Campbell and Libby were steadfast in their reluctance to negotiate with FLOC, meaning that members of the organization upheld the strike each harvest season and the year-round consumer boycott remained in place. The multi-year conflict intensified in 1983 when FLOC leaders and members engaged in a very public display of civil disobedience that was undergirded with demonstrations of religious devotion.

On July 7, 1983, FLOC began their "March for Justice." The following day, Akron's *Beacon Journal* reported on the beginning of this event: "Some 200 strong, with red flags and black banners drooping in a balmy dusk, they stopped traffic and crossed the Maumee River's main bridge in Toledo. Only 558 miles to go." The article described the bevy of supporters that participated in the first stretch of the march as "farm workers from Texas, nuns from Michigan, Muslims from Toledo, Methodists from Indiana."[68] Upwards of seventy FLOC members and supporters were expected to make the full trek from Toledo, Ohio, to the Campbell Soup Co. headquarters in Camden, New Jersey. The marchers planned on arriving in Philadelphia, Pennsylvania, by August 7, where César Chávez would meet them before crossing over the

Delaware River to Camden where the procession would conclude at the company's headquarters.[69]

In response to the March for Justice, Campbell countered by attempting to discredit FLOC's organizing efforts and dismissing the impact of the boycott. James Moran, public relations manager for Campbell, derided Baldemar Velásquez, asserting, "'He's frustrated because since 1968 he's been trying to form a union. He's failed miserably. This [march] is a desperation move.'" Although Moran further claimed the boycott was unsuccessful and that Campbell was "'having one of its best years ever,'" he did concede that FLOC's march was effectively gaining publicity.[70] As FLOC proceeded eastward, they were greeted, fed, and sheltered along the way by religious groups. On August 1, over three weeks since the march began, they were received in Harrisburg, Pennsylvania, with a dinner and rally at the Lakeside Lutheran Church. That night, the marchers slept at a former orphanage owned by the Catholic diocese. At noon the next day, the procession continued on to the steps of the state capitol where they were welcomed by labor, political, and religious groups.[71]

In the days after FLOC protestors passed through Harrisburg, one of the stops before Philadelphia was in Lebanon where Eric Harrison, a *Philadelphia Inquirer* staff writer, covered the organization closely as its members trudged through Eastern Pennsylvania. Harrison began one article by focusing on Alfonso Salinas, one of the marchers.[72] Throughout this trek, Salinas and some of the other FLOC members displayed crucifix necklaces made of two twigs that a priest in Toledo had given them. Describing the significance of the cross dangling from his neck, Salinas said, "'*Es el símbolo de la marcha*'" ("It's the symbol of the march"). Harrison described that in addition to flags for the United States, Mexico, and FLOC, demonstrations in support of the Midwestern migrant farmworkers included homemade banners of the *Virgen de Guadalupe*, as well as Protestant and Catholic prayers.[73]

During the March for Justice, as well as the longer history of FLOC, faith and the support of religious groups continued to play a significant symbolic and material role. On August 7, when FLOC marchers were approaching Camden, they were met by 100 family members that traveled from Ohio by bus and 200 other supporters, including Chávez. As the growing procession crossed the Benjamin Franklin Bridge and neared Campbell's headquarters, one reporter noted, "Two marchers near the front also held a banner depicting Our Lady of Guadalupe, the farmworkers patron saint. After descending a stairway from the bridge, the marchers were greeted by a delegation of flower-bearing children from Sacred Heart Church in South Camden."[74]

With Sunday church bells ringing, demonstrators traveled a few blocks southeast of the bridge to the Cathedral of the Immaculate Conception where ten clergymen used silver bowls to bathe the feet of some of the marchers.[75]

Finally, the month-long March for Justice ended with an all-night vigil outside the front entrance of Campbell and a closing round of demonstrations at the headquarters the following day. That morning, as Campbell's employees returned to the headquarters following the weekend, FLOC supporters handed flowers and three handwritten petitions to Frank Moore, Campbell's manager of community relations. Moore received the offering but made no comment. Campbell's public relations team did offer to meet with members of FLOC, but union representatives were adamant that any meeting had to be directly with President Richard Gordon McGovern. As Velásquez stated, "'We don't want to meet with people without any authority. . . . We're not interested with the PR people.'"[76] The end of the march marked the beginning of a new chapter in FLOC's struggle against Campbell—one that was increasingly focused on shaping the public opinion of the prominent food company. Sister Pat Drydyk, who would eventually be the first woman to lead the National Farm Worker Ministry, helped influence the ecumenical organization to broaden its reach outside of California and the UFW in order to support FLOC's boycott of Campbell. Reflecting on the importance of the march, Sister Drydyk recalled that with local and major newspapers covering each stage of the march, this episode introduced thousands of people to the farmworker justice movement.[77]

Fernando Cuevas Sr., FLOC's vice president and director of field operations, shared this sentiment. Cuevas was confident that even if Campbell refused to make any concessions regarding their role in the conditions of migrant workers, the publicity from the march would positively impact the boycott in FLOC's favor.[78] At the time of the march, Cuevas had nine children ranging from three years old up to eighteen. As the Cuevas family had not picked tomatoes in the Midwest since the 1978 strike began, they were now based in Winter Garden, Florida, harvesting oranges. Perhaps anticipating an area that would be fertile ground in the public relations battle against Campbell, Cuevas stated that all of his children were forced to contribute to the family by working in fields. Because Campbell was a company with a decades-long history of producing marketing and advertising campaigns targeting children and families, the optics of child workers picking the tomatoes that went into the company's famous soup could be devastating. In response to this claim, Moran, Campbell's manager of public relations, maintained that children did

March on Benjamin Franklin Bridge, 1983. Courtesy of the Toledo Lucas County Public Library and Baldemar Velásquez.

not work on the farms that had contracts to provide tomatoes to the company.[79]

In one particularly memorable picture from the March of Justice, an eleven-year-old Hugo Salinas holds three-year-old Nora Cuevas. Salinas, who is looking intently at an upward angle toward the photographer, is dressed in a "Cream of Exploitation" Campbell boycott shirt. The caption for the photo reads, "Both children work in the fields with their families. Hugo has been in the fields since the age of two."[80] As another publication put it, the presence of young marchers begged the question: Why did these children have to work the fields and protest for better conditions, instead of being able to play like other kids in the country?[81] A few months after the march concluded, this photo would become the focal point for a provocative advertisement campaign that called on the public to "Hear the Children."

On Christmas Day, 1983, FLOC ran advertisements that ranged from a quarter page to a full page in the *New York Times, Detroit Free Press, San Diego Union, Los Angeles Times,* and other large daily newspapers. After the New Year, the *Lansing State Journal* characterized this shifting terrain for the ongoing contest between FLOC and Campbell: "A five-year battle between a tiny farmworkers' union and food giant Campbell Soup Co. has moved from the fields of northwestern Ohio to the pages of some of the nation's largest newspapers."[82] Beneath the photo of eleven-year-old Salinas carrying the three-year-old Cuevas, the advertisement contained bolded, capitalized font stating, "To These Kids, Campbell's Soup Tastes like Blood, Sweat, and Tears."[83] The march to the Camden headquarters and FLOC's "Hear the Children" campaign marked the turning point in the labor organization's confrontation of Campbell Soup Co.

Years later, Cruz Phillips reflected on the significance of this six-month period. As Phillips stated, "The best part . . . [of the campaign] was that it marked the beginning of what was to be 2½ years of support for farmworkers by thousands of new people."[84] While the march garnered FLOC new supporters, the "Hear the Children" campaign formally put Campbell on the defensive. Following the March for Justice, it took organizers and supporters only two months to raise $52,000 for the advertising campaign. Beyond the local solidarity and fundraising, the list of co-chairs for the campaign also indicates the level of support that FLOC was receiving from labor unions, politicians, and civil rights and religious organizations. This included the likes of Owen Bieber, president of the UAW AFL-CIO; César Chávez, president of the UFW AFL-CIO; Congressman John Conyers Jr.; Mario Obledo, president of the League of United Latin American Citizens (LULAC);

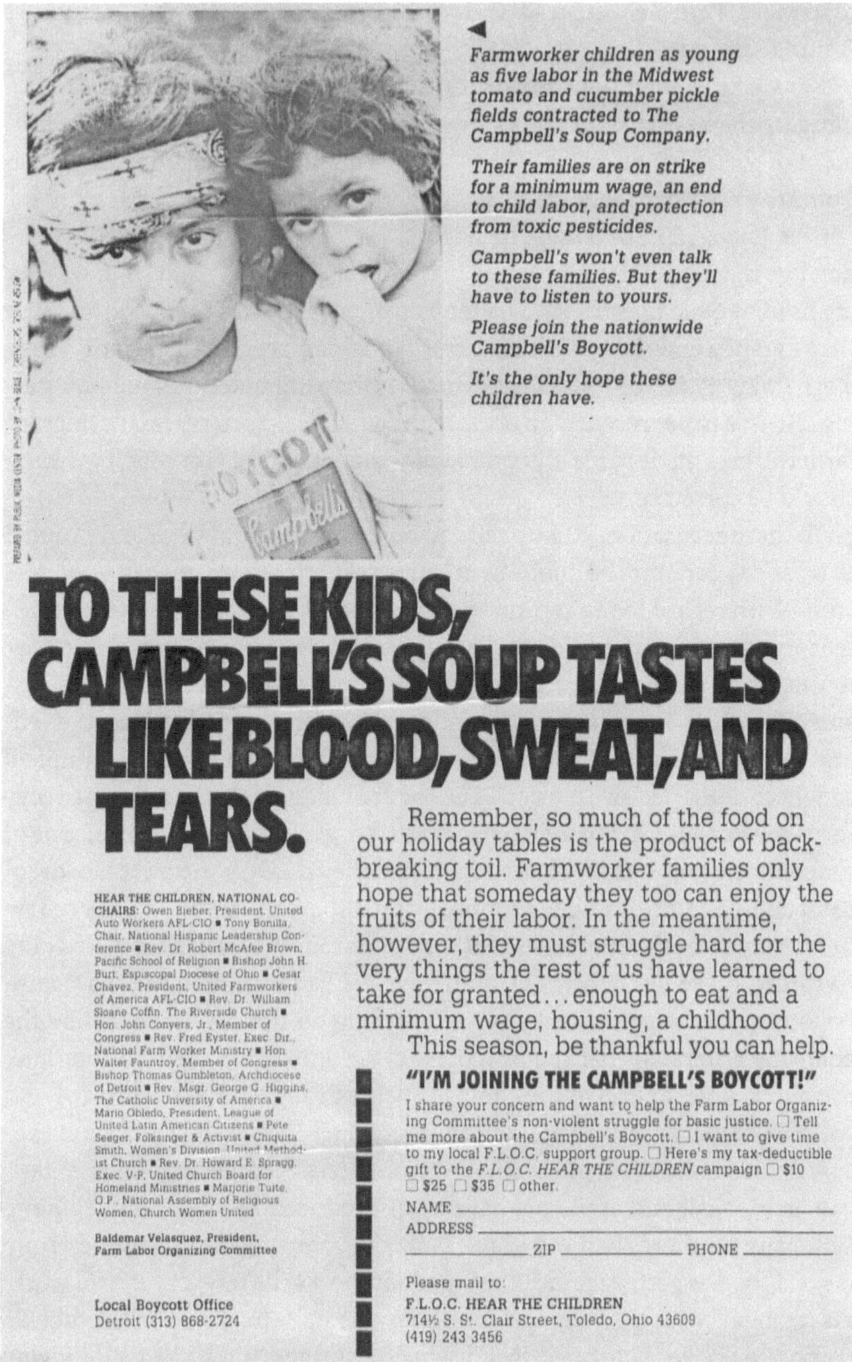

Michigan Farm Worker Ministry: F.L.O.C. Campbells Boycott advertisement work-up. 1980. (47218). Walter P. Reuther Library, Archives of Labor and Urban Affairs, Wayne State University.

folksinger Pete Seeger; and Chiquita Smith of the United Methodist Church, among others.[85]

Sensing the potential damage of FLOC's campaign, Campbell sought to mitigate the harm to their brand by publishing a *New York Times* advertisement of their own on January 1, 1984. In "Fiction vs. Fact," Campbell Soup Company presented four brief "fictions" that they addressed with more extensive "facts." The two most damaging "fictions" to the company were the first two that Campbell confronted in their response: that child labor was being used by Ohio farmers who had tomato contracts with Campbell and that the migrant workers were unsatisfactorily compensated for their labor. Without naming FLOC or Velásquez by name, they intimated as much by stating, "In this paper recently an organization that claims to represent migrant farm workers made some unfortunate misstatements of fact which we think should be corrected."[86]

To these accusations, Campbell's ad denied using child labor and claimed to offer day care for the children on farms that the company had contracts with. With regard to the second "fiction," Campbell pivoted to their consistent argument that they did not directly employ any farmworkers, but rather it was the farmers that were responsible for this. Moreover, Campbell assured *New York Times* readers that migrant workers earned at least the federal minimum wage, if not more. As for the final two fictions, Campbell sought to deal a decisive blow to FLOC by contending that the union had only forty-seven dues-paying members and that organized labor had been one of the company's most outspoken supporters. About FLOC's "Hear the Children" campaign, Scott Rombach, Campbell spokesperson, noted, "'They're trying to play that emotional issue with the children. We felt if they were going to spread those lies to any real audience, we had to respond."[87] As Campbell's response suggests, they were now fully on the defensive. While the company reiterated that the boycott was not impacting their bottom line, the public's perception of the company was shifting dramatically.[88]

In a February 1984 edition of the *Detroit Free Press*, Linda Solomon captured this publicity turn. Solomon commented, "Canned goods as American as baseball and apple pie have been produced by the Campbell Soup Company for more than 100 years. Now the company that advertises 'soup is good food' is getting some bitter medicine—it's the target of a farm workers national boycott." Solomon continues, "At stake for Campbell is its clean corporate image, cultivated by advertising slogans and a corporate giving campaign."[89] One of Campbell's most popular initiatives was the Soup Labels for Education program, which incentivized collecting Campbell's labels. Begun in 1973, participating schools and organizations could exchange the labels for audio-visual equipment, learning aids, art supplies, and gym equipment.[90] Taking into consideration programs like Soup Labels for Education, as well as Campbell's general marketing strategies, FLOC's "Hear the Children" offensive called attention to the hypocrisy of the company and the larger food-processing industry. For a company that consciously promoted itself as a wholesome, child- and family-friendly brand, the accusations of using child labor and underpaying migrant families with dependent children was a scarlet letter. As FLOC continued to gain momentum, a presidential candidate would highlight the organization on one of the country's biggest political stages in the summer of 1984.

"Campbell Signs!"

On July 17, 1984, Reverend Jesse Jackson took center stage and faced a raucous crowd that had packed into San Francisco's Moscone Convention Center for the Democratic National Convention. Three months before Jackson addressed Democratic supporters, the presidential hopeful was seeking to mediate the conflict between FLOC and Campbell. While Jackson described his involvement as one motivated by "action, not advocacy," he did indeed support FLOC's campaign to bargain directly with Campbell.[91] After Jackson endorsed FLOC's efforts on April 14 in Cleveland, Ohio, he communicated this stance to Campbell. This initially yielded a conversation between Jackson and Campbell's vice president of corporate relations, Ray Page. The following month, these conversations advanced to the point where Jackson met with Gordon McGovern, president of Campbell Soup Co., in Washington, DC.[92]

With Jackson's stated interest in mediating this multi-year labor dispute, both FLOC and Campbell coveted the presidential candidate's complete support. To this end, FLOC had already endorsed Jackson and farmworkers were campaigning for the candidate in Ohio and Texas. Conversely, Campbell agreed to put on paper their offer to contribute to medical insurance programs, day care centers, and other initiatives—but stopped short of recognizing the union or getting involved in contract negotiations. Scott Rombach, Campbell spokesperson, claimed that while Jackson came out of their meeting supporting "reconciliation" between the two parties, he did not support the boycott of the company's food products.[93] Although it is difficult to resolve what was said during this closed-door meeting, Jackson would make his public stance unequivocally clear during his address at the DNC.

Around 9:00 in the evening on July 17 at the Moscone Center, Jesse Jackson made his way to the podium as Democratic onlookers roared in applause and raised modest, green signs with Jackson's name in white print. After, Jackson waved and pointed to his supporters, then began his speech. Throughout this address, Jackson emphasized the "rainbow coalition" that had been the centerpiece of his campaign, the importance of Democratic Party unity, and trenchant criticism of Ronald Reagan's presidential term. In a message that encapsulated the voters Jackson sought to draw in throughout his candidacy for the party's nomination, Jackson alliterated, "My constituency is the desperate, the damned, the disinherited, the disrespected, and the despised."[94] Jackson then recounted the patchwork of groups that this coalition—one that crossed ethnic, racial, religious, gender, socioeconomic, sexuality, disability, and age lines—was embracing.

"The Rainbow Coalition is making room for Hispanic Americans who this very night are living under the threat of the Simpson-Mazzoli bill," stated Jackson, referring to the Immigration Reform and Control Act that would eventually be signed into law in 1986. He immediately followed up by asserting that the Rainbow Coalition included "farm workers from Ohio who are fighting the Campbell Soup Company with a boycott to achieve legitimate workers' rights." As soon as Jackson said this, C-SPAN television coverage turned to the audience. There, two people, who were presumably FLOC supporters with prior knowledge that Jackson would be giving the organization recognition during this speech, walked through the crowd carrying two multi-foot-tall banners. The first read "Support Farm Workers" and the second resembled a can of Campbell's soup, with "Boycott Campbell's" at the top and "Cream of Exploitation Soup" at the bottom. Trailing the banner-wielding supporters were a few others with smaller signs branded with the United Farm Workers' trademark eagle logo.[95]

Ultimately, former Vice President Walter F. Mondale won the Democratic Party's nomination on the first ballot, beating out Senator Hart and Jesse Jackson, who received around 31 percent and 12 percent of the delegate votes, respectively. While Jackson's reference to the Campbell boycott and the farmworker movement was brief and just a small part of the "Rainbow Coalition" speech, it was meaningful to the momentum that FLOC was building and now sustaining. Likely feeling somewhat triumphant in the aftermath of the DNC, Baldemar Velásquez declared the financial and political stakes of this moment. According to Velásquez's evaluation, "'When you get a million bucks worth of reference and so on at the Democratic Party convention, the whole world knows it's become a Hispanic political issue.'"[96] Not only did FLOC benefit from the initial television and newspaper publicity, but Jackson's reference to the organization also inspired fresh investigative reporting geared toward individuals who might have caught the reference on C-SPAN but were uninformed about the ongoing labor contest.

Jeremy Iggers recounted this particular moment for the *Detroit Free Press*, writing, "The Campbell soup boycott got a publicity boost at last month's Democratic National Convention. Jesse Jackson endorsed the boycott in his speech, and network tv cameras showed delegates holding placards supporting the boycott." As Iggers perceptively observed, Jackson referred to FLOC's boycott of Campbell without explicitly naming the organization. "So a lot more people know somebody wants them to boycott, but most still don't know who or why," continued Iggers.[97] In this case, Jackson's acknowledgment of the ongoing labor conflict was an entry point for a journalist like Iggers to probe what the Democratic candidate was referring to and to profile some of their members.

For the article, Iggers visited a migrant worker camp near Linwood, Michigan. There, he met a family of eleven from Florida, Higinio and Rebecca Pecina, and their nine children. The eleven members of the Pecina family lived without plumbing in a two-story shack. To make enough money during the two months they spent in Michigan, Higino, Rebecca, and six of their children picked cucumbers. Three of their kids (aged thirteen, eleven, and ten) would be considered child laborers. While in Linwood, the Pecinas were harvesting cucumbers for a farmer selling them to Vlasic Foods, Inc., a subsidiary of Campbell. Ironically, Campbell agreed to acquire Vlasic in 1978, the year that FLOC began their strike and nationwide boycott of the company.[98] Campbell in the meantime maintained their position and continued to deny any responsibility for the circumstances—such as substandard living conditions, poor wages, and child workers—of families like the Pecinas. "'We don't feel we have any business trying to force a union on individual workers who might not want to join a union, and on independent farmers whose workers are not represented by a union,'" stated Rombach, the Campbell spokesperson, as he toed the company line. Even as Campbell stood firm, public opinion was shifting to the point that it was only a matter of time before the company would have to meet with FLOC at the bargaining table.[99]

In May 1985, ten months after the DNC, representatives of FLOC and Campbell, with mediation by the National Council of Churches, quietly made a private agreement that laid out a timeline and framework for ending the multi-year standoff. Campbell publicly disclosed this arrangement the following month, which irritated the FLOC leadership. While Campbell denied there being any ill intent behind the company divulging this information, Velásquez considered this an attempt to undermine the union and their ongoing boycott. Nevertheless, the two parties were still set to go forward with the agreed-upon arrangement. According to this, FLOC and Campbell set July 1 as their deadline for creating an independent commission that could help bring an end to this prolonged dispute. Furthermore, Campbell would encourage the growers that supplied produce to them to send representatives to the commission and John T. Dunlop, a former US secretary of labor and Harvard University economics professor, would direct the commission.[100]

Given his expertise and pragmatism, Dunlop was a prudent choice by representatives of FLOC and Campbell to chair this commission. As the *New York Times* eulogized following his death in 2003, Dunlop was a "foremost labor relations expert and served every president from Franklin D. Roosevelt to Bill Clinton."[101] Appropriately named the Dunlop Commission, this body was formally responsible for several aspects relating to FLOC's future as a recognized union and their relationship with growers and food processors. These responsibilities included overseeing the proceedings for elections that could make FLOC the collective bargaining unit for the farmworkers in Ohio and Michigan, supervising the labor negotiations between the parties, drafting an agricultural collective bargaining act for Ohio and Michigan (likely similar to the California Agricultural Labor Relations Act of 1975), ensuring all parties bargained in good faith, and ensuring mechanisms for enforcing all regulations. In addition to Dunlop, the commission would appoint eight other members—four from a list of FLOC recommendations and four grower representatives from a list provided by Campbell.[102]

By October 1985, concrete mediation talks between the Farm Labor Organizing Committee and growers that supplied Campbell were finally set to begin. Although a three-way contract between FLOC, Campbell, and the growers was anything but finalized, the fact that these talks had finally materialized gave off an air of imminence. As the *Associated Press* expectantly reported, "Union representation could be in effect by next year's growing season on Ohio and Michigan farms."[103] Despite this cautious optimism, FLOC was unrelenting in their commitment to the boycott until a deal was achieved. "I'm not going to call off the boycott until we have a collective bargaining agreement that calls for sweeping changes in the wages and living conditions of farm workers," Velásquez emphatically stated.[104] As FLOC's national boycott was the vehicle that allowed them to finally have the upper hand over Campbell, organizers were completely conscious that it would be premature to end the boycott merely because progress was being made. Just a few months after concrete talks between the parties began, there would be good reason for FLOC to triumphantly call off the boycott.

"For the first time in the Midwest," reported the *Detroit Free Press* in February 1986, "farm workers in Michigan and northwestern Ohio have won collective bargaining agreements with two of the region's food processors, Campbell Soup Co. and its subsidiary, Vlasic Pickle Co."[105] In FLOC's regular newsletter, *Boycott Update,* their major news for the April 1986 edition was that for the first time in seven years, there would *not* be a boycott.[106] For these negotiations, FLOC's bargaining team consisted of Fernando Cuevas Sr., Maria T. Sanchez, and Velásquez. On February 18, FLOC signed their collective bargaining agreement with Vlasic Foods, Inc. (Campbell subsidiary) and cucumber growers under contract to Vlasic.[107] The following day, FLOC formalized their agreement with Campbell Soup Company and the Campbell Tomato Growers Association.[108] Estimates regarding how many FLOC members would benefit from these contracts were between 600 and 800 migrant farmworkers.[109]

According to FLOC's *Boycott Update,* the contract for Ohio's tomato workers would cover around 200 hand-pickers, mechanical harvester workers, and truck drivers for the 1986 harvest season, as well as an additional 200 workers for planting and hoeing the following year. The FLOC members harvesting the tomato fields were designated as wage workers. Thus, with the contract, they were now set to earn $4.50 an hour, up from an average of $3.95 the previous year. The minimum wage would also go up an additional ten cents for the 1987 season. For Michigan's cucumber workers, the new contracts would cover approximately 400 members. In terms of pay rate, cucumber workers were designated as "independent contractors" with a "share basis" whereby the farmworkers and growers split the gross crop value 50/50. While a bonus payment system was also included for the cucumber pickers, this contract preserved the base compensation system that was already in place for farmworkers.[110] How did Campbell benefit from this contract? Well, as their spokesperson stated bluntly, it eased the "'the negative attitude towards our company.'"[111]

The principal significance of these multi-year contracts was union recognition for FLOC as the collective bargaining agent of these workers. In addition to the wage stipulations—wage increases for those employed on Campbell Tomato Growers Association farms and standardizing the cucumber earnings system—there were other important guarantees secured by the contracts with Campbell and Vlasic. These benefits included paid union representatives, health insurance, a forty-eight-hour grievance process, and a paid holiday for Labor Day. FLOC agreed that their union members would not engage in any strikes or lockouts during the duration of the contract. The settlement also authorized the establishment of study committees to review migrant housing and living conditions, day care centers, pesticide use, healthcare and safety, and alternatives to the independent contractor system in the cucumber fields. Finally, each family that was part of the beginning of the Campbell strike in 1978 would be eligible for up to $2,000 in compensation. FLOC organizers had good reason to celebrate this monumental three-way collective bargaining agreement, but for many of them, this contract was hopefully only the first of many to come.[112]

Maria T. Sanchez, who was part of the FLOC bargaining team, recalled the moment after they agreed to the terms with Campbell on February 19. The previous day, when they signed the contract with Vlasic, the FLOC representatives toasted with beer to celebrate the organization's accomplishment. As the Campbell contract was finalized before 8:30 in the morning, coffee seemed to be the more appropriate beverage to consume. Reflecting on this moment, Sanchez remembered that Velásquez, or "Balde" as she referred to him, said, "'Do you know what we've just done? We've just made history and the farm workers are on their way!'" While still thrilled by the outcome of this multi-year struggle, more organizing remained to be done. "For me," Sanchez said, "true victory will come when we have organized all the farm workers in the Midwest and have contracts with Heinz, Hunts, Aunt Jane and all others."[113] Sanchez's ambition and intent to unionize all migrant farmworkers in the Midwest was echoed by Velásquez in the introductory note to workers and supporters in the first collective bargaining agreement booklets.[114] This overwhelming determination to expand these efforts was all the more impressive when considering the national decline of unions in the 1980s.

In their report on the erosion of unions between the late 1960s and the early 1980s, the Economic Policy Institute (EPI) contends that one of the most meaningful indicators has been the dramatic decline in new unionization, across both manufacturing and nonmanufacturing sectors. The key markers of this deterioration were threefold: fewer union elections were held during this period, unions won a smaller share of the elections that were held, and newly organized unions were increasingly unable to secure elusive first contracts. According to the policy analysts for this report, one cause of this decline was increased employer opposition to unions throughout the 1970s. A second source of this erosion was the passage of anti-union legislation and weak labor laws, both of which diminished the bargaining power of unions.[115] In *Knocking on Labor's Door*, Lane Windham, who was also one of the authors for the EPI report, concludes that even though workers still coveted unions, "Employers refused to tolerate unions any longer as profits grew scarce; they fought back and took greater advantage of weak US labor law."[116] Given the challenges that unions were facing during the 1970s and 1980s, it was little surprise how long it took for FLOC to bring Campbell to the bargaining table. Ultimately, the result of FLOC's success was optimism among Midwestern farmworkers and concern for corporate food processors.

When Sanchez, Cuevas Sr., and Velásquez returned to the FLOC office in Toledo and delivered the news of the contract to the staff and supporters, this outcome was an affirmation of their tireless organizing. In what could only be described as a transformative shift in mentality following the collective bargaining agreement, Sanchez explained, "From that moment on we became different people, with reason to be proud and with a bigger reason to continue the struggle."[117] While Sanchez was describing the internalized, personal sense of accomplishment, there was also good reason to believe that FLOC's ability to secure these three-way contracts could produce reverberations for organized labor across the country. Fully aware of the employer and government obstacles that unions and organizers were encountering in the 1980s, FLOC secretary-treasurer Ray Santiago shared his vision for how this victory could revitalize the American labor movement. "Labor does not have to keep going back," proclaimed Santiago. "Labor can go forward if it has a clear plan. We see ourselves where the labor movement saw themselves back at the turn of the twentieth century."[118] As FLOC organizers like Santiago, Sanchez, and Velásquez made explicitly clear, the union had every intention to expand their efforts.

In terms of FLOC's next steps, they had a three-pronged plan for expanding their unionization efforts. First, FLOC had to effectively administer the newly secured contracts. Second, they needed to attempt to bring the remainder of Vlasic's cucumber workers under contract. While FLOC's 1986 contract was momentous, the reality was that it covered only 800 workers, at the most. With around 3,000 workers involved with Campbell and Vlasic and around 70,000 migrant farmworkers in the Great Lakes region, FLOC organizers were fully aware of how much work remained to achieve their ultimate goal of securing contracts for all of the migratory workers sustaining Midwestern agribusiness. Finally, FLOC would be setting their sights on other corporate food processors, such as Heinz. As Heinz clearly sought to avoid the negative impact of a costly consumer boycott, they declared their interest to meet with FLOC representatives on the same day that FLOC and Campbell announced their agreement.[119]

After Campbell agreed to terms with FLOC, Rombach, the company's spokesperson, predicted this contract would have significant implications throughout the region. According to Rombach's assessment, "'It [the contract] will have far-reaching effects on agriculture in the Midwest.'" He continued by predicting, "'The entire food processing industry in the Midwest will have to take a look at what's been done here. There's going to have to be some kind of parity in wages and conditions.'"[120] As Heinz preempted any boycott or strike discussions and expressed their willingness to meeting FLOC organizers, Rombach's evaluation was correct. Food-processing and agribusiness operations in the Midwest were heeding the warning. Between late spring and early summer in 1986, just a few months after FLOC, Campbell, and Vlasic announced their deal, the farmworker organization was already making significant progress in their negotiations with Heinz. Informal discussions began between FLOC and Heinz in June of that year, and rapidly progressed into an August agreement stipulating that the parties would begin formal talks in November with the end goal of having a contract in place for the 1987 harvest season.[121]

The preliminary agreement between FLOC, Heinz, and the Fremont Pickle & Tomato Growers' Association acknowledged the shared concerns of all parties and urged cooperation between them. In April 1987, the parties agreed to the terms and workers ratified the contract. Of the twenty-seven Michigan and Ohio farms that supplied produce for Heinz, FLOC received the requisite support to represent workers on fourteen of them. With this new contract, an additional 500 migrant farmworkers would now have union contracts and be represented by FLOC. Two years after this agreement, FLOC would renegotiate their contract with Campbell. This was followed the next year by contract renewals with both Vlasic and Heinz. Finally, in 1992, Aunt Jane's and Green Bay Food would sign collective bargaining agreements with the union, meaning FLOC now had contracts with all major pickle companies in Northwest Ohio and Southeast Michigan.[122]

Conclusion

Much remains to be written about the history of the Farm Labor Organizing Committee beyond the periodization of this chapter, beyond the Midwest, and beyond the organizing of mostly domestic farmworkers. The purpose of this chapter is not to present a teleological narrative about the progression of FLOC, but rather to present an account of their origins, the critical junctures in their early union history, the organizational approaches they implemented, and an assessment of their accomplishments. The union's ability to secure collective bargaining agreements with Campbell, Vlasic, Heinz, Aunt Jane's, and Green Bay Foods is a central part of the union's legacy. Furthermore, even though Baldemar Velásquez is an influential figure in the history of FLOC, and thus this chapter, he cannot be singularly celebrated for the collective accomplishments. Doing so risks reducing the contributions of the workers and supporters who shared in building this union. Even if this chapter struggles to do so, future studies of FLOC will need to grapple with and elevate the perspectives of the countless others that created and sustained the organization.

The Farm Labor Organizing Committee's accomplishments in the 1980s transformed the landscape of organized labor and agribusiness in the Midwest. Through their long-standing commitment to the consumer boycott, the union was able to apply enough economic pressure to bring corporate food processors and the Midwestern farmers that supplied them to the bargaining table. The organization's impact cannot be overstated. While reactionary anti-union politics, weak labor laws, and neoliberal economic transformations created a pernicious environment for organized labor during the late twentieth century, FLOC began to carve out a foothold in the Midwest and then secure the first three-way contracts between the farmworker organization, growers, and the corporate food giants.

The history of the farmworker movement in the United States is generally associated with the United Farm Workers. While the UFW was immensely effective at advocating for the dignity and humanity of farmworkers, securing union contracts for them in one the country's most powerful agricultural economies, and propelling landmark legislation that established the right for farmworkers in California to collectively bargain, it is misguided to solely associate the farmworker justice movement with the UFW. Reorienting that attention to FLOC offers a drastically different periodization for the farmworker justice movement, and alternate visions for the future of agricultural labor and the role of the Midwest in shaping these developments.

Conclusion

The Permanence of Temporary Farmworkers

The Farm Labor Organizing Committee's 1986 booklet celebrating their momentous collective bargaining agreement with Campbell Soup Company featured an array of congratulatory notes, a timeline of significant events, and photos that captured the prolonged struggle. One of the most prominent aspects of this booklet were the reflections from FLOC organizers, allied organizations, and general supporters. On the first interior page, musician Pete Seeger, a "long-time friend" of FLOC, provided a brief remark. Seeger, a progressive folk musician, had a long history of supporting working-class issues. As the *New York Times* eulogized following his death in 2014, Seeger's "career carried him from singing at labor rallies to the Top 10 . . . and from a conviction for contempt of Congress (after defying the House Un-American Activities Committee in the 1950s) to performing on the steps of the Lincoln Memorial at an inaugural concert for Barack Obama."[1] While exulting the fact that hundreds of Latinx farmworkers in Ohio and Michigan would soon benefit from these new contracts, Seeger also expressed some unease regarding the reluctance of corporate food producers to enter collective bargaining agreements. "The only sad thing," wrote Seeger, "is that it took so many long years of struggle and eventually the increasingly successful boycott of Campbell's products to bring about the agreement." Seeger continued, leveling a more structural criticism, "It is the shame of America that some of the lowest-paid workers are those who pick the food we all eat."[2] This statement captured perhaps the most sardonic feature of the agro-food industry.

Frances Moore Lappé—who has now authored or co-authored nearly two dozen books on food, hunger, environmentalism, and democracy—was another notable FLOC supporter and contributor to their commemorative booklet. In 1984, at the height of FLOC's boycott against Campbell and as the conflict was increasingly spilling into the newspaper headlines, Lappé spent a weekend with the organization. "The experience will always stay with us. While we remember the inhuman conditions in which farm workers have been forced to live, what remains uppermost in our memories is the dignity and courage that shone through in so many people we met."[3] In the end,

FLOC's struggle and that of the previous generations of migrant farmworkers who made their way to the Midwest from Texas, Mexico, and Puerto Rico was about three intertwined values: dignity, worker rights, and justice. There was no singular definition for this, and it took many forms. What exactly this looked like for migrant workers was contingent upon the time period and their place of origin, citizenship status, gender, family status, their number of years following the harvest route, and myriad other circumstances.

In the case of FLOC organizers and rank-and-file members, there were often particular moments during the protracted struggle against Campbell that took on specific significance. For Fernando Cuevas, that was at the beginning of the Campbell strike and boycott in 1978. According to Cuevas, it was then when he realized that "we farm workers could stand up for our own rights. . . . I felt like a new person in a new world, every day stronger and stronger with more hope, dreaming of the day we'd win."[4] As Christian Paiz notes, with regard to Coachella Valley's rank-and-file United Farm Worker members, for precarious farmworkers from different walks of life, participating in strikes and other labor actions was a gamble. For early members like Cuevas, Lucy Duran, and Sara Rios, these were indeed uncertain circumstances.[5] Like the hundreds of farmworkers in Blissfield, Michigan, who organized and secured improved pay for the 1935 harvest, the Latinxs who abandoned exploitative conditions and traveled to Detroit to bring their complaints to Father Clement Kern, the Mexican *braceros* and the Puerto Rican Farm Labor Program participants who contributed to the migrant public sphere, or the Mexican American teenagers who learned music in the fields and practiced in their garage after settling out of the harvest route, FLOC members aspired to improve their circumstances.

Latinx Encounters: How Mexicans, Mexican Americans, and Puerto Ricans Made the Modern Midwest has sought to demonstrate how three groups of Latinxs forged national and transnational networks throughout the Midwest. These were networks of migration, protest, letter writing, music, and labor organizing. Set between the end of World War I and the region's farmworker justice movement of the 1980s, this book has shown how Latinx migrants and agricultural workers shaped the labor regimes, culture, and politics of the twentieth-century US Midwest. Ultimately, *Latinx Encounters* has tried to answer one question: How did agricultural workers in the Midwest redefine migrant power, justice, and rights throughout the twentieth century? Mexican, Mexican American, and Puerto Rican migrants coveted more autonomy in their lives and a more just future for themselves and other farmworkers. This pursuit of migrant justice tells a larger story about the twentieth-century history of guestworker programs, transnational politics, popular culture, and labor organizing.

There remains much to be written about the histories of migrant farmworkers in the United States, the history of the Latinx Midwest, and, as this book has argued, their intersections. At the heart of *Latinx Encounters* are the US-Mexico Bracero Program, the interstate migration of Mexican Americans, and Puerto Rico's Farm Labor Program. Not all of the chapters here have been able to focus on all three groups of Latinxs at the same time. Depending on the time period and the topical focus of a given chapter, it has at times been necessary to privilege the experiences of one group of migrant workers—Mexicans, Mexican Americans, or Puerto Ricans—over another. That was never to suggest that the other groups were no longer present or were inconsequential to that story, but rather it was a choice made for clarity in the content, arguments, and narratives. For example, while "Migrant Rights, Migrant Justice" emphasized FLOC's predominantly Mexican American base, there were figures like Ray Santiago whose path through the organization were left out. Santiago, FLOC's secretaray-treasurer, was a Nuyorican (Puerto Rican from New York). In April 1978, the Puerto Rican organizer, working alongside Mexican Americans, traveled to Indiana University, Bloomington, for a talk by Leonel Castillo, the first Mexican American to head the Immigration and Naturalization Service. There, Santiago questioned Castillo about President Jimmy Carter's immigration agenda and its punitive impact on undocumented workers. Stories like this are indelibly part of this history, even if they are not present here.[6] This is all to underscore that I hope any shortcomings of this book will be generative areas of future inquiry.

While *Latinx Encounters* finishes on a relatively triumphal note in the late 1980s and early 1990s, the pursuit of farmworker justice in the Midwest and beyond remains. The COVID-19 public health crisis was a unique moment when politicians, pundits, and the public in the United States grappled with and reevaluated the meaning of "essential worker." Then, as in other moments throughout twentieth- and twenty-first-century US history, migrant agricultural workers were called upon and marshaled because of their indispensability to the US economy. For all the economic and occupational transformations that have occurred in the United States over the past century, at least one thing remains clear: that migrant workers have been an enduring fixture who have sustained the country's agricultural and food supply chains. On April 22, 2020, when President Donald J. Trump issued his "Proclamation Suspending Entry of Immigrants Who Present Risk to the US Labor Market During the Economic Recovery Following the COVID-19

Outbreak," notably exempt from this executive order were H-2A visa workers. In fact, restrictions on the program were actually reduced, with the Department of Homeland Security stating, "The Department is removing certain limitations on agricultural employers and workers in order to provide agricultural employers with an orderly and timely flow of legal foreign workers, thereby protecting the integrity of the nation's food supply chain and decreasing possible reliance on unauthorized aliens, while encouraging agricultural employer's use of the H-2A program, which protects the rights of US and foreign workers."[7] In one way or another, for an entire century, the federal government, growers, and consumers have deemed Latinx migrant agricultural workers to be "essential" to the economy.

In "Thoughts on the Farm Worker Struggle," Greg Akili lauded the indispensability of migrant farmworkers. Despite their contributions, Akili also criticized Americans for treating them as invisible subjects. Akili asks, "Why? Is it because they are brown, or speak another language or work too close to the land? Where are the rights of the farm worker? What do the farm workers think, want, and feel?"[8] To that end, *Latinx Encounters* has attempted to show the ways that Mexican, Mexican American, and Puerto Rican migrant farmworkers in the Midwest have fought to ensure that they are respected, protected, represented, and understood. Latinx farmworkers in the Midwest advanced migrant and labor justice at large. Even in the face of scarce federal labor protections for agricultural workers, farmworkers very well may be the ones to revitalize the American labor movement, despite being sidelined from it for so long. Their efforts enrich our understanding of the twentieth-century Midwest and illustrate Latinx history's importance for grappling with the past and present of the United States.

Notes

Abbreviations

AHSRE	Archivo Histórico de la Secretaría de Relaciones Exteriores
CKP	Clement Kern Papers
FLOCR	Farm Labor Organizing Committee Records
JSP	Julian Samora Papers
KBP	Ken Barger Papers
LLILAS	Teresa Lozano Long Institute of Latin American Studies
UTA	University of Texas at Austin
WPRL	Walter P. Reuther Library
WSU	Wayne State University

Introduction

1. Dave Marsh, "Looney Toons," *CREEM*, May 1971.

2. "Bob Anderson Rockets to Stardom," *Detroit Free Press*, July 7, 1973. Also see "Seger Comes Stormin' Home Tonight," *Detroit Free Press*, August 28, 1986.

3. See Habell-Pallán, *Loca Motion*, 151; and, Scott Mervis, "Monkees and Mysterians Part of WQED Oldies Spectacular," *Tribune Business News*, May 20, 2010. These are just two references, one scholarly and one journalistic, of the term "punk rock" originating from Marsh's "Looney Toons" article.

4. Marsh, "Looney Toons."

5. "? (Question Mark) & the Mysterians," *Billboard*, https://www.billboard.com/artist/question-mark-the-mysterians/chart-history/hsi/#, accessed February 19, 2020.

6. A note on terminology is needed here. As will likely be clear from the title, as well as the content in this book, I will intentionally be using the term "Latinx" throughout. In this book, I use the term "Latinx" to describe the diverse group of people from various Latin American and Caribbean origins that have migrated, worked, and settled in the United States. Previously, this community has been described in several other ways: Hispanic, Latino/a, and Latin@. Latinx, as well as Latine, are gender neutral terms. I acknowledge that Latinx and Latine are the most recent iterations of these umbrella terms and will likely be followed by other versions in the future. The term Latinx is not embraced by all, but it is useful as a gender-neutral umbrella term. I also use it for brevity, as to reduce the verbosity of constantly saying "Latino/a," "Latino/Latina," or "Mexican, Mexican American, and Puerto Rican." While it may seem ahistorical to use a contemporary term to describe people of previous generations who never used this phrase to identify themselves, as often as possible I will use individuals' nationality or ethnicity. In terms of other terminology, when using the

term "Mexican," I am referring to Mexican nationals. When using the term "*Tejano*," which is a mixture between "*Mexicano*" and "Texan," I am referring to Mexican Americans from Texas. Tejanos were often referred to as Texas-Mexicans and various other iterations. Tejanos/Mexican Americans possess US citizenship. I use "ethnic Mexicans" when referring to Mexicans and Mexican Americans. For people of Puerto Rican descent, I use "Puerto Ricans." Finally, I will be using the term "migrants" and "migration" to describe the movements of Mexicans, Mexican Americans, and Puerto Ricans. As Mexican Americans and Puerto Ricans are US citizens, the terms "immigrants" or "immigration" would not be applicable.

7. Marlon Bishop, "? & The Mysterians: The Migrant Kids Who Inspired Punk Rock," *Latino USA* (podcast), October 13, 2017; also see Alina Simone, "Here's How '96 Tears' Became a Michigan City's Official Rock Anthem," *Public Radio International*, September 26, 2014, https://www.pri.org/stories/2014-09-26/heres-how-96-tears-became-michigan-citys-official-rock-anthem; also see https://michiganrockandrolllegends.com/hall-of-fame/artists/289-question-mark-and-the-mysterians?highlight=WyJtYXJrIiwibWFya2VkIiwibWFya2VoIiwibWFya2VoaW5nIiwibWFya2VocyIsIm1hcmtpbmciLCJtYXJrcyIsIm1hcmsncyIsIm1hcmtvIiwibWFya2VodHMiXQ==, accessed December 3, 2017.

8. Valdés, *Al Norte Agricultural Workers*, 9; Mapes, *Sweet Tyranny*, 122; and Vargas, *Proletarians of the North*, 20–21.

9. Rodriguez, *Tejano Diaspora*, 2.

10. Lori Flores provides an estimate of 73,000 Mexican men and Mireya Loza uses an estimate of 80,000 workers. Loza also emphasizes that if the women and children who participated in this program, but often went uncounted, were included, the number would be significantly higher. Flores, *Grounds for Dreaming*, 42; Loza, "'Let Them Bring Their Families,'" 310.

11. Loza, "'Let Them Bring Their Families,'" 322–23.

12. "Border Opened to Farm Use of Mexican Labor: Help Sought for War Food Program," *Chicago Daily Tribune*, August 7, 1942.

13. Flores, *Grounds for Dreaming*, 42; Loza, *Defiant Braceros*, 2; Rosas, *Abrazando el Espíritu*, 1; Fernández, *Brown in the Windy City*, 30–33; Cohen, *Braceros*, 1–2.

14. Hahamovitch, *No Man's Land*, 5; Bracero History Archive, https://braceroarchive.org/about.

15. Fernández, *Brown in the Windy City*, 25. Also, see Weber, *From South Texas to the Nation*, 216. Weber similarly shows that there was an increase in migration out of Texas during World War II as many Mexican Americans left the state for employment in Northern wartime industries and the fields of the Midwest.

16. Fernández-Jones, *Making the MexiRican City*, 8.

17. Meléndez, *Sponsored Migration*, 36; Fernández, *Brown in the Windy City*, 24; García-Colón, *Colonial Migrants at the Heart of Empire*, 32–33; Suárez Findlay, *We Are Left without a Father Here*, 8; Thomas, *Puerto Rican Citizen*, 6.

18. Pérez, *The Near Northwest Side Story*, 44; Fernández, *Brown in the Windy City*, 24; Fernández-Jones, *Making the MexiRican City*, 24; and Meléndez, *Sponsored Migration*, 64.

19. Meléndez, *Sponsored Migration*, 52.

20. Lourdes Dick, "US Tax Imperialism in Puerto Rico," 61–62.

21. Office of the Executive Secretary, "Act No. 89," *Administrative Bulletin No. 1077*, April 12, 1948.

22. Office of the Executive Secretary, "Act No. 89," *Administrative Bulletin No. 1077*; "Act No. 417," May 14, 1947; García-Colón, *Colonial Migrants at the Heart of Empire*, 62.

23. This was prior to the institution becoming Michigan State University.

24. A. B. Love and H. P. Gaston, "Michigan Emergency Farm Labor, 1943–1947," *Michigan State College Extension Bulletin* 288, December 1947, 5.

25. Love and Gaston, "Michigan Emergency Farm Labor, 1943–1947," 5.

26. The Governor's Study Commission on Migratory Labor, "Migrants in Michigan: A Handbook on Migratory, Seasonal, Agricultural Workers in Michigan," September 1954, 6.

27. Commission on Migratory Labor, "Migrants in Michigan," 9.

28. Commission on Migratory Labor, "Migrants in Michigan," 10.

29. Texas-Michigan Public Health Service Migrant Project, "Third Interim Report: Michigan Phase," 1, Bancroft Library, National Council of Agricultural Life and Labor, Carton 15, Folder 26.

30. Legislative Service Bureau, "A Report on Migrant Labor in Michigan," September 1965, 2.

31. Michigan Civil Rights Commission (MCRC), "Report and Recommendations on the Status of Migratory Farm Labor in Michigan," 1968, 2, Centro Archives, Records of the Office of the Government of Puerto Rico in the United States, Farm Labor Program (FLP), Box 2486, Folder 15.

32. Love and Gaston, "Michigan Emergency Farm Labor, 1943–1947," 28–29.

33. Martínez-Matsuda, *Migrant Citizenship*, 6.

34. There is an extensive list of literature that either focuses directly or indirectly on the United Farm Workers, as well as their leading figures: César Chávez and Dolores Huerta. Some of these works include: Flores, *Grounds for Dreaming*; Flores, *Awaiting their Feast*; Paiz, *Strikers of Coachella*; Garcia, *From the Jaws of Victory*; Pitti, *The Devil in Silicon Valley*; Pawel, *The Union of Their Dreams*; Ganz, *Why David Sometimes Wins*; and Bardacke, *Trampling Out the Vintage*. This list is not exhaustive, but does capture the extent to which the UFW and its leadership have been the subject of study.

35. State of Michigan Legislative Council, "Minimum Wage Law of 1964," Act 154 of 1964, www.legislature.mi.gov, accessed December 12, 2024.

36. MCRC, "Report and Recommendations on the Status of Migratory Farm Labor in Michigan," 1968, 2.

37. Padilla, *Latino Ethnic Consciousness*; Fernández, *Brown in the Windy City*; Fernández-Jones, *Making the MexiRican City*; and González, *Strangers No Longer* are some of the notable works.

38. Francisco Espinosa Q. and Uvaldo García R. to Marcelino Mendoza, Box 1, Folder 1, Clement Kern Papers (CKP), Archives of Labor and Urban Affairs, Walter P. Reuther Library (WPRL).

39. González, *Strangers No Longer*, 22.

40. Fernández, *Brown in the Windy City*; Fernández-Jones, *Making the MexiRican City*; González, *Strangers No Longer*. According to the US Census, in 2020, there were 35.9

million Mexicans and 5.6 million Puerto Ricans living in the United States. The next largest group was Salvadorans with 2.3 million residents. US Census Bureau, "Growing in Numbers," September 13, 2024, https://www.census.gov/library/visualizations/2024/comm/growing-in-numbers.html. The Pew Research Center's data for 2021 has the numbers for Mexicans and Puerto Ricans at 37.2 million and 5.8 million, respectively. Mohamad Moslimani, Mark Hugo Lopez, and Luis Noe-Bustamante, "11 Facts about Hispanic Origin Groups in the US," Pew Research Center, August 16, 2023, https://www.pewresearch.org/short-reads/2023/08/16/11-facts-about-hispanic-origin-groups-in-the-us/.

41. Amezcua, *Making Mexican Chicago*, 4.

42. Monographs on the Latinx Midwest include: Padilla, *Latino Ethnic Consciousness*; Valdés, *Al Norte*; Valdés, *Barrios Norteños*; Vargas, *Proletarians of the North*; Pérez, *The Near Northwest Side Story*; Arredondo, *Mexican Chicago*; Gordillo, *Mexican Women and the Other Side of Immigration*; Rodriguez, *Tejano Diaspora*; Rúa, *A Grounded Identidad*; Fernández, *Brown in the Windy City*; Innis-Jiménez, *Steel Barrio*; Suárez Findlay, *We Are Left Without A Father Here*; Vega, *Latino Heartland*; Delgadillo, *Latina Lives in Milwaukee*; Flores, *The Mexican Revolution in Chicago*; Kanter, *Chicago Católico*; Amezcua, *Making Mexican Chicago*; Velázquez, *Puerto Rican Chicago*; Fernández-Jones, *Making the MexiRican City*; González, *Strangers No Longer*; Olmstead, *Making Michigan Home*; and, Staudenmaier, *White, Black, Brown*. In-progress books by Emiliano Aguilar, Carolina Ortega, and Nico Soto promise to make important contributions to the field.

43. "Fly from Puerto Rico: Airlift Providing Michigan with Sugar Beet Work Crews," *Battle Creek Inquirer*, June 18, 1950.

44. Márquez, *Making the Latino South*, 5.

Chapter One

1. "*Aviso Importante a los Trabajadores del Betabel*," *La Prensa*, April 1, 1947, 2.

2. Useful studies for understanding the intersections of ethnic Mexican labor contractors, Texas's Emigrant Agent Act, and contestations over mobility include: Weber, *From South Texas to the Nation*, 58–101; Salinas, *Managed Migrations*, 114–37; Montejano, *Anglos and Mexicans in the Making of Texas*, 197–217; McWilliams, *Ill Fares the Land*, 3–12, 257–81; Taylor, "Mexican Labor in the United States," 293–464; and Taylor, *An American-Mexican Frontier*. For more on the early twentieth-century circuits of ethnic Mexican farmworkers in Michigan, see Valdés, *Al Norte*, VII–88; Vargas, *Proletarians of the North*, 1–34; and Mapes, *Sweet Tyranny*, 122–65. Useful for understanding the circulation of labor and politics between Texas and the Midwest will be Rodriguez, *Tejano Diaspora*.

3. Hahamovitch, *The Fruits of Their Labor*, 51.

4. Just one example of this is the case of Julio de la Peña. Although he was responsible for transporting migrant farmworkers from Texas to Findlay, Ohio, he was employed by the Great Lakes Sugar Company, which had refineries in both Michigan and Ohio. In addition to the money that de la Peña made for the interstate transportation of workers during the 1940 harvest season, he also earned $431 for hauling sugar beets to the refineries and a salary of $90 per month for his services as a "translator" during

the season (around seven months). See US Congress, House, Select Committee Investigating National Defense Migration, National Defense Migration, Part 19: 7810–12; and Valdés, *Al Norte*, 75.

5. For just a few examples of braceros that worked for Mexican American crew leaders, see Violeta Domínguez, "Rodolfo Cruz Figueroa," in Bracero History Archive, Item #134, http://braceroarchive.org/items/show/134 (accessed June 23, 2021); Jackie Martínez, "Lorenzo González," in Bracero History Archive, Item #379, http://braceroarchive.org/items/show/379 (accessed June 23, 2021); Laureano Martinez, "Lorenzo Maynes Castillo," in Bracero History Archive, Item #70, http://braceroarchive.org/items/show/70 (accessed June 23, 2021); and for examples of bracero fieldworkers that became crew leaders, see Steve Velásquez, "José Hernández Romero," in Bracero History Archive, Item #157, http://braceroarchive.org/items/show/157 (accessed June 23, 2021); Myrna Parra-Mantilla, "Eduardo De Santiago," in Bracero History Archive, Item #45, http://braceroarchive.org/items/show/45 (accessed June 27, 2021); and Chew, Selfa, "Jesús Martínez," in Bracero History Archive, Item #231, http://braceroarchive.org/items/show/231 (accessed June 27, 2021).

6. The Farm Labor Program will be discussed extensively in the following chapter.

7. Vargas, *Proletarians of the North*, 3–34. Also see Valdés, *Al Norte*, 4–29.

8. Valdés, *Al Norte*, 74.

9. Valdés, *Al Norte*, 74. Valdés describes a handful of interest groups (liberal politicians, women's groups, religious groups, journalists, and labor unions) that were concerned with a range of issues (labor and living conditions, migrant health, children's education, etc.) related to the agricultural migrants entering the Midwest. For Valdés's full description of the "migrant problem," refer to 73–87.

10. Hahamovitch, *The Fruits of Their Labor*, 9–53; Peck, *Reinventing Free Labor*; and Peck, "Reinventing Free Labor," 848–71. For more on *padrones*, also refer to Higbie, *Indispensable Outcasts*, 53–55, 108. For different examples of non-*padrón* intermediaries, see Ngai, "'A Slight Knowledge of the Barbarian Language,'" 5–32; and Barrett, *Work and Community in the Jungle*, 27–28.

11. Hahamovitch, *The Fruits of Their Labor*, 41–42; Peck, *Reinventing Free Labor*, 228.

12. Peck, *Reinventing Free Labor*, 195.

13. For just a few specific examples of contract jumping, see: Rosas, *Abrazando el Espíritu*, 86; and Valdés, *Al Norte*, 102. Although braceros abandoning their contracts was a relatively common occurrence, it was not a decision that was made lightly. Doing so revoked their status to legally work and reside in the United States. For more on abandoning bracero contracts and the resulting shift in legal status, see Ngai, *Impossible Subjects*, 146–47; and Flores, *Grounds for Dreaming*, 90–91.

14. Flores, *Grounds for Dreaming*, 6.

15. Select works on panethnic identity include Padilla, *Latino Ethnic Consciousness*; De Genova and Ramos-Zayas, *Latino Crossings*; Fernández, *Brown in the Windy City*; and Fernández, "Becoming Latino."

16. Weber, *From South Texas to the Nation*, 50.

17. Valdés, *Al Norte*, 9; Mapes, *Sweet Tyranny*, 122; Vargas, *Proletarians of the North*, 20–21.

18. Valdés, "*Betabeleros*," 551–52.

19. Mapes, *Sweet Tyranny*, 144. Also see Valdés, *Al Norte*, 11; Vargas, *Proletarians of the North*, 29.

20. Ngai, *Impossible Subjects*, 21–55. For more on these debates and how they relate to sugar beet and agricultural labor in Michigan, see Mapes, *Sweet Tyranny*, 143–45. It is also important to note that just because there were no numerical restrictions placed on immigrants from Mexico, this did not mean that Mexicans were unaffected by this legislation. Mae Ngai, Adam Goodman, and John Weber point out that after July 1, 1924, the legislation mandated the deportation of anyone who entered the United States without an inspection or who overstayed a visa, regardless of how long the person may have been a resident of the United States. Furthermore, Congress decided to establish the Border Patrol that same year. Collectively, the 1924 Immigration Act deeply impacted processes of Mexican immigration and contributed to the creation of the category of "illegal aliens." See Ngai, *Impossible Subjects*, 50–58; Goodman, *The Deportation Machine*, 39; and Weber, *From South Texas to the Nation*, 109.

21. Paul S. Taylor highlights how Michigan's sugar companies were reportedly in need of 6,000 ethnic Mexican workers from Texas. See, Taylor, "Mexican Labor in the United States," 141; Valdés, *Al Norte*, 10–11.

22. Balderrama and Rodríguez, *Decade of Betrayal*, 1.

23. Balderrama and Rodríguez, *Decade of Betrayal*, 150–51. Although it is difficult to determine the official number of repatriates during this period, Balderrama and Rodríguez present one million repatriates as the "conservative middle ground."

24. This hope was due largely to programs such as the Works Progress Administration, the Civilian Conservation Corps, and the Farm Security Administration, as well as the possible protections offered by the 1934 Jones-Costigan Act and the Sugar Beet Act of 1937. See Mapes, *Sweet Tyranny*, 216. For more on the Farm Security Administration and ethnic Mexicans, see Martínez-Matsuda, "For Labor and Democracy."

25. Valdés, *Al Norte*, 38–48.

26. For a study examining the tenuous relationship between organized labor, specifically the AFL and eventually the AFL-CIO (American Federation of Labor-Congress of Industrial Organizations), and farmworkers, see Hazelton, *Labor's Outcasts*.

27. United State Department of Labor, "Labor Unionism in American Agriculture," Bulletin No. 836 (United States Government Printing Office, 1945), 383; Mapes, *Sweet Tyranny*, 229–30; Valdés, *Al Norte*, 42.

28. Mapes, *Sweet Tyranny*, 231; Valdés, *Al Norte*, 45.

29. Mapes, *Sweet Tyranny*, 229–31.

30. Select Committee to Investigate the Interstate Migration of Destitute Citizens, Part 3, US House of Representatives (United States Government Printing Office, 1941), 1272.

31. Valdés, *Al Norte*, 45–46.

32. For select works that examine the Bracero Program, see Loza, *Defiant Braceros*; Cohen, *Braceros*; Flores, *Grounds for Dreaming*; Calavita, *Inside the State*; Mitchell, *They Saved the Crops*; Rosas, *Abrazando el Espíritu*; and Weise, *Corazón de Dixie*, among other works.

33. Weber, *From South Texas to the Nation*, 200–206.

34. Weber, *From South Texas to the Nation*, 216.

35. "Frank Cortez: 'Guadalupana,'" *La Prensa,* November 15, 1934, 6; "Frank Cortez," *La Prensa,* June 6, 1940, 5.

36. McWilliams, *Ill Fares the Land,* 260. With this spectacular account deriving from McWilliams's interview with Cortez, there is a chance that Cortez may have embellished some of the details. Yet, most of the information about the number of workers recruited, transportation conditions, medical examinations, and Cortez's compensation are verifiable in one way or another through articles in *La Prensa* or the findings of congressional hearings. As Cortez was a well-known labor contractor, more can be found on him in: Weber, *From South Texas to the Nation,* 59–61; and Valdés, *Al Norte,* 54.

37. Select Committee to Investigate the Interstate Migration of Destitute Citizens, Part 3, 1272–86.

38. Select Committee to Investigate the Interstate Migration of Destitute Citizens, Part 3, 1272–86.

39. Select Committee to Investigate the Interstate Migration of Destitute Citizens, Part 5, 1870.

40. McWilliams, *Ill Fares the Land,* 261–62; Select Committee to Investigate the Interstate Migration of Destitute Citizens, Part 5, 1858–59. Also see Weber, *From South Texas to the Nation,* 59. For more on Latinxs, race, and public health, see Molina, *Fit to be Citizens?*; and Mckiernan-González, *Fevered Measures*.

41. Truman Commission on Migratory Labor, Saginaw, Michigan, Proceedings for September 11, 1950, Statement of Max Henderson, 185, Harry S. Truman Presidential Library.

42. Truman Commission on Migratory Labor, Saginaw, Michigan, Proceedings for September 11, 1950, Statement of Max Henderson, 187–88, Harry S. Truman Presidential Library. Also see Bob Pearson, "Crew Leader Is Dictator In State Cherry Orchards," *Detroit Free Press,* July 23, 1962, 3.

43. For example, if the blocking, thinning, and hoeing of sugar beets is finished by mid-to-late June, workers are not needed again until September to finish the harvesting. Thus, from the end of June until early September, migrant workers are recontracted to work on cucumber, cherry, or agricultural farms. Truman Commission on Migratory Labor, Saginaw, Michigan, Proceedings for September 11, 1950, Statement of Max Henderson, 188, Harry S. Truman Presidential Library.

44. Truman Commission on Migratory Labor, Saginaw, Michigan, Proceedings for September 12, 1950, Statement of Felipe Gonzalez, 483, Harry S. Truman Presidential Library.

45. Summer 1948 Questionnaire on Migratory Labor, National Council of Agricultural Life and Labor, Collection, Carton 1, Folder 34, Bancroft Library, University of California, Berkeley.

46. Summer 1948 Questionnaire on Migratory Labor.

47. "William Lieserson," *Pittsburgh Press,* February 20, 1957, 12.

48. Truman Commission on Migratory Labor, Saginaw, Michigan, Proceedings for September 11, 1950, Statement of Max Henderson, 186–87, Harry S. Truman Presidential Library.

49. Hearings Before the Select Committee Investigating National Defense Migration, Detroit Hearings, September 23–25, 1941, Part 19 (US Government Printing

Office, 1941), 7778, 7944; "Agents Work Valley Area Report Says," *Valley Morning Star*, April 23, 1942, 8; "Law Denies Rail Unit's Job Control," *Brownsville Herald*, May 2, 1942, 6; "Recruiting of Employed Labor Banned," *The Monitor*, April 25, 1943, 2; "Valley Workers Being Recruited," *Brownsville Herald*, April 20, 1944, 7.

50. Summer 1948 Questionnaire on Migratory Labor.

51. Truman Commission on Migratory Labor, Saginaw, Michigan, Proceedings for September 11, 1950, Statement of Harry Markle, 28, Harry S. Truman Presidential Library.

52. "Views Vary on Work on Michigan Farms: Numerous Assessments Irk Mexicans," *Detroit Free Press*, May 31, 1948, 3.

53. "Views Vary on Work on Michigan Farms," *Detroit Free Press*, May 31, 1948, 3.

54. Some examples of what crew leaders might be referred to are: "the captain," "dictator," "tribal chief," and the "judge and jury."

55. "Views Vary on Work on Michigan Farms," *Detroit Free Press*, May 31, 1948, 3.

56. Hearings Before the Select Committee to Investigate the Interstate Migration of Destitute Citizens, Oklahoma City Hearings, September 19–20, 1940, Part 5 (US Government Printing Office, 1941), 1843.

57. Montejano, *Anglos and Mexicans in the Making of Texas, 1836–1986*, 197.

58. Senate Bill No. 127, Sess. Of 1929 (Tex. 1929), https://lrl.texas.gov/scanned/sessionLaws/41-2/SB_127_CH_96.pdf; "Emigrant Agent Tax Bill Passed by the Senate Last Night," *Brownsville Herald*, May 16, 1929, 1; "Injunction Being Sought on Tax of Labor Agents," *Corsicana Daily Sun*, May 24, 1929, 11.

59. "State Labor Law Operation Halted by Temporary Writ," *El Paso Times*, June 2, 1929, 31; "Sugar Company Given Injunction in Labor Case," *Austin American*, June 2, 1929, 2; "Amendment Passed for Emigrant Tax Bill," *Fort Worth Star-Telegram*, June 11, 1929, 4.

60. Senate Bill No. 127; US House of Representatives, Select Committee to Investigate the Interstate Migration of Destitute Citizens, 1300–1301; Montejano, *Anglos and Mexicans in the Making of Texas, 1836–1986*, 211.

61. US Department of Labor, Bureau of Labor Statistics, Laws Relating to Employment Agencies in the United States as of July 1, 1937, Bulletin No. 630 (US Government Printing Office, 1937), 11.

62. The Farm Placement Service operated under the Texas State Employment Service.

63. Hearings Before the Select Committee to Investigate the Interstate Migration of Destitute Citizens, Oklahoma City Hearings, 1843.

64. Hearings Before the Select Committee to Investigate the Interstate Migration of Destitute Citizens, Chicago Hearings, August 19–21, 1940, Part 3 (US Government Printing Office, 1940), 1311–12.

65. Hearings Before the Select Committee to Investigate the Interstate Migration of Destitute Citizens, Chicago Hearings, 1315–16.

66. Migratory labor constantly required Latinxs to travel across national, state, and local lines. Not only were they traveling from their places of permanent residence to Michigan, but, often, migrant farmworkers also had to travel from their living camps to the fields that could be dozens of miles away. While generally understood that agricultural labor was a particularly grueling occupation, we have yet to fully comprehend

the variety of ways in which migrants who were in between locations had to risk their bodies—one of which was through their traveling and transportation. Regardless of the distance that migrants had to travel, there was significant risk involved. Once migrants arrived at their living grounds, there was still typically more travel involved in getting to the fields for work. In a written statement left in the possession of Father Kern, Tomas Ledesma, a Mexican bracero contracted to work the beet fields, described the various distances that workers would have to travel from the living quarters to the fields. See 1948 Affidavit of Tomas Ledesma, WPRL, CKP, Box 1, Folder 2.

67. Statement by Gerardo Hernandez Pau, 1948, Reuther Library, Clement Kern Collection, Box 1, Folder 2.

68. Truman Commission on Migratory Labor, Saginaw, Michigan, Proceedings for September 12, 1950, Statement of Monsignor Harold Boulton, 544, Harry S. Truman Presidential Library.

69. See September 12, 1953 from Consul Josefe to the Mexican Consul in El Paso, Texas, Folder 1451/2, *Archivo Histórico de la Secretaría de Relaciones Exteriores (AHSRE)*. During this 1953 harvest season, a bracero by the name of Abelino Acosta Peinado was contracted by Lang & Sons, Inc. of Fremont, Michigan, and was recontracted to Trailback Plantation. The vehicle that was transporting Peinado and six other braceros from Michigan to Missouri flipped along the way and Peinado died from the accident.

70. Statement by Unnamed Bracero, 1948, MCKC, Box 1, Folder 2, WPRL, WSU.

71. Salinas, *Managed Migrations*, 116–17.

72. Because workers were paid by the weight of the crops they picked, as well as the quality or "class" of those crops, consistently altering the weight of the picked crops could result in a large amount of lost earnings over the course of a season. Salinas, *Managed Migrations*, 114–37.

73. A third option would be that this bracero had worked in Michigan and therefore may have been familiar with Kern, but the bracero's statement, which is a narrative of their entire migrant journey this harvest season, vividly describes hearing on the radio and in newspapers that bracero contracts would be available in Monterrey. It leads me to infer that this was their first time seeking a bracero contract.

74. 1948 Telegram from Mexican Consul of St. Louis to Trailback Plantation, Folder 1454/1, *AHSRE*.

75. Castillo and Salinas went to the consulate in McAllen, Texas, who then informed the consul in St. Louis, Missouri.

76. 1948 Telegram from Mexican Consul of St. Louis to Trailback Plantation, Folder 1454-1, *AHSRE*. Also see Statement by Unnamed Bracero, 1948, MCKC, Box 1, Folder 2, WRL, Wayne State University.

77. For more on the intersections of the Bracero Program and Operation Bootstrap (the Farm Labor Program was one component of Operation Bootstrap), see Fernández, "Of Immigrants and Migrants."

Chapter Two

1. "37 of 65 on Plane Saved in Atlantic: Bodies of 8 Found—Little Hope for Remaining Migrant Workers on Transport," *New York Times*, June 7, 1950, 1; "Sharks Filled Sea!

Rescue of 37 Described," *Chicago Daily Tribune*, June 7, 1950, 1; and "Destroyer Rescues in Plane Sea Tragedy," *Los Angeles Times*, June 7, 1950, 1.

2. "37 on Crashed Plane Rescued from Atlantic," *Detroit Free Press*, June 7, 1950, 1, 15. It should also be noted that this was the fifth plane crash involving Puerto Ricans since 1947, with a probable death toll of 151.

3. Walter W. Ruch, "Air Lift of Puerto Ricans Averts Wide Beet Crop Loss in Michigan," *New York Times*, June 18, 1950, 1, 55.

4. Molina, Martinez HoSang, and Gutiérrez, *Relational Formations of Race*, 2. Through this relational approach, scholars can examine the broad implications of racial formation, citizenship, and Latinx identity. Not only does this approach make visible the conflicts and collaborations that occur among marginalized groups, but it can also connect seemingly disparate historical processes to unveil how race, power, and inclusion/exclusion function. Also see Molina, *How Race is Made in America*; and Carpio, *Collisions at the Crossroads*.

5. Guerrero, *Nuevo South*, 16.

6. McDonald, "A Fair Deal for Immigrants?," 206–8.

7. Truman Commission on Migratory Labor, Saginaw, Michigan, Proceedings for September 11, 1950, 2, Harry S. Truman Presidential Library.

8. Robinson, "Taking the Fair Deal to the Fields," 383–84; US Department of Agriculture, "Termination of the Bracero Program: Some Effects on Farm Labor and Migrant Housing Needs," Agricultural Economic Report No. 77, 4–6.

9. The President's Commission on Migratory Labor, "Migratory Labor in American Agriculture: Report of the President's Commission on Migratory Labor," March 26, 1951, VII; "Migrant Hearings Widen," *New York Times*, August 20, 1950, 47; Robinson, "Taking the Fair Deal to the Fields," 385.

10. The President's Commission on Migratory Labor, "Migratory Labor in American Agriculture, 69; Robinson, "Taking the Fair Deal to the Fields," 388.

11. United States Department of Agriculture, "Termination of the Bracero Program: Some Effects on Farm Labor and Migrant Housing Needs," Agricultural Economic Report No. 77 (1965), 5.

12. United States Department of Agriculture, "Termination of the Bracero Program," 5.

13. The President's Commission on Migratory Labor, "Migratory Labor in American Agriculture," III.

14. The President's Commission on Migratory Labor, "Migratory Labor in American Agriculture," X.

15. Robinson, "Taking the Fair Deal to the Fields," 394.

16. Robinson, "Taking the Fair Deal to the Fields," 393; Creagan, "Public Law 78," 542–43.

17. *An Act To Amend the Agricultural Act of 1949*, Public Law 78, *US Statutes at Large* 65 (1951): 119–21; Robinson, "Taking the Fair Deal to the Fields," 394.

18. For context, "Migratory Labor in American Agriculture," the official report of the Truman Commission on migratory labor, contains over 170 "wetback" references. This includes an entire chapter of the report, "The Wetback Invasion—Illegal Alien Labor in American Agriculture." Perhaps the landmark document relating to the

"wetback crisis" is "What Price Wetbacks?," a 1953 report by the American G. I. Forum of Texas and the Texas State Federation of Labor (AFL). Operation Wetback was the Immigration and Naturalization Service's 1954 militarized deportation campaign. For more on this, see Amezcua, *Making Mexican Chicago*, 19–60; Mitchell, *They Saved the Crops*, 233–56; Kang, *The INS on the Line*, 139–67; Hernández, *Migra!*, 171–95; Hernández, "The Crimes and Consequences of Illegal Immigration," 421–44; Molina, *How Race is Made in America*, 112–38; Weber, *From South Texas to the Nation*, 210–17; Goodman, *The Deportation Machine*, 37–72; Flores, *Grounds for Dreaming*, 75–107; Goodman, "Bananas North, Deportees South," 949–74; and Patiño, *Raza Sí, Migra No*, 38–41, among other works.

19. This bill amended section 8 of the Immigration Act of 1917, which the Supreme Court had rejected in 1948 for its vagueness. See Kang, *The INS on the Line*, 143.

20. Kang, *The INS on the Line*, 143.

21. *An Act To Assist in Preventing Aliens from Entering or Remaining in the United States Illegally*, Public Law 283, *US Statutes at Large* 66 (1952): 26; Robinson, "Taking the Fair Deal to the Fields," 396.

22. US Department of Agriculture, "Termination of the Bracero Program," 5; Creagan, "Public Law 78," 544–45.

23. Duany, "A Transnational Colonial Migration," 227–78.

24. Duany, "A Transnational Colonial Migration," 227–78.

25. Glazer and Moynihan, *Beyond the Melting Pot*, 95.

26. Glazer and Moynihan, *Beyond the Melting Pot*, 95–96; Ayala and Bernabe, *Puerto Rico in the American Century*, 179; Duany, "A Transnational Colonial Migration," 232–33.

27. Glazer and Moynihan, *Beyond the Melting Pot*, 93; Ayala and Bernabe, *Puerto Rico in the American Century*, 179.

28. Truman Commission on Migratory Labor, Saginaw, Michigan, Proceedings for September 11, 1950, Statement of Fred L. Crawford, 9–10, Harry S. Truman Presidential Library.

29. García-Colón, *Colonial Migrants at the Heart of Empire*, 5.

30. Duany, "A Transnational Colonial Migration," 231–36.

31. Truman Commission on Migratory Labor, Saginaw, Michigan, Proceedings for September 11, 1950, Statement of Fred L. Crawford, 10, Harry S. Truman Presidential Library.

32. "Stoop" labor refers to the stooped position needed for picking some of the crops.

33. Scott, *Degrees of Freedom*; Merleaux, *Sugar and Civilization*; Ayala, *American Sugar Kingdom*; and Mapes, *Sweet Tyranny*.

34. Truman Commission on Migratory Labor, Saginaw, Michigan, Proceedings for September 11, 1950, Statement of Fred L. Crawford, 12, Harry S. Truman Presidential Library.

35. J. F. Thaden, "Migratory Beet Workers in Michigan," by J. F. Thaden of the Section of Sociology, 3–8, Carton 1, Folder 35, National Council of Agricultural Life and Labor, University of California, Berkeley.

36. Cohen, *Braceros*, 119.

37. Truman Commission on Migratory Labor, Saginaw, Michigan, Proceedings for September 12, 1950, Statement of Dr. Frederick Leeder, 492, Harry S. Truman Presidential Library.

38. Cohen, *Braceros*, 99.

39. Truman Commission on Migratory Labor, Saginaw, Michigan, Proceedings for September 12, 1950, Statement of R. L. Loftin, 399, Harry S. Truman Presidential Library.

40. Molina, *Fit to be Citizens?*, 179.

41. Frank Morris, "Puerto Rican Colony Grows in Saginaw Valley," *Detroit Times*, MCKC, Box 1, Folder 11, WPRL, WSU.

42. Morris, "Puerto Rican Colony Grows in Saginaw Valley."

43. Langer, et al., "Epidemiology of Tuberculosis in the United States," 693–702. Even in 1953, there were still 52.6 cases of tuberculosis per 100,000 persons; "Tuberculosis Toll Less: Total of 57,005 Deaths in 1943 Continued Downward Trend," *New York Times*, July 6, 1945, 13.

44. Truman Commission on Migratory Labor, Saginaw, Michigan, Proceedings for September 12, 1950, Statement of Dr. Frederick Leeder, 492, Harry S. Truman Presidential Library.

45. In one case, a group of sixty-five workers were packed into a truck that only had a maximum capacity of twenty-five. A truck with that many workers was unusual, but it was common for these trucks to carry at least twenty workers. September 1954 letter from Alberto Becerra Sierra to Ralph Strong, *AHSRE*, Box PACT 32, Folder 3.

46. J. F. Thaden, "Migratory Beet Workers in Michigan" by J. F. Thaden of the Section of Sociology, 5–6, Carton 1, Folder 35, National Council of Agricultural Life and Labor, University of California, Berkeley.

47. Hearings Before the Select Committee to Investigate the Interstate Migration of Destitute Citizens, Oklahoma City Hearings, 1858.

48. Hugh Williamson, "South Texas Tuberculosis Toll Heavy," *The Monitor*, April 29, 1941, 10.

49. "Tuberculosis and Hospital Sanatoriums Act 177 of 1925," www.legislature.mi.gov/documents/mcl/archive/2014/April/mcl-Act-177-of-1925.pdf; "Tuberculosis Toll Less: Total of 57,005 Deaths in 1943 Continued Downward Trend," *New York Times*, July 6, 1945, 13.

50. Hearings Before the Select Committee Investigating National Defense Migration, Detroit Hearings, 7794–95.

51. Truman Commission on Migratory Labor, Saginaw, Michigan, Proceedings for September 11, 1950, Statement of A. B. Love, 80, Harry S. Truman Presidential Library.

52. Truman Commission on Migratory Labor, Saginaw, Michigan, Proceedings for September 12, 1950, Statement of Edgar Johnston, 515, Harry S. Truman Presidential Library.

53. Truman Commission on Migratory Labor, Saginaw, Michigan, Proceedings for September 12, 1950, Statement of Norman Hughes, 529, Harry S. Truman Presidential Library.

54. Truman Commission on Migratory Labor, Saginaw, Michigan, Proceedings for September 12, 1950, Statement of Norman Hughes, 535, Harry S. Truman Presidential Library.

55. Truman Commission on Migratory Labor, Saginaw, Michigan, Proceedings for September 12, 1950, Statement of S. L. Durham, 291, Harry S. Truman Presidential Library.

56. Truman Commission on Migratory Labor, Saginaw, Michigan, Proceedings for September 12, 1950, Statement of S. L. Durham, 291, Harry S. Truman Presidential Library.

57. Truman Commission on Migratory Labor, Saginaw, Michigan, Proceedings for September 12, 1950, Statement of Harold Gough, 325, Harry S. Truman Presidential Library.

58. "Puerto Rican Colony Grows in Saginaw Valley," *Detroit Times*, June 14, 1950.

59. Truman Commission on Migratory Labor, Saginaw, Michigan, Proceedings for September 12, 1950, Statement of Norman Hughes, 531–33, Harry S. Truman Presidential Library.

60. Truman Commission on Migratory Labor, Saginaw, Michigan, Proceedings for September 12, 1950, Statement of Harold Gough, 324, Harry S. Truman Presidential Library.

61. Truman Commission on Migratory Labor, Saginaw, Michigan, Proceedings for September 12, 1950, Statement of Harold Gough, 324, Harry S. Truman Presidential Library.

62. Statement of Gerardo Hernandez Pau, Father Clement Kern Collections, Box 1, Folder 2, WPRL.

63. Carpio, *Collisions at the Crossroads*, 238.

64. Truman Commission on Migratory Labor, Saginaw, Michigan, Proceedings for September 11, 1950, Statement of Max Henderson, 164, Harry S. Truman Presidential Library.

65. Truman Commission on Migratory Labor, Saginaw, Michigan, Proceedings for September 12, 1950, Statement of Father Clement Kern, 423, Harry S. Truman Presidential Library.

66. Statement of Eduardo Morales, Monsignor Clement Kern Collections, Box 1, Folder 2, WPRL.

67. Truman Commission on Migratory Labor, Saginaw, Michigan, Proceedings for September 12, 1950, Statement of Santos Cintron, 444–54. Also see Statement of Father Clement Kern, 428–29, Harry S. Truman Presidential Library.

68. Truman Commission on Migratory Labor, Saginaw, Michigan, Proceedings for September 12, 1950, Statement of S. L. Durham, 294–95, Harry S. Truman Presidential Library.

69. Truman Commission on Migratory Labor, Saginaw, Michigan, Proceedings for September 12, 1950, Statement of Harold Gough, 325, Harry S. Truman Presidential Library.

70. "American Atrocities," *Gothic*, December 1, 1950, Kern Collection, Box 1, Folder 11, WPRL.

71. "American Atrocities."

72. "His Wage 'Minus,' Migrant Relates," *New York Times*, September 13, 1950, 30.

73. "Translation of Eduardo Morales' Statement," Kern Collection, Box 1, Folder 2, WPRL.

74. "Migrant Workers Crowd Miserable Hovels in Beet Fields of Saginaw Area," *Detroit Free Press*, May 30, 1948, 1.

75. "Minutes of Farm Placement Section of State Farm Advisory Committee Meeting." February 6, 1948, Kern Collection, Box 1, Folder 13, WPRL.

76. Molina, *How Race is Made in America*, 38.

77. "Our 'Good Neighbor' Policy—At Home," Kern Collection, Box 1, Folder 11, WPRL.

78. "Wages Discussed at US Beet Parley: Officials Meet in City for Study of Work Conditions in State," *Detroit Free Press*, January 4, 1949, 13.

79. "American Atrocities."

80. "Excerpts from Frank Edwards' Broadcast on Mutual Broadcasting System," July 12, 1950, Kern Collection, Box 1, Folder 10, WPRL.

81. Hahamovich, *No Man's Land*, 3.

82. Kern Collection, Box 1, Folder 10, WPRL; folder includes letters of correspondence between government officials referring to Puerto Ricans by identification numbers.

83. "Letter from Medical Superintendent," November 15, 1950, Kern Collection, Box 1, Folder 10, WPRL.

84. "Letter from Medical Superintendent."

Chapter Three

1. Francisco Espinosa Q. and Uvaldo García R. to Marcelino Mendoza, Box 1, Folder 1, Clement Kern Papers, WPRL.

2. Espinosa and García to Mendoza, Box 1, Folder 1, CKP, WPRL.

3. "Detroit 1900–Present," Michigan Newspaper History, http://michigannewspaperhistory.pbworks.com/w/page/43753140/Detroit%201900-present, accessed February 2, 2020.

4. Espinosa and García to Mendoza, Box 1, Folder 1, CKP, WPRL.

5. For literacy rates in Mexico, see World Bank, World Development Indicators database, National Center of Education Statistics, National Assessment of Adult Literacy; for Puerto Rico, see US Department of Commerce, "Characteristics of the Population of Puerto Rico," 1950 Census of Populations, April 1, 1950.

6. As of 2025, *La Unión Cívica Mexicana* was still operational serving Saginaw's Mexican and Latinx community.

7. *"La Voz del Público," La Prensa*, January 8, 1954, 2; *"La Voz del Público: Una Miradita," La Prensa*, September 11, 1958, 8; *"La Voz del Público: Ahora Es Tiempo," La Prensa*, March 5, 1959, 10.

8. *"La Voz del Público," La Prensa*, March 6, 1954, 2.

9. Habermas, *The Structural Transformation of the Public Sphere*, 27.

10. Habermas, *The Structural Transformation of the Public Sphere*, 51. Also see Picatto, "Public Sphere in Latin America," 167–68.

11. Habermas, *The Structural Transformation of the Public Sphere*, 56.

12. Picatto, "Public Sphere in Latin America," 169.

13. Piccato, "Public Sphere in Latin America," 167–68.

14. Weise, *Corazón de Dixie*, 98.

15. January 15, 1948 Letter from Thomas Keehn to Sarah Hepburn, National Council on Agricultural Life and Labor, Bancroft Library, Carton 2, Folder 15.

16. Weise, *Corazón de Dixie*, 10.

17. June 18, 1953 Letter from Consul Michel to Consul Josefé, 1, *AHSRE*, Box PACT 11, Folder 5.

18. June 18, 1953 Letter from Consul Michel to Consul Josefé, 1–2, *AHSRE*, Box PACT 11, Folder 5.

19. October 27, 1952 Letter from Consul Josefé to Ralph Holton, *AHSRE*, Box PACT 11, Folder 5.

20. October 27, 1952 Letter from Consul Josefé to Ralph Holton, *AHSRE*, Box PACT 11, Folder 5.

21. "Good Neighbors Get Together Here: Bracero Contract Seen as Great Benefit to Workers from Mexico," December 5, 1949, article from unknown newspaper, *AHSRE*, Box 1454, Folder 1.

22. "Hi Amigos! They Came to Help Us Win the War. Now They're Going Back Home as Good-Will Ambassadors," Rita Halle Kleeman, *AHSRE*, Box 1451, Folder 22.

23. June 18, 1953 Letter from Consul Michel to Consul Josefé, 1, *AHSRE*, Box PACT 11, Folder 5.

24. June 18, 1953 Letter from Consul Michel to Consul Josefé, 1, *AHSRE*, Box PACT 11, Folder 5.

25. "Se Remiten 4 cheques de Braceros," September 26, 1953, *AHSRE*, Box 1451, Folder 2.

26. "Informe del Señor Carl Davenport al Departamento de Trabajo de los Estados Unidos, Oficina Regional en Cleveland, Ohio," 1, *AHSRE*, Box 1451, Folder 2.

27. "Informe del Señor Carl Davenport al Departamento de Trabajo de los Estados Unidos, Oficina Regional en Cleveland, Ohio," 1, *AHSRE*, Box 1451, Folder 2.

28. "Informe del Señor Carl Davenport al Departamento de Trabajo de los Estados Unidos, Oficina Regional en Cleveland, Ohio," 6, *AHSRE*, Box 1451, Folder 2.

29. "Informe del Señor Carl Davenport al Departamento de Trabajo de los Estados Unidos, Oficina Regional en Cleveland, Ohio," 2, *AHSRE*, Box 1451, Folder 2.

30. August 21, 1953 Letter from Pedro Miranda Gómez to Omar Josefé, *SRE*, Box 1451, Folder 2.

31. "Informe del Señor Carl Davenport al Departamento de Trabajo de los Estados Unidos, Oficina Regional en Cleveland, Ohio," 6, *AHSRE*, Box 1451, Folder 2.

32. August 12, 1953 report by Gabriel Torres and Emery Torres, *AHSRE*, Box 1451, Folder 2, 4.

33. August 12, 1953 report by Gabriel Torres and Emery Torres, *AHSRE*, Box 1451, Folder 2, 5.

34. "Informe del Señor Carl Davenport al Departamento de Trabajo de los Estados Unidos, Oficina Regional en Cleveland, Ohio," 4, *AHSRE*, Box 1451, Folder 2.

35. "Informe del Señor Carl Davenport al Departamento de Trabajo de los Estados Unidos, Oficina Regional en Cleveland, Ohio," 5, *AHSRE*, Box 1451, Folder 2.

36. "Informe del Señor Carl Davenport al Departamento de Trabajo de los Estados Unidos, Oficina Regional en Cleveland, Ohio," 5, *AHSRE*, Box 1451, Folder 2.

37. August 29, 1965 Memo from Guadalupe Ruiz to Tony Vega, Farm Labor Program, Centro Archives, Box 969, Folder 1.

38. 1948 Summer Questionnaire on Migratory Labor, National Council on Agricultural Life and Labor, Bancroft Library, Carton 1, Folder 34.

39. "Informe del Señor Carl Davenport al Departamento de Trabajo de los Estados Unidos, Oficina Regional en Cleveland, Ohio," 5, *AHSRE*, Box 1451, Folder 2.

40. See the November 3, 1914 edition of *La Prensa* for an example of the wide array of items covered in the pages of the newspaper.

41. Morales, "*Tejas, Afuera de México*," 62–64.

42. "Denuncian Abusos Cometidos por un Contratador de Braceros en Michigan: Un Compatriota se Queja de que el Consul Mexicano De Detroit Los Desatiende," *La Prensa*, September 25, 1956.

43. "Denuncian Abusos Cometidos por un Contratador de Braceros en Michigan."

44. "Denuncian Abusos Cometidos por un Contratador de Braceros en Michigan."

45. September 26, 1957 Letter from *AHSRE* to Consul Josefé, *AHSRE*, Box PACT 11, Folder 5.

46. "Field Hands Feel Honored: Puerto Ricans Thank People of Michigan," *Detroit Free Press*, July 30, 1950.

47. See, for example, Bud Lanker, "Solve Beet Crop Problem: Employers Praise Puerto Rican Labor," *Detroit Free Press*, July 18, 1950.

48. "Dorvillier Column for Immediate Release," Box 1, Folder 11, CKP, WPRL.

49. "Field Hands Feel Honored."

50. Pérez, *The Near Northwest Side Story*, 71–79.

51. Luis Sánchez Cappa, "*Gobierno Trae 230 Obreros Despedidos EU*," *El Mundo*, September 9, 1964, 1, 18.

52. In the Matter of I. Miller Pickles, Inc., Judge Edward Benson's Opinion Regarding Priority Wage Claim of the Secretary of Labor of the Commonwealth of Puerto Rico, Centro Archives, Collection of Farm Labor Program, Box 948, Folder 12; Cappa, "*Gobierno Trae 230 Obreros Despedidos EU*," 1, 18.

53. In the Matter of I. Miller Pickles, Inc., Judge Edward Benson's Opinion Regarding Priority Wage Claim of the Secretary of Labor of the Commonwealth of Puerto Rico.

54. In the Matter of I. Miller Pickles, Inc., Allowance of Claim #17 of Puerto Rican Agricultural Workers Insurance Fund, Centro Archives, Collection of Farm Labor Program, Box 948, Folder 12.

55. In the Matter of I. Miller Pickles, Inc., Petition for Review, Centro Archives, Collection of Farm Labor Program, Box 948, Folder 12.

56. "*Patrono Quebro en EU: Trabajo Reparte Compensación A Bracero Broiquas Desplazados*," *El Mundo*, August 27, 1968, 3.

57. "Puerto Rico Acts to Protect Labor; Spurs Campaign to Require Contracts on US Farms," *New York Times*, April 30, 1967, 70.

58. "*Patrono Quebro en EU*," 3; "Puerto Rico Acts to Protect Labor," 70.

59. *El Mundo* reported that the check was for $74.49. The wage claim of $18,719.30 divided evenly among 260 workers would amount to $71.99 though. "*Patrono Quebro*

en EU," 3; and "Puerto Rico Acts to Protect Labor," 70. Violation of Commonwealth Law 87 was a misdemeanor crime that could result in a fine of up to $500 for first-time offenders or a prison sentence of up to six months, or both. See *Gobierno de Puerto Rico, Departamento del Trabajo y Recursos Humanos, "Ley Núm. 87 de 22 de Junio de 1962, Según Enmendada, Conocida como Ley para Regular el Reclutamiento y la Contratación de Trabajadores para Realizar Labores fuera de Puerto Rico."*

60. See Lake Erie Operation Annual Report, 1963–1964, Centro Archives, Farm Labor Program, Box 2173, Folder 24. Also see July 1966 Monthly Report, Centro Archives, Farm Labor Program, Box 2412, Folder 16.

61. November 4, 1965, Michigan's Image in Puerto Rico, Centro Archives, Farm Labor Program, Box 965, Folder 19.

62. September 9, 1965 Letter from Anthony Vega to Matilde Fernandez; Also see September 17, 1965 Letter from Matilde Fernandez to Anthony Vega, Centro Archives, Farm Labor Program, Box 915, Folder 2.

63. August 30, 1965 Progress Report from Guadalupe Ruiz to Anthony Vega, Centro Archives, Farm Labor Program, Box 903, Folder 20.

64. October 20, 1965 Progress Report from Guadalupe Ruiz to Anthony Vega, Centro Archives, Farm Labor Program, Box 903, Folder 20.

65. October 20, 1965 Progress Report from Guadalupe Ruiz to Anthony Vega.

66. September 3, 1965 Letter from Harry Vazquez Gallardo to Anthony Vega; Transmittal Slip from Anthony Vega to Guadalupe Ruiz, Centro Archives, Farm Labor Program, Box 903, Folder 20.

67. Letter from Enrique Ayala to WMDD radio station, Centro Archives, Farm Labor Program, Box 903, Folder 2.

Chapter Four

1. "Dave Marsh," Rock's Back Pages Library, https://www.rocksbackpages.com/Library/Writer/dave-marsh, accessed October 25, 2024.

2. John Smyntek, "Is Rock Music Dead?," *Detroit Free Press*, October 25, 1981.

3. For more on Question Mark and the Mysterians, see Behr, "? and the Mysterians (1966)," 21–28; Habell-Palan, *Loca Motion*, 147–80; and Greene, "Not Your Punk," 307–25.

4. Scott Mervis, "Monkees and Mysterians Part of WQED Oldies Spectacular," *Tribune Business News*, May 20, 2010.

5. Alan Nester, "No Questions, It's a Mystery, But Is It Bigger than Nostalgia?," *The Globe and Mail*, May 14, 1996M, D5.

6. https://www.michiganrockandrolllegends.com/mi-rock-a-roll-hall-of-fame/184-mrrl-mission-statement, accessed November 7, 2018. This link is now broken and the quote is no longer on the website's mission statement, https://michiganrockandrolllegends.com/about/36-mrrl-mission-statement, accessed October 3, 2025.

7. "'96 Tears' 50th Anniversary," *Mi Gente*, October 2016, 10.

8. This is an online article about Question Mark and the Mysterians regarding their induction to the Michigan Rock and Roll Legends Hall of Fame. https://michiganrockandrolllegends.com/hall-of-fame/artists/289-question-mark-and-the-mysterians

?highlight=WyJtYXJrIiwibWFya2VkIiwibWFya2VoIiwibWFya2VoaW5nIiwibWFya2VocyIsIm1hcmtpbmciLCJtYXJrcyIsIm1hcmsncyIsIm1hcmtvIiwibWFya2VodH-MiXQ==, accessed October 3, 2025.

9. Ramsey, *Race Music*, 46. Also see, Grossman, *Land of Hope*; Najuma Stewart, *Migrating to the Moves*; and Baldwin, *Chicago's New Negroes*, just to name a few examples.

10. "Discover Freddy Fender," Country Music Hall of Fame and Museum, https://www.countrymusichalloffame.org/learn/teacher-resource-portal/social-studies/discover-freddy-fender, accessed September 20, 2025; Teresa Palomo Acosta, "Freddy Fender: The Icon of Rock-and-Roll, Country, and Tejano Music," Texas State Historical Association, https://www.tshaonline.org/handbook/entries/huerta-baldemar-freddy-fender, accessed September 17, 2025; Steven Loza, "Freddy Fender (Baldemar Garza Huerta)," *Grove Music Online*, November 26, 2013, https://doi.org/10.1093/gmo/9781561592630.article.A2262304, accessed September 16, 2025; "Freddy Fender," *Billboard*, https://www.billboard.com/artist/freddy-fender/chart-history/hsi/, accessed September 21, 2025; "Past Winners and Nominees," Country Music Association Awards, https://cmaawards.com/past-winners-and-nominees/, accessed September 21, 2025; Academy of Country Music, https://www.acmcountry.com/winners?awardTitle=Freddy+Fender&awardCategory=&awardYear=&actionButton=Submit, accessed September 21, 2025.

11. Guernica and Aldoy, "Freddy Fender–Baldemar Huerta," 37–38.

12. Huerta-Fender, *Wasted Days and Wasted Nights*, 27.

13. Dave Zurawik, "Success Was '96 Tears,'" *Detroit Free Press*, February 12, 1977, 2C.

14. Marlon Bishop, "? & The Mysterians: The Migrant Kids Who Inspired Punk Rock," *Latino USA* (podcast), October 13, 2017. Also see Alina Simone, "Here's How '96 Tears' Became a Michigan City's Official Rock Anthem," *Public Radio International*, September 26, 2014, https://www.pri.org/stories/2014-09-26/heres-how-96-tears-became-michigan-citys-official-rock-anthem. Also see https://michiganrockandrolllegends.com/hall-of-fame/artists/289-question-mark-and-the mysterians?highlight=WyJtYXJrIiwibWFya2VkIiwibWFya2VoIiwibWFya2VoaW5nIiwibWFya2VocyIsIm1hcmtpbmciLCJtYXJrcyIsIm1hcmsncyIsIm1hcmtvIiwibWFya2VodHMiXQ==.

15. "'96 Tears' 50th Anniversary," 14.

16. "'96 Tears' 50th Anniversary," 14.

17. Bishop, "? & The Mysterians."

18. Daily Paulson, "? and the Mysterians," 167–69; also see https://michiganrockandrolllegends.com/hall-of-fame/artists/289-question-mark-and-the-mysterians?highlight=WyJtYXJrIiwibWFya2VkIiwibWFya2VoIiwibWFya2VoaW5nIiwibWFya2VocyIsIm1hcmtpbmciLCJtYXJrcyIsIm1hcmsncyIsIm1hcmtvIiwibWFya2VodHMiXQ==; Mervis, "Monkees and Mysterians."

19. "Screen: A Double Bill: 'Watsui' Arrives with 'The Mysterians,'" *New York Times*, July 2, 1959, 15.

20. "Bob Anderson Rockets to Stardom," *Detroit Free Press*, July 7, 1973, 7A. Also see "Seger Comes Stormin' Home Tonight," *Detroit Free Press*, August 28, 1986, 4B.

21. Thompson, "Detroit's Play-It-Extra-Loud Rock 'n' Roll Scene."

22. "'96 Tears' 50th Anniversary," 8.

23. "Show of Faith," *The Guardian*, October 24, 1998, D17.

24. "'96 Tears' 50th Anniversary," 12–13.

25. US Bureau of the Census, *Nineteenth Census of the United States: 1970*, Report on Census Tracts for Detroit, Mich. (US Government Printing Office, 1972), https://www2.census.gov/library/publications/decennial/1970/phc-1/39204513p6ch09.pdf; US Bureau of the Census, *Nineteenth Census of the United States: 1970*, Report on Census Tracts for Grand Rapids, Mich. (US Government Printing Office, 1972), https://www2.census.gov/prod2/decennial/documents/39204513p8ch06.pdf; US Bureau of the Census, *Nineteenth Census of the United States: 1970*, Report on Census Tracts for Flint, Mich. (US Government Printing Office, 1972), https://www2.census.gov/library/publications/decennial/1970/phc-1/39204513p7ch12.pdf; US Bureau of the Census, *Nineteenth Census of the United States: 1970*, Report on Census Tracts for Saginaw, Mich. (US Government Printing Office, 1972), https://www2.census.gov/library/publications/decennial/1970/phc-1/39204513p18ch07.pdf.

26. "'96 Tears' 50th Anniversary," 14.

27. "Show of Faith," D17.

28. "'96 Tears' 50th Anniversary," 10. Also see https://michiganrockandrolllegends.com/hall-of-fame/artists/289-question-mark-and-the-mysterians?highlight=WyJtYXJrIiwibWFya2VkIiwibWFya2VoIiwibWFya2VoaW5nIiwibWFya2VocyIsIm1hcmtpbmciLCJtYXJrcyIsIm1hcmsncyIsIm1hcmtvIiwibWFya2VodHMiXQ==. Also see, "Definitive List of the Greatest 500 Songs of All Time," *Rolling Stone*, April 7, 2011, https://www.rollingstone.com/music/music-lists/500-greatest-songs-of-all-time-151127/.

29. "Show of Faith," D17.

30. "'96 Tears' 50th Anniversary," 6.

31. "'96 Tears' 50th Anniversary," 10.

32. Bloomfield, *Legendary Locals of Bay City, Michigan*, 92. Also see Holtzapple, *Music Makers*, 20; https://michiganrockandrolllegends.com/hall-of-fame/artists/289-question-mark-and-the-mysterians?highlight=WyJtYXJrIiwibWFya2VkIiwibWFya2VoIiwibWFya2VoaW5nIiwibWFya2VocyIsIm1hcmtpbmciLCJtYXJrcyIsIm1hcmsncyIsIm1hcmtvIiwibWFya2VodHMiXQ==.

33. Thompson, "Detroit's Play-It-Extra-Loud Rock 'n' Roll Scene."

34. "Show of Faith," D17. Also see https://michiganrockandrolllegends.com/hall-of-fame/artists/289-question-mark-and-the-mysterians?highlight=WyJtYXJrIiwibWFya2VkIiwibWFya2VoIiwibWFya2VoaW5nIiwibWFya2VocyIsIm1hcmtpbmciLCJtYXJrcyIsIm1hcmsncyIsIm1hcmtvIiwibWFya2VodHMiXQ==; Daily Paulson, "? and the Mysterians," 167–69.

35. Thompson, "Detroit's Play-It-Extra-Loud Rock 'n' Roll Scene."

36. "'96 Tears' 50th Anniversary," 10.

37. Simone, "Here's How '96 Tears' Became a Michigan City's Official Rock Anthem."

38. Oral history conducted with Yolanda Gonzalez by Juan Mora, December 17, 2018.

39. Flory, *I Hear a Symphony*, 1–2. Also see Rudinow, *Soul Music*.

40. Sue White, "Fifty Years Later, Question Mark and the Mysterians as Mysterious as Ever," *M Live*, October 13, 2012, https://www.mlive.com/news/saginaw/index.ssf/2012/10/fifty_years_later_question_mar.html, accessed February 19, 2019.

41. "*Forman un Nuevo Club Latinoamericano en Saginaw, Michigan*," *La Prensa*, February 10, 1952, 4. Also see "Second Report of Governor's Commission on Migrant Labor," August 1966, 1, Reuther Library; Oral History with Yolanda Gonzalez by Juan Mora.

42. *As I Walk through the Valley*, directed by Ronnie Garza and Charlie Vela, 2017. Also see Oral History with Yolanda Gonzalez by Juan Mora.

43. Olmstead, *Los Mexicanos de Michigan*, 241.

44. Harris and Peters, *Motor City Rock and Roll*, 41.

45. Nester, "No Questions, It's a Mystery," D5. Also see Dave Zurawik, "Success Was '96 Tears,'" *Detroit Free Press*, February 12, 1977, 2C.

46. "'96 Tears' 50th Anniversary," 10.

47. "'96 Tears' 50th Anniversary," 14.

48. Judy Wax and Doris Jarrell, "Romney Tightens Rules: Grand Rapids Hit By Sniper Attacks," *Detroit Free Press*, July 27, 1967, 9A. Also see, "'96 Tears' 50th Anniversary," 14.

49. "'96 Tears' 50th Anniversary," 12–14. Also see Oral History conducted with Yolanda Gonzalez by Juan Mora.

50. "'96 Tears' 50th Anniversary," 14.

51. Carson, *Grit, Noise, and Revolution*, 150.

52. J. R. Jones, "One Hit, 30 Years, 96 Tears," *Chicago Reader*, https://www.chicagoreader.com/chicago/one-hit-30-years-96-tears/Content?oid=894821, accessed January 8, 2019.

53. Melanie Cole, "Where Are They Now?," *Hispanic*, October 1997, 44. Also see Jones, "One Hit, 30 Years, 96 Tears"; "Neil Bogart, Entertainment Executive, Dead at 39," *New York Times*, May 9, 1982.

54. "Charge Two With Glue Sniffing," *Traverse City Record Eagle*, April 3, 1968, 16.

55. Shapiro, *The Yale Book of Quotations*, 492.

56. Bishop, "? & The Mysterians."

57. Thompson, "Detroit's Play-It-Extra-Loud Rock 'n' Roll Scene."

58. "'96 Tears' 50th Anniversary," 13.

59. "? (Question Mark) & the Mysterians," *Billboard*, https://www.billboard.com/artist/question-mark-the-mysterians/chart-history/hsi/#, accessed January 8, 2019.

60. Carson, *Grit, Noise, and Revolution*, 86; also see "96 Tears," Official Charts, https://www.officialcharts.com/search/singles/96-tears/, accessed January 15, 2018.

61. Also see "Definitive List of the Greatest 500 Songs of All Time," *Rolling Stone*, April 7, 2011, https://www.rollingstone.com/music/music-lists/500-greatest-songs-of-all-time-151127/; "This List May Rock You," *New York Times*, September 3, 1995, E5.

62. Solis, "I Did It My Way," 315.

63. Michelle Faul and Jeff Karoub, "Cult Star Seeks to Resolve Lost SAfrican Royalties," *Associated Press*, February 23, 2013, https://apnews.com/movies-arts-and-entertainment-general-news-c976f0a16dd9497d951944e63c2a9b0f.

64. "Rodriguez: A Ghetto Dylan," *Big Fat Magazine*, May 1970, https://blog.sugarman.org/2020/11/17/rodriguez-a-ghetto-dylan-big-fat-magazine-may-1970/.

65. "Eva's Memories," South African Rock Encyclopedia, http://sugarman.org/rodmemories2.html#bio, accessed September 16, 2025; "Remembering Sixto Rodriguez, South Africa's Surprise Superstar," *National Public Radio*, August 12, 2023, https://www.npr.org/2023/08/12/1193612057/remembering-sixto-rodriguez-south-africas-surprise-superstar; Laura Payne, "Sixto Rodriguez," *Britannica*, https://www.britannica.com/biography/Rodriguez, accessed September 17, 2025.

66. Mike Duffy, "Part Good, Part Junk—All Punk," *Detroit Free Press*, August 23, 1976, 11C.

67. Wayne Robins, "The Lines' New Wave Rock Has an Intellectual Bent," *Newsday*, February 23, 1980, A26.

68. Allan Kozinn, "Classical Music Meets Pop Culture in New Renditions and Revivals," *New York Times*, October 7, 1988, C1.

69. Mike Downey, "An 18-Stop Tour of 'Dizzyland,'" *Detroit Free Press*, March 3, 1982, H.

70. "'96 Tears' 50th Anniversary," 6. Also see Oral History with Yolanda Gonzalez by Juan Mora.

71. Oral History with Yolanda Gonzalez by Juan Mora.

72. "'96 Tears' 50th Anniversary," 12–13.

73. Dan Santella, "Lillie Gonzalez, Founder of El Pato Restaurants, Passes Away at 98," *Brownsville Herald*, https://www.brownsvilleherald.com/news/valley/lillie-a-gonzalez-founder-of-el-pato-restaurants-passes-away/article_6d6f97ba-dfca-11e3-a93e-0017a43b2370.html, accessed December 11, 2018.

74. Yolanda Gonzalez explained that Jose Gonzalez opened several stores around the Saginaw area, but the original *El Pato* was the one he kept. Members of his family moved north to Saginaw to work and assist with the businesses. Gonzalez gave one store to his brother and another one to a nephew of his. The *El Pato* restaurant was likely one such business.

75. Oral History with Yolanda Gonzalez by Juan Mora.

76. "*Escuche la Hora Mexicana*," *Gladiador*, June 25, 1964. Also see Oral History with Yolanda Gonzalez by Juan Mora. The only other historical reference I can find regarding Luna is his presence in the October 30, 1980 entry in the daily diary of President Jimmy Carter. During a visit to Saginaw Valley State College, Carter met with Luna, who was then chairman of the Labor Council for Latin America. See Jimmy Carter, "The Daily Diary of President Jimmy Carter, October 30, 1980," in the Jimmy Carter Presidential Library and Museum, https://www.jimmycarterlibrary.gov/assets/documents/diary/1980/d103080t.pdf.

77. Oral History with Yolanda Gonzalez by Juan Mora.

78. Oral History with Yolanda Gonzalez by Juan Mora. Also see Peña, *The Texas-Mexican Conjunto*, 90.

79. "'96 Tears' 50th Anniversary," 12–13.

80. Peña, *The Texas-Mexican Conjunto*, 2–3.

81. Peña, *The Texas-Mexican Conjunto*, 92.

82. Peña, *The Texas-Mexican Conjunto*, 70–72.

83. This is speculation, but it appears intentional for their slogan to address their target group as the "Latin American People," rather than just solely Mexicans, which, similarly to the "Latin American Program" on WBCM, the newspaper could have done. This is likely acknowledging Tejanos or Mexican Americans who were maybe not Mexican nationals, as well as potentially Puerto Ricans and other smaller Latinx groups in town.

84. "Representative de Gladiador en Alma," *Gladiador*, June 25, 1964.

85. Texas Conjunto Music Hall of Fame and Museum, http://www.texasconjunto music.org/past_inductees03.html, accessed February 6, 2019.

86. "*Gran Baile*," *Latin Times*, August 18, 1966.

87. "All-Star Attraction 'Live on Stage,'" *Detroit Free Press*, January 22, 1967, 7B.

88. Peña, *The Texas-Mexican Conjunto*, 106. Also see Ragland, *Música Norteña*, 116–17.

89. Eduardo Martinez, "Lillie A. Gonzalez and Her Role in Bego," Pharr from Heaven (blog), June 13, 2014, http://pharrfromheaven.blogspot.com/2014/06/lillie-gonzalez-and-her-role-in-bego.html. Also see Chris Bishop, "Pa-Go-Go Discography," Garage Hangover (blog), February 8, 2011, https://www.garagehangover.com/pa-go-go-discography/; Agustin Garza, "Conjunto Bernal," The Schwartz Frontera Collection of Mexican and Mexican American Recordings, http://frontera.library.ucla.edu/artists/conjunto-bernal, accessed December 11, 2018.

90. There are also references to "Pa-Go-Go" standing for Pato (Jose/Lillie), Gonzales (Rudy Tee), and Gonzalez (Manuel).

91. *As I Walk through the Valley*, directed by Ronnie Garza and Charlie Vela, 2017. Also see Oral History with Yolanda Gonzalez by Juan Mora; Margaret Moser, "A Browner Shade of Black: Blazing Trails of Chicano Soul," *Austin Chronicle*, February 28, 2007, https://www.austinchronicle.com/music/2007-12-28/575535/.

92. Adam Tutor, "Rudy Tee Joins King Pelican, Relives Classic Sound," *San Antonio Report*, May 6, 2016, https://therivardreport.com/rudy-tee-joins-king-pelican-relives-classic-sound/. Also see "West Side Sound Pioneer Gets Animated," *My San Antonio*, September 28, 2015, https://www.mysanantonio.com/entertainment/music-stage/article/West-Side-Sound-pioneer-gets-animated-6512387.php; Bishop, "Pa-Go-Go Discography"; "Pa-Go-Go," The Schwartz Frontera Collection of Mexican and Mexican American Recordings.

Chapter Five

1. Tim Mattimoe, "Chavez Backs FLOC Strike and Boycott," *Catholic Chronicle*, August 10, 1979, Farm Labor Organizing Committee Records (FLOCR), Box 5, Folder 13, WPRL, WSU.

2. Mattimoe, "Chavez Backs FLOC Strike and Boycott."

3. Luther Jackson, "Tomato Field Labor Rumblings," *Detroit Free Press*, June 8, 1979, 15. Also see, "Farm Workers Plan Boycotts," *Detroit Free Press*, June 15, 1979, 12.

4. Jennifer Gavin, "Ohio Union Hopes to Add Michigan Farmworkers," *Times Herald*, August 5, 1979, 8E.

5. Ed Zdrojewski, "Farm Bureau Doubts Chavez Claim: He's In State to Bolster Union, Berrien Chief Says," *Herald-Palladium*, November 16, 1979, 12. Also see

"Chavez: Farm Unions in State Far Off," *Lansing State Journal*, November 15, 1979, 18. Chávez is likely referring to the need for legislation similar to California's Agricultural Labor Relations Act of 1975. The Act gave agricultural workers in the state similar rights to those of nonagricultural workers in private industry under the National Labor Relations Act. For more, see https://repository.uchastings.edu/cgi/viewcontent.cgi?article=1833&context=ca_ballot_props#:~:text=The%20Agricultural%20Labor%20Relations%20Act,participate%20in%20lawful%20union%20activities.

6. Zdrojewski, "Farm Bureau Doubts Chavez Claim," 12.

7. "Chavez: Farm Unions in State Far Off," 18.

8. Collective Bargaining Agreement between FLOC and Campbell Soup Company and Campbell Tomato Growers Association (Feb. 19, 1986–Jan. 31, 1989), 1, Ken Barger Papers (KBP), Box 1, Folder 1, WPRL, WSU.

9. Collective Bargaining Agreement between FLOC and Campbell Soup Company and Campbell Tomato Growers Association.

10. Collective Bargaining Agreement between FLOC and Campbell Soup Company and Campbell Tomato Growers Association.

11. Collective Bargaining Agreement Between Green Bay Food and FLOC Endorsed by Dean Foods Company (Jan. 1, 1992–Dec. 31, 1994), 21, KBP, Box 1, Folder 1, WPRL, WSU.

12. Barger and Reza, *The Farm Labor Movement in the Midwest*, XI–XII.

13. "Farm Union Eyes Berrien Workers: Berrien Springs Major Target for Migrant Labor Organization," *Herald-Palladium*, March 29, 1983, 22. Also see Ed Zdrojewski, "FLOC Union May Target S. Michigan," *Herald-Palladium*, February 18, 1983, 15.

14. "Ohio Migrants Trek to Jersey," *Lansing State Journal*, August 8, 1983, 3; Suzanne Wood, "Uniting for the Future: Hispanic Leadership Group Marches to Capitol to Deliver New Agenda, Make Calls for Unity," *Lansing State Journal*, June 16, 1990, 1A, 2A.

15. "Report of the President of FLOC, Baldemar Velasquez, to the Fifth Constitutional Convention," KBP, Box 1, Folder 2, WPRL, WSU.

16. Garcia, *From the Jaws of Victory*, 31.

17. Garcia, *From the Jaws of Victory*, 36–40.

18. Garcia, *From the Jaws of Victory*, 41–43. Also see "Workers United: The Delano Grape Strike and Boycott," National Park Service, https://www.nps.gov/articles/000/workers-united-the-delano-grape-strike-and-boycott.htm, accessed February 14, 2023.

19. Garcia, *From the Jaws of Victory*, 41.

20. Garcia, *From the Jaws of Victory*, 41.

21. Griswold del Castillo, "César Chávez, the United Farm Workers and Mexican Immigration," 36.

22. Garcia, *From the Jaws of Victory*, 110–11.

23. William S. Welt, "Cesar Chavez in the City of Unions: Of UAWs, UFWs, Teamsters and Exceedingly Sour Grapes," *Detroit Free Press*, June 9, 1974, 7.

24. Garcia, *From the Jaws of Victory*, 113–14.

25. Welt, "Cesar Chavez in the City of Unions," 7.

26. Pat Vogt, "AFL-CIO Pledges Support: Chavez Promises Drive to Unionize Michigan," *The Packer*, June 19, 1971. UFW Office of the President: Cesar Chavez Collection, Part 2, Box 34, Folder 41, WPRL, WSU.

27. For more on the wavering amount of support that the UAW and AFL-CIO provided to the UFW, see Garcia, *From the Jaws of Victory*, 75–144.

28. Hazelton, *Labor's Outcasts*, 10.

29. Bill Osinski, "Child of Migrant Camps Matures as Labor Movement Force," *Detroit Free Press*, September 16, 1990, 1F, 7F. Also see Barger and Reza, *The Farm Labor Movement in the Midwest*, 54.

30. Osinski, "Child of Migrant Camps Matures as Labor Movement Force," 1F, 7F.

31. Osinski, "Child of Migrant Camps Matures as Labor Movement Force," 1F, 7F. Also see Barger and Reza, *The Farm Labor Movement in the Midwest*, 54.

32. Valdés, "From Following the Crops to Chasing the Corporations," 46.

33. December 1972 Newsletter, FLOCR, Box 6, Folder 62, WPRL, WSU.

34. Valdés, "From Following the Crops to Chasing the Corporations," 48. Also see Barger and Reza, *The Farm Labor Movement in the Midwest*, 57–58.

35. FLOC's collective bargaining agreements state thirty-three growers signed contracts with FLOC, which is also the number that Barger and Reza cite. Alternatively, Valdés's chapter says it was twenty-two growers.

36. Valdés, "From Following the Crops to Chasing the Corporations," 48. Also see Barger and Reza, *The Farm Labor Movement in the Midwest*, 57–58.

37. Barger and Reza, *The Farm Labor Movement in the Midwest*, 58.

38. Barger and Reza, *The Farm Labor Movement in the Midwest*, 58.

39. Valdés, "From Following the Crops to Chasing the Corporations," 49.

40. Valdés, "From Following the Crops to Chasing the Corporations," 49–50; Barger and Reza, *The Farm Labor Movement in the Midwest*, 59; December 1972 Newsletter, FLOCR, Box 6, Folder 62, WPRL, WSU.

41. "FLOC: The Second Five Years," *Nuestra Lucha*, November–December 1977, 1, FLOCR, Box 3, Folder 37, WPRL, WSU.

42. Undated 1972–1973 Newsletter, FLOCR, Box 6, Folder 62, WPRL, WSU.

43. December 1972 Newsletter, FLOCR, Box 6, Folder 62, WPRL, WSU.

44. "FLOC—Ten Years of Struggle," *South Side Express*, April 1978, 4–5, FLOCR, Box 3, Folder 37, WPRL, WSU.

45. August 1973 Newsletter, FLOCR, Box 6, Folder 62, WPRL, WSU.

46. "Benito Lopez with March Organizers" (photo), Indiana Historical Society, https://images.indianahistory.org/digital/collection/p16797coll38/id/353, accessed March 3, 2023.

47. "Victory for Indiana Farmworkers," *Nuestra Lucha*, October 1976, 1, 4, FLOCR, Box 5, Folder 20, WPRL, WSU. Also see Valdés, "From Following the Crops to Chasing the Corporations," 50–51; "Strike Ends at Morgan Cannery," *Huntington Herald-Press*, September 8, 1976, Julian Samora Papers (JSP), Box 14, Folder 21, LLILAS Benson, University of Texas at Austin (UTA).

48. "Migrants, Morgan Reach Stalemate," *Huntington Herald-Press*, August 27, 1976, JSP, Box 14, Folder 21, LLILAS Benson, UTA; "Strike Ends at Morgan Cannery," *Huntington Herald-Press*, September 8, 1976, JSP, Box 14, Folder 21, LLILAS Benson, UTA; "Victory for Indiana Farmworkers," 1, 4.

49. "Indiana Farm Workers," *The Militant*, September 17, 1976, JSP, Box 14, Folder 21, LLILAS Benson, UTA.

50. "Victory for Indiana Farmworkers," 4.

51. "Strike Ends at Morgan Cannery"; Untitled images and captions, *Huntington Herald-Press*, September 5, 1976, JSP, Box 14, Folder 21, LLILAS Benson, UTA. Also see "Indiana Farm Workers."

52. "Victory for Indiana Farmworkers," 4; "Strike Ends at Morgan Cannery."

53. Barger and Reza, *The Farm Labor Movement in the Midwest*, 60.

54. "Chavez—UFW Endorses FLOC," *Nuestra Lucha*, July 1977, 1, FLOCR, Box 3, Folder 37, WPRL, WSU.

55. "FLOC Takes Aim on Canneries," *Putnam County Sentinel*, September 15, 1976, JSP, Box 14, Folder 21, LLILAS Benson, UTA.

56. "FLOC—Ten Years of Struggle," *Nuestra Lucha*, August 1977, 1, FLOCR, Box 3, Folder 37, WPRL, WSU.

57. "Chavez—UFW Endorses FLOC," 1.

58. "Migrants to Strike?," *Herald-Palladium*, July 25, 1978, 12; "Aimed at Growers: Migrants Vow Cannery Strike," *Herald-Palladium*, July 28, 1978, 22; "FLOC Anticipates Strike," *Nuestra Lucha*, July–September 1978, 1, 4, FLOCR, Box 5, Folder 20, WPRL, WSU.

59. "FLOC Anticipates Strike," *Nuestra Lucha*, July–September 1978, 4, FLOCR, Box 5, Folder 20, WPRL, WSU.

60. "FLOC Anticipates Strike," 4; "Migrants Firm in Demands," *Herald-Palladium*, August 30, 1978, 8; "Tomato Strike to Continue; Boycott to Begin," *Nuestra Lucha*, December 1978–January 1979, 4, FLOCR, Box 6, Folder 68, WPRL, WSU.

61. "Tomato Strike to Continue," 1, 3.

62. "Tomato Strike to Continue," 3.

63. "Pickers Demand Boycott," *Lansing State Journal*, September 10, 1978, 10.

64. "Farm Workers Plan Boycotts," *Detroit Free Press*, June 15, 1979, 12; Luther Jackson, "Tomato Field Labor Rumblings," *Detroit Free Press*, June 8, 1979, 15.

65. "Midwest Farmworker Convention," *Nuestra Lucha*, July 1979, 1, FLOCR, Box 6, Folder 68, WPRL, WSU.

66. "Letters . . . ," *Nuestra Lucha*, July 1979, 2, FLOCR, Box 6, Folder 68, WPRL, WSU.

67. "Church Groups Support FLOC," *Nuestra Lucha*, August 1979, 6, FLOCR, Box 6, Folder 68, WPRL, WSU.

68. Virginia Wlegand, "Campbell's Is Targeted by Migrants," *Beacon Journal*, July 8, 1983, FLOCR, Box 5, Folder 14, WPRL, WSU.

69. Wlegand, "Campbell's Is Targeted by Migrants."

70. Lowman S. Henry, "No Soup! Farm Workers Protest Campbell Fields," *Greensburg Standard-Observer*, July 23, 1983, FLOCR, Box 5, Folder 14, WPRL, WSU.

71. Eric Harrison, "Marchers Lay Blame on Campbell," *Philadelphia Inquirer*, August 3, 1983, 1B and 4B, FLOCR, Box 5, Folder 14, WPRL, WSU.

72. Although the voices of rank-and-file members, like Salinas, are only sparsely integrated into this chapter, these will be a larger emphasis in a future project I will be pursuing about FLOC.

73. Eric Harrison, "Farm Workers' Long Trek to Camden Reflects the Passion of a 5-Year Struggle," *Philadelphia Inquirer*, August 7, 1983, 3F, FLOCR, Box 5, Folder 14, WPRL, WSU.

74. James A. Walsh, "Farm Laborers Arrive," *Courier-Post*, August 8, 1983, FLOCR, Box 5, Folder 14, WPRL, WSU.

75. Walsh, "Farm Laborers Arrive"; Eric Harrison, "Ohio Farm Workers' March Comes to an End in Camden," *Philadelphia Inquirer*, August 8, 1983, 1B, FLOCR, Box 5, Folder 14, WPRL, WSU; "Migrants Ending Trek to Campbell Soup Co.," *Detroit Free Press*, August 9, 1983, 25; "Migrants End March for Wages," *Lansing State Journal*, August 9, 1983, 2.

76. Patrick Breslin, "Farm Workers Take Boycott Push to Campbell's, Decline Meeting," *Philadelphia Inquirer*, August 9, 1983, FLOCR, Box 5, Folder 14, WPRL, WSU.

77. Sister Pat Drydyk, "Partners in Struggle—the NFWM" and "The March for Justice," Farm Labor Organizing Committee: Campbell's Signs!, February 1986, FLOCR, Box 24, Folder 54, WPRL, WSU; also see "Pat Drydyk," National Farm Worker Ministry, https://nfwm.org/50for50/artwork/pat-drydyk, accessed October 2, 2025.

78. Breslin, "Farm Workers Take Boycott Push to Campbell's, Decline Meeting"; "Migrants End March for Wages," 2.

79. "Migrants End March for Wages," 2.

80. "Young Marchers," *Tribune-Review*, July 23, 1983, FLOCR, Box 1, Folder 2, WPRL, WSU.

81. "FLOC Marches 530 Miles to Campbell's Company," *Frente a Frente*, August/September 1983, FLOCR, Box 5, Folder 14, WPRL, WSU.

82. "Campbell in the Soup with Tiny Farm Union," *Lansing State Journal*, January 5, 1984, 6.

83. Untitled Advertisement, *New York Times*, December 25, 1983, E10.

84. Cruz Phillips, "The Children Were Heard," Farm Labor Organizing Committee: Campbell's Signs!, February 1986, FLOCR, Box 24, Folder 54, WPRL, WSU.

85. Untitled Advertisement, *New York Times*, December 25, 1983, E10.

86. "Fiction vs. Fact: A Message from Campbell Soup Company," *New York Times*, January 1, 1984, E5.

87. Alan L. Adler, "Union, Campbell Fight Spills into Newspapers," *Herald-Palladium*, January 6, 1984, 17.

88. See Adler, "Union, Campbell Fight Spills into Newspapers," 17. Rombach asserts that the boycott was not hurting the company and that they were receiving few letters of complaint in the mail.

89. Linda Solomon, "Company's Reputation Pitted against Workers' Boycott," *Detroit Free Press*, February 16, 1984, 5A.

90. Solomon, "Company's Reputation Pitted against Workers' Boycott," 5A. Also see "Campbell Ends Labels for Education Program," Food Processing, https://www.foodprocessing.com/business-of-food-beverage/business-strategies/news/11314115/campbell-ends-labels-for-education-program, accessed October 2, 2025.

91. "Jackson Huddles with Parties in Dispute," *Del Rio News Herald*, April 25, 1984, 17.

92. "Jackson Huddles with Parties in Dispute," 17; "Jackson, Soup Firm President Meet," *Daily Advocate*, May 3, 1984, 3.

93. "Jackson, Soup Firm President Meet," 3.

94. "Address before the Democratic National Convention," The Pilgrimage of Jesse Jackson, *Frontline*, July 18, 1984, https://www.pbs.org/wgbh/pages/frontline/jesse/speeches/jesse84speech.html.

95. "Address before the Democratic National Convention"; also see https://www.c-span.org/clip/public-affairs-event/user-clip-jesse-jackson-1984-democratic-national-convention-speech-complete/4787462, accessed October 3, 2025.

96. Sue Cross, "Boycott vs. Campbell Soup Goes On," *Gettysburg Times*, July 31, 1984.

97. Jeremy Iggers, "Whos and Whys of Campbell Boycott," *Detroit Free Press*, August 22, 1984.

98. "Campbell and Vlasic Agree to F. T. C. Plan," *New York Times*, May 19, 1978, D4. In 1978, Campbell agreed to acquire Vlasic for $33 million in stock.

99. Iggers, "Whos and Whys of Campbell Boycott."

100. "Campbell Soup Co. Denies Charge by Farm Labor Union Leader," *Gettysburg Times*, June 20, 1985; "Campbell Disclosure Angers Union," *Times Herald*, June 19, 1985.

101. Steven Greenhouse, "John Dunlop, 89, Dies; Labor Expert Served 11 Presidents," *New York Times*, October 4, 2003.

102. "Msgr. Higgins Seeks Fairness and Justice for Farmworkers," *Catholic Advance*, August 15, 1985; "Dunlop Names Four to Farm Labor Panel," *The Blade*, August 1, 1985; 169th Convention of the Diocese of Ohio, "Report of the Special Committee to Study Migrant Farm Labor in the Diocese of Ohio," FLOCR, Box 18, Folder 15, WPRL, WSU.

103. "Migrants Unionize," *Daily Advocate*, October 16, 1985.

104. Kim Moody, "Campbell Boycott Continues, Ohio Farm Union Says," *Labor Notes*, KBP, Box 1, Folder 10, WPRL, WSU.

105. Deborah Kaplan, "Farm Workers Win Pact with Processors," *Detroit Free Press*, February 20, 1986.

106. "Campbell Signs Contracts Boycott Suspended," *Boycott Update*, April 1986, KBP, Box 1, Folder 11, WPRL, WSU.

107. The official contract between FLOC, Vlasic, and the growers states that the contract was agreed to on March 15, but all other reports and news have February 18 as the date of the contract.

108. While there were varying reports about exactly how many growers signed these contracts, it was between 28 and 32 farmers. FLOC's official collective bargaining agreement with Vlasic states that 28 tomato and pickle growers signed contracts; other outlets like the *Detroit Free Press* and the Illinois Farm Worker Ministry reported 32 signatories. See Kaplan, "Farm Workers Win Pact with Processors"; Illinois Farm Worker Ministry, "Victory in the Fields of the Midwest!," FLOCR, Box 4, Folder 33, WPRL, WSU; "Collective Bargaining Agreement Between Farm Labor Organizing Committee and Vlasic Food, Inc. and Growers Under Contract to Vlasic Food, Inc.," KBP, Box 1, Folder 1, WPRL, WSU.

109. "Collective Bargaining Agreement Between Farm Labor Organizing Committee and Vlasic Food, Inc. and Growers Under Contract to Vlasic Food, Inc."; "Campbell Signs Contracts Boycott Suspended"; Illinois Farm Worker Ministry, "Victory in

the Fields of the Midwest!"; Helen Fogel, "Religious Groups' Pressure Key to Farm Contracts," *Detroit Free Press*, February 21, 1986.

110. "Campbell Signs Contracts Boycott Suspended"; Illinois Farm Worker Ministry, "Victory in the Fields of the Midwest!"; Robert de Boer, "FLOC Signs Contract with Campbell, Growers on Rights of Farmworkers," *Toledo Blade*, February 20, 1986; Fogel, "Religious Groups' Pressure Key to Farm Contracts"; Kaplan, "Farm Workers Win Pact with Processors."

111. Illinois Farm Worker Ministry, "Victory in the Fields of the Midwest!"

112. "Collective Bargaining Agreement Between Farm Labor Organizing Committee and Vlasic Food, Inc. and Growers Under Contract to Vlasic Food, Inc.,"; Fogel, "Religious Groups' Pressure Key to Farm Contracts"; Judith Tyler, "Farmworkers' Victory Ends Campbell's Boycott," *Frontline*, April 14, 1986; "Campbell Signs Contracts Boycott Suspended"; "FLOC Signs Contract with Campbell, Growers on Rights of Farmworkers."

113. Maria T. Sanchez, "Victory!," Farm Labor Organizing Committee: Campbell's Signs!, February 1986, FLOCR, Box 24, Folder 54, WPRL, WSU.

114. "Collective Bargaining Agreement Between Farm Labor Organizing Committee and Vlasic Food, Inc. and Growers Under Contract to Vlasic Food, Inc."; "Collective Bargaining Agreement Between Farm Labor Organizing Committee and Campbell Soup Company and Campbell Tomato Growers Association," KBP, Box 1, Folder 1, WPRL, WSU. In the collective bargaining agreement, Velásquez writes, "This is only on our first contract. Our struggle for complete justice and dignity is not over yet. There are many things still to be done, and many workers who still don't enjoy the benefits of a contract."

115. Lawrence Mishel, Lynn Rhinehart, Lane Windham, "Explaining the Erosion of Private-Sector Unions," *Economic Policy Institute*, November 18, 2020, 7, https://www.epi.org/unequalpower/publications/private-sector-unions-corporate-legal-erosion/.

116. Windham, *Knocking on Labor's Door*, 178.

117. Sanchez, "Victory!"

118. Tyler, "Farmworkers' Victory Ends Campbell's Boycott."

119. "What Comes Next For FLOC?," KBP, Box 1, Folder 11, WPRL, WSU; Illinois Farm Worker Ministry, "Heinz a Target," FLOCR, Box 4, Folder 33, WPRL, WSU; Don Hopey, "Heinz, Farmworkers, Growers Reach Agreement on Labor Pact," *Pittsburgh Press*, April 9, 1987, KBP, Box 1, Folder 11, WPRL, WSU.

120. Kaplan, "Farm Workers Win Pact with Processors."

121. "Talk to Begin with Heinz," September 1986, KBP, Box 1, Folder 11, WPRL, WSU.

122. John Nichols, "FLOC, Heinz Growers Agree on Farm Workers Contract," *The Blade*, April 9, 1987, KBP, Box 1, Folder 11, WPRL, WSU; John Saunders, "Heinz Farm Workers OK Pact," *Detroit Free Press*, April 10, 1987; Hopey, "Heinz, Farmworkers, Growers Reach Agreement on Labor Pact"; Collective Bargaining Agreement Between Green Bay Food and FLOC Endorsed by Dean Foods Company, KBP, Box 1, Folder 1, WPRL, WSU; Collective Bargaining Agreement Between Aunt Jane's and FLOC Endorsed by Dean Foods Company, KBP, Box 1, Folder 1, WPRL, WSU.

Conclusion

1. Jon Pareles, "Pete Seeger, Champion of Folk Music and Social Change, Dies at 94," *New York Times*, January 28, 2014.

2. Pete Seeger, "From a Long-Time Friend," Farm Labor Organizing Committee: Campbell's Signs!, February 1986, FLOCR, Box 24, Folder 54, WPRL, WSU.

3. Frances Moore Lappé, "Dignity and Courage," Farm Labor Organizing Committee: Campbell's Signs!, February 1986, FLOCR, Box 24, Folder 54, WPRL, WSU.

4. Fernando Cuevas, "New Hope—The '78 Strike," Farm Labor Organizing Committee: Campbell's Signs!, February 1986, FLOCR, Box 24, Folder 54, WPRL, WSU.

5. For an example of this with the United Farm Workers in California, see Paiz, *Strikers of Coachella*, 278.

6. "FLOC Attends Conferences on Undocumented," *Nuestra Lucha*, February–June 1978, 6–7, FLOCR, Box 5, Folder 20, WPRL, WSU; "Brief Look at the Puerto Rican Labor Movement: Its Importance to the Political Status of Puerto Rico," *Nuestra Lucha*, September–October 1977, 9, FLOCR, Box 3, Folder 37, WPRL, WSU.

7. US Department of Homeland Security, US Citizenship and Immigration Services, Temporary Final Rule, "Temporary Changes to Requirements Affecting H-2A Nonimmigrants Due to the COVID-19 National Emergency," *Federal Register* 85, no. 76 (April 20, 2020): 21739–745, https://www.govinfo.gov/content/pkg/FR-2020-04-20/pdf/2020-08356.pdf; US President, Proclamation, "Suspension of Entry of Immigrants Who Present Risk to the United States Labor Market During the Economic Recovery Following the Novel Coronavirus Outbreak, 2020, Proclamation 10014 of April 22, 2020," *Federal Register* 85, no. 81 (April 27, 2020): 23441, https://www.whitehouse.gov/presidential-actions/proclamation-suspending-entry-immigrants-present-risk-u-s-labor-market-economic-recovery-following-covid-19-outbreak/; Liz Crampton, "Farm Workers to Be Exempt from Trump's Immigration Ban," *Politico*, April 21, 2020, https://www.politico.com/news/2020/04/21/farm-workers-exempt-trumps-immigration-ban-198039.

8. Greg Akili, "Thoughts on the Farm Worker Struggle," Farm Labor Organizing Committee: Campbell's Signs!, February 1986, FLOCR, Box 24, Folder 54, WPRL, WSU.

Bibliography

Archives

Ann Arbor, MI
- Bentley Historical Library, University of Michigan

Austin, TX
- LLILAS Benson Latin American Studies and Collections, University of Texas at Austin
  - Julian Samora Papers

Berkeley, CA
- Bancroft Library, University of California, Berkeley
  - National Council of Agricultural Life and Labor Records
    - Paul S. Taylor Papers

College Park, MD
- National Archives and Records Administration
  - General Records of the Department of Labor
  - Records of the Manpower Commission
  - Records of the Office of the Secretary of Agriculture

Detroit, MI
- Archives of Labor and Urban Affairs, Walter P. Reuther Library, Wayne State University
  - Agricultural Workers History Collection
    - Clement Kern Papers
    - Edgar Johnston Collection
  - Farm Labor Organizing Committee Records
    - Ken Barger Papers
- Detroit Public Library

Distrito Federal, México
- *Archivo General de la Nación*
- *Archivo Histórico de la Secretaría de Relaciones Exteriores* (AHSRE)

East Lansing, MI
- Michigan State University Special Collections

Independence, Missouri
- Harry S. Truman Presidential Library
  - Records of the President's Commission on Migratory Labor

New York, NY
- Centro Library and Archives, Silberman School of Social Work at Hunter College
  - Records of the Office of the Government of Puerto Rico in the United States, Farm Labor Program

Palo Alto, CA
Stanford University Special Collections
Ernesto Galarza Papers
San Juan, Puerto Rico
Archivo General de Puerto Rico
Washington, DC
Library of Congress
The National Association for the Advancement of Colored People Records
The National Consumers League Records
National Museum of American History Archives Center

Online Archive

Bracero History Archive

Periodicals

Associated Press
Austin American
Austin Chronicle
Battle Creek Inquirer
Beacon Journal
Big Fat Magazine
Blade
Brownsville Herald
Catholic Advance
Chicago Daily Tribune
Chicago Reader
Corsicana Daily Sun
Courier-Post
CREEM
Daily Advocate
Del Rio News Herald
Detroit Free Press
Detroit Times
El Mundo
El Paso Times
Fort Worth Star-Telegram
Frente a Frente
Gettysburg Times
Gladiador
Globe and Mail
Greensburg Standard-Observer
Guardian
Herald-Palladium
Hispanic
Huntington Herald-Press
Labor Notes
Lansing State Journal
La Prensa
Latin Times
Los Angeles Times
Mi Gente
The Militant
MLive
Monitor
New York Times
Nuestra Lucha
Packer
Philadelphia Inquirer
Pittsburgh Press
Putnam County Sentinel
San Antonio Report
South Side Express
Times Herald
Toledo Blade
Traverse City Record Eagle
Tribune Business News
Tribune-Review
Valley Morning Star

Books and Articles

Alamillo, José M. *Making Lemonade out of Lemons: Mexican American Labor and Leisure in a California Town, 1880–1960*. University of Illinois Press, 2006.

Amezcua, Mike. *Making Mexican Chicago: From Postwar Settlement to the Age of Gentrification*. University of Chicago Press, 2022.

Arredondo, Gabriella F. *Mexican Chicago: Race, Identity, and Nation, 1916–39*. University of Illinois Press, 2008.

Ayala, César. *American Sugar Kingdom: The Plantation Economy of the Spanish Caribbean, 1898–1934*. University of North Carolina Press, 1999.

Ayala, César, and Rafael Bernabe. *Puerto Rico in the American Century: A History since 1898*. University of North Carolina Press, 2007.

Balderrama, Francisco E., and Raymond Rodríguez. *Decade of Betrayal: Mexican Repatriation in the 1930s*. University of New Mexico Press, 1995.

Baldwin, Davarian L. *Chicago's New Negroes: Modernity, the Great Migration, and Black Urban Life*. University of North Carolina Press, 2007.

Bardacke, Frank. *Trampling Out the Vintage: Cesar Chavez and the Two Souls of the United Farm Workers*. Verso Books, 2011.

Barger, W. K., and Ernesto M. Reza. *The Farm Labor Movement in the Midwest: Social Change and Adaptation among Migrant Farmworkers*. University of Texas Press, 1994.

Barrett, James R. *Work and Community in the Jungle: Chicago's Packinghouse Workers, 1894–1922*. University of Illinois Press, 1987.

Behr, Adam. "? and the Mysterians (1966)." In *One-Hit Wonders: An Oblique History of Popular Music*, edited by Sarah Hill, 21–28. Bloomsbury Academic, 2022.

Bloomfield, Ron. *Legendary Locals of Bay City, Michigan*. Arcadia Publishing, 2012.

Brantley, Allyson P. *Brewing a Boycott: How a Grassroots Coalition Fought Coors and Remade American Consumer Activism*. University of North Carolina Press, 2021.

Briggs, Laura. *Reproducing Empire: Race, Sex, Science, and U.S. Imperialism in Puerto Rico*. University of California Press, 2002.

Burgos, Adrian, Jr. *Playing America's Game: Baseball, Latinos, and the Color Line*. University of California Press, 2007.

Cadava, Geraldo L. *Standing on Common Ground: The Making of a Sunbelt Borderland*. Harvard University Press, 2013.

Calavita, Kitty. *Inside the State: The Bracero Program, Immigration, and the I. N. S.* Routledge, 1992.

Camarillo, Albert. *Chicanos in a Changing Society: From Mexican Pueblos to American Barrios in Santa Barbara and Southern California, 1848–1930*. Harvard University Press, 1979.

Carpio, Genevieve. *Collisions at the Crossroads: How Place and Mobility Make Race*. University of California Press, 2019.

Carson, David A. *Grit, Noise, and Revolution: The Birth of Detroit Rock 'n' Roll*. University of Michigan Press, 2005.

Cohen, Deborah. *Braceros: Migrant Citizens and Transnational Subjects in the Postwar United States and Mexico*. University of North Carolina Press, 2011.

Creagan, James F. "Public Law 78: A Tangle for Domestic and International Relations." *Journal of Inter-American Studies* 7, no. 4 (October 1965): 542–43.

Daily Paulson, Linda. "? and the Mysterians." In *Contemporary Musicians: Profiles of People in Music*, edited by Leigh Ann DeRemer, 167–69. Gale Group, 2002.

De Genova, Nicholas, and Ana Y. Ramos-Zayas. *Latino Crossings: Mexicans, Puerto Ricans, and the Politics of Race and Citizenship*. Routledge Press, 2003.

Delgadillo, Theresa. *Latina Lives in Milwaukee*. University of Illinois Press, 2015.

Duany, Jorge. "A Transnational Colonial Migration: Puerto Rico's Farm Labor Program." *NWIG: New West Indian Guide* 84, no. 3/4 (2010): 227–78.

Fernández, Johanna. *The Young Lords: A Radical History*. University of North Carolina Press, 2022.

Fernández, Lilia. *Brown in the Windy City: Mexicans and Puerto Ricans in Postwar Chicago*. University of Chicago Press, 2012.

———. "Of Immigrants and Migrants: Mexican and Puerto Rican Labor Migration in Comparative Perspective, 1942–1964." *Journal of American Ethnic History* 2, no. 3 (Spring 2010): 6–39.

Fernández-Jones, Delia. "Becoming Latino: Mexican and Puerto Rican Community Formation in Grand Rapids, Michigan, 1926–1964." *Michigan Historical Review* 39 (Spring 2013): 71–100.

———. *Making the MexiRican City: Migration, Placemaking, and Activism in Grand Rapids, Michigan*. University of Illinois Press, 2023.

Findlay, Eileen J. Suárez. *We Are Left Without a Father Here: Masculinity, Domesticity, and Migration in Postwar Puerto Rico*. Duke University Press, 2014.

Fink, Leon. *The Maya of Morganton: Work and Community in the Nuevo South*. University of North Carolina Press, 2003.

Flores, John H. *The Mexican Revolution in Chicago: Immigration Politics from the Early Twentieth Century to the Cold War*. University of Illinois Press, 2018.

Flores, Lori A. *Awaiting Their Feast: Latinx Food Workers and Activism from World War II to COVID-19*. University of North Carolina Press, 2025.

———. *Grounds for Dreaming: Mexican Americans, Mexican Immigrants, and the California Farmworker Movement*. Yale University Press, 2016.

Flory, Andrew. *I Hear a Symphony: Motown and Crossover R&B*. University of Michigan Press, 2017.

Galarza, Ernesto. *Merchants of Labor: The Mexican Bracero Story*. McNally and Loftin, 1964.

Ganz, Marshall. *Why David Sometimes Wins: Leadership, Organization, and Strategy in the California Farm Worker Movement*. Oxford University Press, 2009.

Garcia, Matt. *From the Jaws of Victory: The Triumph and Tragedy of Cesar Chavez and the Farm Worker Movement*. University of California Press, 2014.

———. *A World of its Own: Race, Labor, and Citrus in the Making of Greater Los Angeles*. University of North Carolina Press, 2001.

García-Colón, Ismael. *Colonial Migrants at the Heart of Empire: Puerto Rican Workers on U.S. Farms*. University of California Press, 2020.

Glazer, Nathan, and Daniel Patrick Moynihan. *Beyond the Melting Pot: The Negroes, Puerto Ricans, Jews, Italians, and Irish of New York City*. Massachusetts Institute of Technology Press, 1963.

Gómez-Quiñones, Juan. *Mexican American Labor: 1790–1990*. University of New Mexico Press, 1994.

González, Sergio M. *Strangers No Longer: Latino Belonging and Faith in Twentieth-Century Wisconsin*. University of Illinois Press, 2024.

Goodman, Adam. "Bananas North, Deportees South: Punishment, Profits, and the Human Costs of the Business of Deportation." *Journal of American History* 106, no. 4 (March 2020): 949–74.

———. *The Deportation Machine: America's Long History of Expelling Immigrants*. Princeton University Press, 2020.

Gordillo, Luz María. *Mexican Women and the Other Side of Immigration: Engendering Transnational Ties*. University of Texas Press, 2010.

Greene, Shane. "Not Your Punk." In *PUNK! Las Américas Edition*, edited by Olga Rodríguez-Ulloa, Rodrigo Quijano, and Shane Greene, 307–25. University of Chicago Press, 2021.

Griswold del Castillo, Richard. "César Chávez, the United Farm Workers and Mexican Immigration." *Rio Bravo: Journal of the Borderlands* 2, no.1 (Fall 1992): 36.

Grossman, James R. *Land of Hope: Chicago, Black Southerners, and the Great Migration*. University of Chicago Press, 1989.

Guerin-Gonzales, Camille. *Mexican Workers and American Dreams: Immigration, Repatriation, and California Farm Labor, 1900–1939*. Rutgers University Press, 1994.

Guernica, Antonio José, and Sonia Aldoy. "Freddy Fender—Baldemar Huerta." *Agenda* 7, no. 3 (May/June 1977): 37–38.

Guerrero, Perla M. *Nuevo South: Latinas/os, Asians, and the Remaking of Place*. University of Texas Press, 2017.

Habell-Pallán, Michelle. *Loca Motion: The Travels of Chicana and Latina Popular Culture*. New York University Press, 2005.

Habermas, Jürgen. *The Structural Transformation of the Public Sphere: An Inquiry into a Category of Bourgeois Society*. Translated by Thomas Burger. MIT Press, 1989.

Hahamovitch, Cindy. *The Fruits of Their Labor: Atlantic Coast Farmworkers and the Making of Migrant Poverty 1870–1945*. University of North Carolina Press, 1997.

———. *No Man's Land: Jamaican Guestworkers in America and the Global History of Deportable Labor*. Princeton University Press, 2011.

Harris, Bob, and John Douglas Peters. *Motor City Rock and Roll: The 1960s and 1970s*. Arcadia Publishing, 2008.

Hazelton, Andrew J. *Labor's Outcasts: Migrant Farmworkers and Unions in North America, 1934–1966*. University of Illinois Press, 2022.

Hernández, Kelly Lytle. "The Crimes and Consequences of Illegal Immigration: A Cross-Border Examination of Operation Wetback, 1943 to 1954." *Western History Quarterly* 37 (Winter 2006): 421–44.

———. *Migra! A History of the U.S. Border Patrol*. University of California Press, 2010.

Hernández, Sonia. *For a Just and Better World: Engendering Anarchism in the Mexican Borderlands, 1900–1938*. University of Illinois Press, 2021.

———. *Working Women into the Borderlands*. Texas A&M University Press, 2014.

Higbie, Frank Tobias. *Indispensable Outcasts: Hobo Workers and Community in the American Midwest, 1880–1930*. University of Illinois Press, 2003.

Hinojosa, Felipe. *Apostles of Change: Latino Radical Politics, Church Occupations, and the Fight to Save the Barrio*. University of Texas Press, 2022.

Holtzapple, William R. *Music Makers from Mid Michigan and Surrounding Areas, 1940s Thru 1970s: Who Were They?* Kawkawlin, 2006.

Huerta-Fender, Tammy Lorraine. *Wasted Days and Wasted Nights: Freddy Fender—A Meteoric Rise to Stardom*. Xlibris Book Publishing, 2017.

Innis-Jiménez, Michael. *Steel Barrio: The Great Mexican Migration to South Chicago, 1915–1940*. New York University Press, 2013.

Kang, S. Deborah. *The INS on the Line: Making Immigration Law on the US-Mexico Border, 1917–1954*. Oxford University Press, 2017.

Kanter, Deborah E. *Chicago Católico: Making Catholic Parishes Mexican*. University of Illinois Press, 2020.

Langer, A. J., Thomas R. Navin, Carla A. Winston, and Philip LoBue. "Epidemiology of Tuberculosis in the United States." *Clinics in Chest Medicine* 40, no. 4 (December 2019): 693–702.

Lim, Julian. *Porous Borders: Multiracial Migrations and the Law in the U.S.-Mexico Borderlands*. University of North Carolina Press, 2020.

Lourdes Dick, Diane. "U.S. Tax Imperialism in Puerto Rico." *American University Law Review* 65, no. 1 (2015).

Loza, Mireya. *Defiant Braceros: How Migrant Workers Fought for Racial, Sexual, and Political Freedom*. University of North Carolina Press, 2016.

———. "'Let Them Bring Their Families': The Experiences of the First Mexican Guest Workers, 1917–1922." *Journal of American History* 109, no. 2 (2022): 310–23.

Mantler, Gordon K. *The Multiracial Promise: Harold Washington's Chicago and the Democratic Struggle in Reagan's America*. University of North Carolina Press, 2023.

Mapes, Kathleen. *Sweet Tyranny: Migrant Labor, Industrial Agriculture, and Imperial Politics*. University of Illinois Press, 2009.

Márquez, Cecilia. *Making the Latino South: A History of Racial Formation*. University of North Carolina Press, 2023.

Martínez-Matsuda, Verónica. "For Labor and Democracy: The Farm Security Administration's Competing Visions for Farm Workers' Socioeconomic Reform and Civil Rights in the 1940s." *Journal of American History* 106, no. 2 (September 2019): 338–61.

———. *Migrant Citizenship: Race, Rights, and Reform in the U.S. Farm Labor Camp Program*. University of Pennsylvania Press, 2020.

McDonald, Jason. "A Fair Deal for Immigrants? The Truman Administration and Immigration Policy Reform." *Immigrants & Minorities* 32, no. 2 (January 2014): 206–8.

Mckiernan-González, John. *Fevered Measures: Public Health and Race at the Texas-Mexico Border, 1848–1942*. Duke University Press, 2012.

McNamara, Sarah. *Ybor City: Crucible of the Latina South*. University of North Carolina Press, 2023.

McWilliams, Carey. *Ill Fares the Land: Migrants and Migratory Labor in the United States*. Barnes & Noble, Inc., 1941.

Meléndez, Edgardo. *Sponsored Migration: The State and Puerto Rican Postwar Migration to the United States*. The Ohio State University Press, 2017.

Merleaux, April. *Sugar and Civilization: American Empire and the Cultural Politics of Sweetness*. University of North Carolina Press, 2015.
Mitchell, Don. *They Saved the Crops: Labor, Landscape, and the Struggle over Industrial Farming in Bracero Era California*. University of Georgia Press, 2012.
Molina, Natalia, *Fit to be Citizens? Public Health and Race in Los Angeles, 1879–1939*. University of California Press, 2006.
———. *How Race is Made in America: Immigration, Citizenship, and the Historical Power of Racial Scripts*. University of California Press, 2014.
Molina, Natalia, Daniel Martinez HoSang, and Ramón A. Gutiérrez. *Relational Formations of Race: Theory, Method, and Practice*. University of California Press, 2019.
Montejano, David. *Anglos and Mexicans in the Making of Texas, 1836–1986*. University of Texas Press, 1987.
Montgomery, David. *The Fall of the House of Labor: The Workplace, the State, and American Labor Activism*. Cambridge University Press, 1987.
Morales, Daniel. "*Tejas, Afuera de México*: Newspapers, the Mexican Government, *Mutualistas*, and Migrants in San Antonio, 1910–1940." *Journal of American Ethnic History* 40, no. 2 (Winter 2021): 62–64.
Mora-Torres, Juan. *The Making of the Mexican Border: The State, Capitalism, and Society in Nuevo León, 1848–1910*. University of Texas Press, 2001.
Najuma Stewart, Jacqueline. *Migrating to the Movies: Cinema and Black Urban Modernity*. University of California Pres, 2005.
Ngai, Mae M. *Impossible Subjects: Illegal Aliens and the Making of Modern America*. Princeton University Press, 2004.
———. "'A Slight Knowledge of the Barbarian Language': Chinese Interpreters in Late-Nineteenth and Early-Twentieth-Century America." *Journal of American Ethnic History* 30, no. 2 (Winter 2011): 5–32.
Olmstead, Brett. *Making Michigan Home: Mexican Americans Bridging the Rural-Urban Experience*. University of Illinois Press, 2025.
Padilla, Felix M. *Latino Ethnic Consciousness: The Case of Mexican Americans and Puerto Ricans in Chicago*. University of Notre Dame Press, 1985.
Paiz, Christian O. *Strikers of Coachella: A Rank-and-File History of the UFW Movement*. University of North Carolina Press, 2023.
Patiño, Jimmy. *Raza Sí, Migra No: Chicano Struggles for Immigrant Rights in San Diego*. University of North Carolina Press, 2017.
Pawel, Miriam. *The Union of Their Dreams: Power, Hope, and Struggle in Cesar Chavez's Farm Worker Movement*. Bloomsbury Press, 2009.
Peck, Gunther. "Reinventing Free Labor: Immigrant Padrones and Contract Laborers in North America, 1885–1925." *Journal of American History* 83, no. 3 (December 1996): 848–71.
———. *Reinventing Free Labor: Padrones and Immigrant Workers in the North American West, 1880–1930*. Cambridge University Press, 2000.
Peña, Manuel H. *The Texas-Mexican Conjunto: History of a Working-Class Music*. University of Texas Press, 1985.
Perales, Monica. *Smeltertown: Making and Remembering a Southwest Border Community*. University of North Carolina Press, 2010.

Pérez, Gina M. *The Near Northwest Side Story: Migration, Displacement, and Puerto Rican Families*. University of California Press, 2004.

Picatto, Pablo. "Public Sphere in Latin America: A Map of the Historiography." *Social History* 35, no. 2 (May 2010): 167–68.

Pitti, Stephen J. *The Devil in Silicon Valley: Northern California, Race, and Mexican Americans*. Princeton University Press, 2003.

Poblete, Joanna. *Islanders in the Empire: Filipino and Puerto Rican Laborers in Hawai'i*. University of Illinois Press, 2014.

Povitz, Lana Dee. *Stirrings: How Activist New Yorkers Ignited a Movement for Food Justice*. University of North Carolina Press, 2019.

Ragland, Catherine. *Música Norteña: Mexican Americans Creating a Nation between Nations*. Temple University Press, 2009.

Ramsey, Guthrie P. *Race Music: Black Cultures from Bebop to Hip-Hop*. University of California Press, 2004.

Robinson, Robert S. "Taking the Fair Deal to the Fields: Truman's Commission on Migratory Labor, Public Law 78, and the Bracero Program, 1950–1952." *Agricultural History* 84, no. 3 (Summer 2010): 381–402.

Rodriguez, Marc Simon. *Tejano Diaspora: Mexican Americanism and Ethnic Politics in Texas and Wisconsin*. University of North Carolina Press, 2011.

Rosas, Ana Elizabeth. *Abrazando el Espíritu: Bracero Families Confront the US-Mexico Border*. University of California Press, 2014.

Rúa, Mérida M. *A Grounded Identidad: Making New Lives in Chicago's Puerto Rican Neighborhoods*. Oxford University Press, 2012.

Rudinow, Joel. *Soul Music: Tracking the Spiritual Roots of Pop from Plato to Motown*. University of Michigan Press, 2010.

Ruiz, Vicki L. *Cannery Women, Cannery Lives: Mexican Women, Unionization, and the California Food Processing Industry, 1930–1950*. University of New Mexico Press, 1987.

Salinas, Cristina. *Managed Migrations: Growers, Farmworkers, and Border Enforcement in the Twentieth Century*. University of Texas Press, 2018.

Sanchez, George J. *Becoming Mexican American: Ethnicity, Culture, and Identity in Chicano Los Angeles, 1900–1945*. Oxford University Press, 1993.

Sandoval-Strausz, Andrew K. *Barrio America: How Latino Immigrants Saved the American City*. Basic Books, 2019.

Scott, Rebecca. *Degrees of Freedom: Louisiana and Cuba after Slavery*. Harvard University Press, 2008.

Shapiro, Fred R. *The Yale Book of Quotations*. Yale University Press, 2006.

Solis, Gabriel. "I Did It My Way: Rock and the Logic of Covers." *Popular Music and Society* 33, no. 3 (July 2010): 315.

Staudenmaier, Michael. *White, Black, Brown: Becoming Puerto Rican in Chicago*. University of North Carolina Press, 2026.

Suárez Findlay, Eileen J. *We Are Left without a Father Here: Masculinity, Domesticity, and Migration in Postwar Puerto Rico*. Duke University Press, 2014.

Taylor, Paul S. *An American-Mexican Frontier: Nueces County, Texas*. Russell and Russell, 1934.

———. "Mexican Labor in the United States: Dimmit County, Winter Garden District, South Texas." *University of California Publication in Economics* 6, no. 5 (1930): 293–464.

Thomas, Lorrin. *Puerto Rican Citizen: History and Political Identity in Twentieth-Century New York City*. University of Chicago Press, 2010.

Thompson, James. "Detroit's Play-It-Extra-Loud Rock 'n' Roll Scene: Garage Bands Thrived in the Motor City in Mid-60s." *Goldmine* 26, no. 4 (February 25, 2000).

Valdés, Dionicio (Dennis) N. *Al Norte Agricultural Workers in the Great Lakes Region, 1917–1970*. University of Texas Press, 1991.

———. *Barrios Norteños: St. Paul and Midwestern Mexican Communities in the Twentieth Century*. University of Texas Press, 2000.

———. "*Betabeleros*: The Formation of an Agricultural Proletariat in the Midwest, 1897–1930." *Labor History* 30, no. 4 (2007): 536–62.

———. "From Following the Crops to Chasing the Corporations: The Farm Labor Organizing Committee." In *The Chicano Struggle: Analyses of Past and Present Efforts*, edited by John A. García, Teresa Córdova, Juan Ramon García, and the National Association for Chicano Studies. Bilingual Press, 1984.

Vargas, Zaragos. *Proletarians of the North: A History of Mexican Industrial Workers in Detroit and the Midwest, 1917–1933*. University of California Press, 1993.

Vega, Sujey. *Latino Heartland: Of Borders and Belonging in the Midwest*. New York University Press, 2015.

Velázquez, Mirelsie. *Puerto Rican Chicago: Schooling the City, 1940–1977*. University of Illinois Press, 2022.

Weber, John. *From South Texas to the Nation: The Exploitation of Mexican Labor in the Twentieth Century*. University of North Carolina Press, 2015.

Weise, Julie M. *Corazón de Dixie: Mexicans in the US South since 1910*. University of North Carolina Press, 2015.

Whalen, Carmen Theresa. *From Puerto Rico to Philadelphia: Puerto Rican Workers and Postwar Economies*. Temple University Press, 2001.

Windham, Lane. *Knocking on Labor's Door: Union Organizing in the 1970s and the Roots of a New Economic Divide*. University of North Carolina Press, 2017.

Index

Italic page numbers refer to illustrations.

* 9 7 8 1 4 6 9 6 9 3 8 5 9 *